Practical Shooting
Beyond Fundamentals

Brian Enos

Photography and design by Kris Kunkler

Practical Shooting: Beyond Fundamentals is published in the United States by Zediker Publishing, P.O. Box 426, Clifton, CO 81520

ISBN 978-0-9626925-0-5

First printing, June 1990
Second printing, July 1991
Third printing, February 2000
Fourth printing, August 2000
Fifth printing, July 2001
Sixth printing, July 2002
Seventh printing, February 2003
Eighth printing, February 2004
Ninth printing, January 2005
Tenth printing, November 2005
Eleventh printing, August 2006
Twelfth printing, March 2007
Thirteenth printing, July 2008
Fourteenth printing, December 2009
Fifteenth printing, November 2010

PRINTED IN THE UNITED STATES OF AMERICA

TABLE OF CONTENTS

I'd like to dedicate this book to the creative shooter. The shooter who isn't bound by any ideas or traditions. The shooter who is always looking within himself to discover the limitless ability that is always there. We're all on the same road.

FOREWORD

By Rob Leatham
6-time National IPSC Champion
3-time World IPSC Champion

I've known Brian longer than anybody else, as far as other shooters go. We met in 1979, at a shooting match, right where you're supposed to meet. It was a steel match held in a pit in Gilbert, Arizona, and somebody showed up who nobody knew. It was Brian, and what set him apart from us was that he *never* missed a target. We'd make up for accuracy by shooting enough shots that *eventually* we'd hit everything. But Brian stepped up and went *ding, ding, ding*, and we were making fun of him because here's somebody who's hitting the targets... At this point this was unheard of amongst ourselves. You didn't shoot the targets, you shot *at* the targets. After the match he wanted to see my gun and I wanted to find out who this guy was, and that started it off.

What makes Brian really stand out is that he's one of the very few *logistical* tacticians in the game. Some people can shoot and they have no idea why they're doing it or how they're doing it, and that's really not a problem. But what you find out is to actually repair the mistakes you make you have to go through an analytical phase to understand exactly not only what you are doing but the things that you're probably not doing, which is where most all the problems are. And Brian was one of the first people who went beyond *hold the gun like this, look at the sights, squeeze the trigger,* and the same basic line you've heard forever. Back when everyone else was experimenting with checkering, Brian was trying to figure out what you really should pay attention to and what you shouldn't pay attention to, what is important and what isn't important. There are still probably only five or six people who really know how to tell you what is happening while you're shooting. You can ask Brian and he probably knows *exactly* how it happens, not just what he *thinks* makes it happen.

In 1982-83, we (I say "we" because he and I have been together for the entire time of our shooting careers, so it will be the empirical "we") went through an experimental phase where we were basically rebelling. We didn't trust anything we were doing, and we felt like it was time to try everything, whether we liked it or not—cross-draw holsters, finger on and off the trigger guard, and anything else we could think of. Plus, we started putting a lot of emphasis on what we looked at—not just looking at the sights, but trying to notice the things that we saw when we shot.

I still have a box of parts and pieces from the experimental phase days. We realized that the score changes we were getting from the guns were very minimal. We were finding that you'd have the greatest gun in the world and the difference it made was fractional compared to if you went to a match and missed *one* shot. Now it seems so clear, but when we were going through the phase it seemed like we couldn't figure anything out. Then we went to the 1983 IPSC Nationals and realized it all of a sudden, in a flash. We were sitting there at the match thinking that we'd been to a couple of Nationals and each year we messed everything up, so this year let's really ignore the scores—let's just shoot each event as well as we can at the time. And that was the year we went one/two, but there was an incredible difference between our scores, which were very close, and everybody else's. They were a whole class behind us. That was the waking-up year.

And we didn't invent anything. All we did was put two and two together and got four; it's become very obvious to us and I guess it's just a little harder for some people to count it up. We probably spent more time in 1982 and 1983 talking and thinking than any two people in the world. The way it would work is that I'd load all night the night before, and then we'd go shooting all day long, and then we'd talk shooting until we were falling asleep early into the morning hours. At some point it turns into philosophy where you find out that you're not really shooting, you're simply doing *something*. And it's really not important what the actual means are. Now it's come to a point, almost full circle, where I couldn't care less how I hold the gun. There are reasons why one way may be preferable, but the benefits for that are so much less than for what you *should* be thinking about. Shooting is something that you must prepare for, and the preparation time is more important than the time when you're on the line, because on the line you can't do anything but what you're going to do.

I liken it to going to school. You go to class to learn the material so you can take the test. And the test will show what you know, and more importantly, what you don't know. And it's the same for a match. When you go to a match, what you know is shown every time you shoot. That means that if you mess up, that is what you were prepared to do. To this day, there are still only a handful of people who have spent the time preparing to put in a good performance. A guy will walk off the line and say, "I can do better than that." Bull! The bottom line is that you do what you're prepared to do.

People do need to know how to hold the gun and know how the stance works, but what keeps me busy in my classes is trying to help my students learn how to think. They say, "Rob holds his hands like this...," and they don't know that the reason I hold my hands like this is *not* to make myself look that way. The end result is not to hold the gun that way; holding the gun that way is the end result of doing something else. I think of it like this: I could build a machine that could shoot better than I could until something went wrong with it. And then the rest of the day it would miss because it's not going to adjust for anything. That is the only place where we as biological units are superior to things we can build. We can adapt and improve and modify and change. And the changes aren't going to come on the outside, they're going to come on the inside.

We take all this for granted because we've done this now for 10 years, and not to sound cocky, but we can do things that someone who hasn't shot too much can't even begin to do. So they come out and see us do these things and ask the question, "How do you do that?" I've found that it's a whole lot harder to explain to somebody what you're doing than it is to just do it. I can shoot an *El Presidente* in 5 seconds and then talk to you for 15 minutes to explain what happened. This is where Brian excels. He has spent the hundreds and hundreds of hours figuring out what happened.

If you want to improve, you are first going to have to recognize that you are deficient—there are some things that you don't know. And you've got to get the ego out of the way. If someone is very good at something, but not good at everything, they often don't feel that they have to be good at anything else, and I've found that they're extremely difficult to teach. But what makes you good at anything is exactly the same thing. And the person who is good at one thing and not at something else has missed the point. He has within his ability to be successful at whatever he wants. And the problem is that people aren't able to benefit from what they have. They limit themselves.

Some people who go to Bianchi say they can't shoot fast, and some who go to the Steel Challenge say they can't shoot accurately, and what it generally comes down to is that they're not really interested in the other thing. It has nothing to do with the fact of whether they can do it or not—they've decided that they don't care about learning it, and that's an honest evaluation—but to say I can't shoot accurately or I can't shoot fast, that's telling yourself that you can't do something when all it takes is a refocus of the same basic fundamentals. Shooting is shooting and I do not care what it is. No matter what the game is, you want to let the shot go when the gun is lined up sufficiently accurately to get what you need out of the shot. Whether that means hitting a clay bird, hitting an X, or nipping the edge of a 12-inch disk at 10 yards, the whole trick is to *only do what you have to do*. That's what it all comes down to. That's shooting. And that's what you're going to learn about here.

And the point is not to become so good at one thing that you're unstoppable. The point is to become so good at teaching yourself to do everything that there's nothing that you can't learn. Therefore, all you have to do is to put the effort in and you can't be stopped at *anything*. I tell a student that when he goes to a match and he's not scared of anything, he's already won. Whether or not you have the physical skills is not even the point. A lot of people will never develop them. The point is that if you walk up and look at the course of fire and there isn't a thing there that you cannot do—and this isn't just from telling yourself this, but from something that you realize—if you can walk up and say *I can do all this,* you've won!

Brian and I are both trying to achieve perfection as shooters. And we've come to realize that there's not a lot of latitude in how you get that done, and I'm not talking physical here. I'm talking about the attitude you need to have—there's not much latitude in how you approach your shooting if you want to let yourself do as well as you can. You also have to realize that the only person who can ever stress you hard enough is *you*. If you only work to other people's expectations, you can only be as good as they are. If someone tells you 5 seconds is fast and you truly believe it, you will never go faster than that. Just to keep the level you're at, you've got to keep breaking ground, you've got to push. If you just try to hold your ground, you're going to slip. If I had to encapsulate all shooting, I would say that it is nothing more than an experiment to learn from. This book will help you learn how you learn. It will help you prepare for shooting. If you've been shooting for a while, you'll see that you already have the answers within you. You just need to take a look at yourself and see the limitations you've created. That's the ground that you're going to have to continue to break for as long as you shoot.

In the whole world, there is only one person who I would allow to talk to my students, and that is Brian. He's the only one who I feel has not just put in the superficial effort, but who has put in the true effort to figure any of this out—not just the pieces of if, not even just the whole thing, but *anything*. There's nobody else out there I could say, "Okay, listen to him."

PREFACE

I wrote this book because I wanted to share with you some things I've learned that have helped me understand shooting, and, more importantly, the things I know will help me continue to improve.

But this isn't all there is to shooting, especially from my perspective. I learn, and hope to improve, on every shot I fire. What is in this book, though, are the concepts, ideas, and whatever else we could call them, that I will continue to follow to realize that improvement. Although this will make more sense to you after you've read the book through, that in no way means that I'm finished with the experience and feel that every aspect of shooting is organized into some huge, can't-miss system. I don't claim to know all there is to know about shooting, but I believe that I do know where the answers are. What you'll come to understand is that the things I believe are important to shooting performance almost guarantee that my shooting will change constantly.

I am not a self-taught shooter, but I am a self-realized shooter. I did not have an instructor, per se. I have refined my shooting from inputs from many different sources. I've incorporated ideas from bullseye shooting, shotgunning, trick shooting, golf, martial arts, and even motorcycle racing. My sources are as diverse as John Satterwhite, Bill Blankenship, Ed McGivern, Bruce Lee, and a lot of other people whose names I didn't catch. I can't even guess at the hours I've spent trying to make sense of different bits and pieces of ideas I got from those inputs—trying to relate them to the whole of shooting—and have discovered that they all relate, in some way. Some directly, some indirectly, some not at all.

Although there are a legion of mechanics contained in this book, I didn't just set out to write a "how-to" manual. There's no denying the importance of mechanics because a good technique helps you to experience the more advanced facets of shooting. But it's only important that you develop your technique so that you can take yourself beyond it.

The omission of any and all defensive tactics or use of handguns for anything but target sports was entirely intentional. I'll leave the street stuff to the other guys. To me, shooting is a sport, nothing more, nothing less. But practical pistol shooting does teach a life-saving skill. If I had to save myself or someone else from drowning, I'd much rather be an Olympic swimmer. That's the same correlation

I make with practical pistol shooting. Practical shooting develops high-speed gun handling ability and refines everything to such a reflexive level that I'm confident of my ability to shoot. Learning tactics is a different story, and I don't confuse the two.

If this book comes across as being a little different from what you're used to seeing in shooting books, so much the better. What helped lead to my ideas on shooting instruction, and to the development of this book, was an observation I made over and over: here I am, a shooter who has never swung a club, reading golf books to improve my shooting. Likewise, other athletes, such as Bruce Lee, who perhaps had never held a gun, showed me through their work some parallels I incorporated in my pistol shooting. Just like any other sport, shooting involves speed, timing, coordination, and all other such things almost categorically omitted from discussions of competitive shooting. Sports performance, in its essence, knows nothing of the boundaries we often corral it with. It's a goal of mine that skiers, tennis players, or any athlete, could read this book and benefit from its contents. This book is about performance. It happens to deal with shooting directly.

I dedicated this book to the open-minded, creative shooter. That's the one who just enjoys shooting and enjoys learning about shooting—whether it's shooting a rifle, shooting a pistol at high speed, shooting a pistol with precision, shooting skeet or trap, or just any type of shooting at all, because it basically is all the same. There are technical differences, but the attitude it takes to be successful in shooting and to enjoy and learn from it—no matter what type of shooting it is—is the same.

This book is directly geared to the practical pistol shooter who is interested in improving his shooting skills, whether he's defense-oriented or competition-oriented. We all shoot for different reasons, but when you get right down to it, the aspects of the shooting are no different. I am tired of all the friction between "martial artists" and "gamesmen" and trap shooters who don't talk to skeet shooters and IPSC guys who won't shoot steel—*because it's all so much fun*. Every style of shooting is fun, and whether you enjoy it or not it shouldn't hurt another person's enjoyment of it. I wrote this book for the real shooter who doesn't take away from anybody else and wants to improve his own skill.

INTRODUCTION

This is a book about *shooting*. A lot has been written about firing, but not much about shooting. And there's a big difference between the two. Firing ability is not what separates levels of shooters. My success as a shooter came from learning to see my own limitations, discovering why they existed, and then finding ways to break free of them. And I will do that continually for as long as I shoot.

You can shoot without thought, without effort, and without limitations. You first have to understand those limitations, and that's what this book is about.

The whole purpose of this book is to help you expose your own limitations. The point of view that you need to cultivate is not one of learning new things or of even learning to shoot—it's in shedding away your own obstructions to the knowledge that you already have. The things that let you shoot to your maximum potential, and the things that make that potential unlimited, are already a part of your life. You really don't need to *know* anything else; you only need to understand how things that you do and experience every day apply to your shooting. You've already learned how to do many things that are just as complex as firing a pistol at high speed—driving a car for instance—and you'll see how the approach you follow to do those things can be the same one you take for shooting.

I don't want to come off from my descriptions in this book as being steeped in transcendental reincarnation or anything like that. Any pattern or idea that you follow is just another man's or another group's philosophy. We'll attempt to get beyond ideas and systems so that you can function creatively as was your original nature. Adhering to someone else's system or a pattern through which you're supposed to direct your mind is, to me, just something else to think about. I don't want to be in a trance; I want total animation.

The more organized my overall picture of shooting becomes, the more I realize that things all change constantly. I may not be shooting the same way next year as I did this year, and certainly I don't shoot the same way I did, say, five years ago. But, even so, I know that I'll be applying the same concepts and searching for the same results as I'll outline in this book. The directions those searches take me might change, but that's what I want: no limitations.

There are plenty of ideas in this book on techniques, gun handling, strategy, equipment, and a lot more specific information about what I've learned about practical pistol shooting. But I hope that you'll see that my advice is only intended to be your starting point and your guide, not your Bible. You'll learn how to figure out your own details. If you're a beginning or intermediate shooter, you might want to take a shortcut through my experience, because you can bet that I've probably tried whatever you might be thinking about trying. But regardless of your level, I believe that you'll benefit from understanding some of the concepts—and misconceptions—behind the modern practical pistol technique. Some ideas will support your shooting and some won't. But you'll see that mechanics are developed and refined through achieving the right attitude about shooting. If you know where you want to go, you will find a way to get there. But it can't work the other way around.

You'll learn how to use awareness and observation in your shooting to show you the technical improvements that might be limiting your ability to fire the pistol. You'll learn how just relaxing and observing what the gun is doing will direct your body to support the wishes of your mind. And you have to let yourself realize that it *just happens;* you don't stop on a discovery and concentrate on that. You're not using the body's process of opening up and making these discoveries as a route to learning more mechanics or going deeper into mechanics; that's an easy trap. Don't make your artificially-created knowledge become a truth that you have to live by. It's so easy to trap yourself in your own little creations.

The beginner will see how important it is to integrate the mind and body when he's building his shooting skills. Hopefully, after reading this book, the beginning shooter will not suffer through as many set-backs and re-builds as most Masters have. By following the ideas in this book, especially in the *Development* section, he won't have to learn from his mistakes as much as he can learn from his experiments, and that means that he'll learn faster and that he'll continue to learn.

The intermediate shooter will also be able to better understand the relationships of mind, body, and performance. The *Tools Of Shooting* section will add greatly to his understanding of the modern technique; there may be some information there that will improve his skills, which in turn may help give him the confidence to move on to applying those skills. The *Specific Challenges* section will give him some insights into more efficient ways to deal with the advanced aspects of practical shooting. But mostly, the intermediate shooter needs to be aware of some of the traps he might be in right now. Once he can identify those traps, and learn ways to go beyond his own limitations, he'll be able to progress faster and farther than he might have thought possible.

Finally, I'd like the advanced shooters to use what's in here to break through what I believe are their biggest barriers. There are many good shooters who can't overcome their own self-imposed limitations. They are already much better shooters than they think they are. I don't claim to have a system, in that "system" could be defined to mean a step-by-step, do this, do that procedure that will lead to championships. You'll learn that the "system" is in not having a system. The difference between me and other Masters is not in the way I grip the gun. The answer is never in more mechanics or in different mechanics. You need to get over the idea that you can somehow *know* how to shoot. The mechanics only exist to help you go beyond them. There is a level of shooting that goes beyond mechanics and strategies and all the other intellectual bits of knowledge we can cultivate. You'll find ways to experience that level.

I've always tried to eliminate contradictions in my shooting. You have to think about shooting or your skills won't improve. But then you have to not think about your shooting or your performance won't improve. That sounds like a contradiction, but it's really not. You need to get past the whole cause and effect idea that if you do something then something else will happen. It really doesn't work that way. There's a level where the causes and effects are the same thing and actually become nothing at all.

It's difficult to just open up and allow your awareness and intuition to consume your shooting because we're not comfortable with *not* thinking about shooting. We've been led to believe that shooting is so difficult that we can't shoot just as easily as we can do anything else. Shooting is a process, but, in actuality, it's a practice. You must take steps to improve your shooting or you'll resign yourself to staying at the level where you are now. But the steps you take must end in your passing over them.

A phrase you're going to read a lot in this book is, "And I'll talk more about that later on..." Once you've turned the last page and closed the cover, hopefully all the things that I talked about will fit together for you. Almost everything in this book comes down to being able to do three things that you, and I, will absolutely have to do for as long as we shoot—and for each shot we fire.

Locate the target. Get the gun on the target. Keep the gun on the target while you fire the shot.

That's about it. Being able to do these three things in any and all circumstances, and for every shot you fire, means being aware of different things that relate to different circumstances. Keeping these three things in mind when you're reading will help you follow my perspective. You'll see that pretty much everything I say in each section is directly related to finding the target, getting the gun on the target, and holding the gun on the target when it fires. Understanding your current relationship with those three things will, hopefully, also show you where your limitations are—and allow you to intuit ways to surpass them.

How To Read This Book

To learn from this book, just like to learn anything else, you've got to have the right attitude about it. If you immediately reject something you don't believe could be true or don't believe could work—and you don't try it—then you're not going to learn anything from this book.

You need to examine everything in this book, roll it over in your mind, and let those things that you read give rise to new ideas of your own, things that you can try on your own. And then, on your own, you can discover whether or not that particular idea works or doesn't work for you or whether or not it suits your personality. A lot of the things I say may not work for you, and some of the things I don't do may work better for you, but make those determinations through careful testing and analysis and observation of your own personality and what suits you. Don't accept anything I say as being any kind of gospel just because I've done this or done that. Don't reject anything I say just because you've heard someone else say that that's not the way it works. Just read it and examine it. *Try it.* See how it works for you.

And pay attention to everything that you do, everything that you try, everything that you think about. When it's all said and done, if you just want to sit down and talk about the shooting to someone, you need to understand every single thing that you do; you need to know why you're doing everything that you do; you need to know why you know everything that you know.

There are a few great natural athletes who may not understand everything that they do, but they can do it. I'm not a natural athlete; I'm not a natural shooter. For me, the whole thing has been a process of determination. I enjoy this immensely, and I just stick with it—I never give up. I never feel that I'm as good as I can be. And it's that attitude that's made me understand everything that I do.

But during the actual shooting, you have to know when to let all the knowledge that you've accumulated and all the things that you've learned go and just let it happen.

This book is going to hopefully show you how to turn your knowledge into action.

Eventually you'll understand that everything that you do is dependent on your own attitude. And you're responsible for every single function you have when you're shooting. If you're shooting too fast, shooting too slow, if you can't hit any targets, if you're tense or worried—every single problem you'll have *you* have to deal with, and you can solve it if you just pay attention to yourself.

It probably could be accurately said that you may have already determined what you're going to get out of this book before you read it, and again, I'm talking about the attitude that you're going to read it with. So open up your mind when you're reading and be aware of your own attitude and how you process the information that comes to you from this book.

SAFETY

Pay attention! Safety is pretty much common sense, but no matter how long you've been shooting or competing, safety can never be taken for granted. You should have safe gun handling down to a reflex, but please stop every now and then and review what you need to keep in mind.

Never make any distinction between the safety practices you must follow at a match and those you follow in practice or in dry-firing at home. When it comes to safety, it's always "for real."

Always wear shooting glasses that carry the proper certification for impact resistance. Hearing protection is a given. If you shoot steel, make sure that the target faces are relatively free from damage. A smooth plate usually just causes the bullet to flatten and slide off straight to the ground. A plate that has a partial bullet hole in it can cause the lead splatter to come back your way. And anytime you're not actually in the process of engaging a target, the trigger finger is outside the trigger guard.

The .38 Super has brought a new safety awareness to the game: high pressure ammunition. It's up to each shooter to take responsibility for his loads. There isn't any actual load data in this book for that reason. The guns I use are expertly built and fitted and can handle the extra pressure that comes with major loads. But things like barrel lengths, quality of workmanship, and component differences all make it necessary for each shooter to develop his own load in his own gun. I'd never shoot anyone else's major loads in my gun; and I would never allow another shooter to use my loads.

There are a lot of advanced gun handling techniques covered in this book. I have safely practiced all the techniques I describe literally thousands of times through dry-firing before I ever take them to the range, and I suggest that you do the same.

But the most important thing I can say about safety is that *guns are always loaded.* No matter what you do, never point a gun at anything that you wouldn't mind shooting. A lot of people won't understand the significance of this advice, but they will if they've seen as many accidental discharges as I have. If you're around guns and around shooters as much as I am, eventually you're going to see an AD. As long as the gun is pointed in a safe direction, it will scare you good and you'll learn a lot from it, but that's the worst that comes out of it. Take this advice now so you won't have to learn it from seeing an AD.

Section 1: AWARENESS & FOCUS

I begin this book with what might be thought of as an advanced topic: the shooter's attitude. (Attitude, as I intend it to mean, will soon be replaced with the more accurate description of a shooter's relationship with *awareness* and *focus.)* Although this is usually the "last chapter" for most people, to me, it's the first thing to understand. Without the proper attitude there can never be improvement. Throughout this book, I'll use the terms *awareness* and *focus*. Because these concepts are central to your understanding of everything that's to come in the following pages, it's vital that you get and keep a very clear understanding of what they mean to me, and to you, before reading any further. Go over this section carefully. Stop and consider what you're reading. Experience it and visualize it from your own perspective. Keep in mind that whenever "mental" this or that is discussed, it has to relate *to your own mind.* It's pointless to ever try to copy someone else's attitude. Like Bruce Lee said, "It's easy to teach someone the skills, but it's difficult to teach them their own attitude."

**Observe the shooting, as it is happening.
Let the shooting tell you its story.**

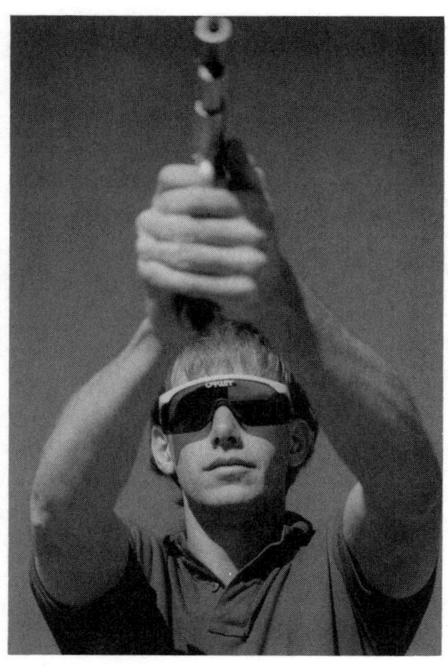

If you can be aware of what's happening as you are shooting—not analyze it, judge it, or consciously try to change it—*just be aware of what you're doing and of what you're seeing,* there is no limit to your potential.

AWARENESS

Awareness. Awareness is everything and it's nothing at all. Awareness means everything to your performance, but it's not in the performance itself. Basically, awareness in shooting is an opening up of your mind, your vision, and all your senses to accept and observe things that are happening while you're shooting—*at the instant they are happening.* Awareness removes you from what just happened or what might happen. Awareness is almost a "third-person" perspective in that it's not directed, almost detached from fact. It is, though, pure reality because awareness shows you exactly what's going on at any one moment. Awareness is observation without thought or judgement. Awareness allows all inputs from your observation to enter your mind. If you could step out of your own skin and look at your shooting as you're engaged in it—not judging, only watching—you may witness awareness as a reality. I have yet to look down on myself as I shoot a stage, but that's about the feeling I have when I'm in a state of awareness.

If we can just look at something without judging or evaluating it, we are seeing it in its purest, actual form. Awareness allows you to see things exactly as they are at any instant. Awareness allows you to fully experience any given moment, and all given moments. Awareness allows you to experience without retaining the experience in memory. Once something has been experienced, there is immediately something else to be experienced. Any memory of the first experience can't be carried along to the next or that next experience—the one that matters right now—can't be fully engaged in. Awareness carries with it no burden of past experiences; it only shows what *is*. Awareness lets the shooter simply observe the constantly changing relationships between himself, the gun, and the targets.

During the shooting, the inputs from this observation are monitored by the shooter's intuition, not by his conscious mind. When the conscious mind is engaged, what's happening before us cannot be fully experienced for what, in fact, it is. When the conscious mind is engaged, you're operating through a filter or screen—a screen of your own knowledge—that limits you to your past experience or your future understanding of something through your past experience, and you're not actually viewing the situation in its clarity.

You don't work *on* your attitude; you work *within* your attitude. Attitude is not something you add in or work on after everything else is learned. With the right attitude, learning is continuous.

When you meet a person for the first time and you're interested in learning about them, your mind is totally open and receptive to every input you get from them—the way they move, think, talk, act, look. But when you meet a friend you may not have seen in a while, but one who you've known for years, in that situation you're not viewing your friend the same way you did the new acquaintance. You're not totally open; you've built up an image about your friend that's become a screen that you see him through. You are limited only to your knowledge of past experiences. He may have undergone a radical change since you saw him last, and because of your viewing him through this screen of images and ideas you've built around him, you may not even be aware of the change. He may be a totally different person, but you still see him in the same old way. Think about how this applies to your whole life—your shooting included.

I've been asked a lot of times what separates a shooter who continues to stay on top and continues to finish well, such as my friend, Rob Leatham, from the other guys who come and go. The difference is that a shooter like Rob understands that he never *really* learns anything. Rob continues to learn every time he shoots. His mind is always open; every time he fires, his mind is always ready to incorporate anything new that he learns. Whereas shooters who haven't been able to stay on top have built themselves up to a certain point and have learned and mastered the fundamentals or ideas that have helped them get there—they have refined their filters—but then they stop and don't retain the open-mindedness that allowed them to get to that point. Even if you're good enough to win a national championship in some event, if you're not careful and your mind does not stay open, you'll stay at that same, stagnant point...where guys like Rob will pass you by.

FOCUS

Focus is a finite occurrence that exists in the infinite realm of awareness. Focus is your filter for all the inputs your observation brings in; however, focus is *not* a filter you've built from your past experience. Focus monitors your inputs right at the moment they're coming in—in real time. The difference between a screen of focus and the screen of past experience is that a screen built only from your own knowledge of the past blocks observations from entering your mind. Focus doesn't block anything—it only alerts you to the important inputs your observation brings in. In the example of your seeing a friend who's gone through a radical change, but not noticing it, if you looked at him with a present tense focus—as if you were seeing him for the first time—you

Strive to shoot with a calm, relaxed body and an alert, attentive mind. Observe the shooting—as it is happening.

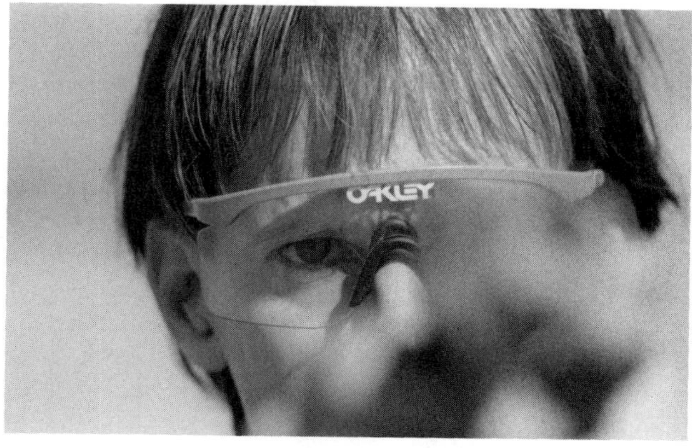

would have immediately noticed the change. Focus shows you everything. You should look at the shooting—*each time you shoot*—the same way.

Focus could be defined as having a flexible preoccupation with anything that will affect your shooting performance. Focus is simply paying attention to things your awareness shows you are happening, as they are happening. Focus brings subjectivity to the objectivity of awareness. Awareness makes focus possible; focus engages awareness.

With all the things that are going on when you're shooting a stage at a match, you might wonder how you can open yourself up to observe everything without becoming distracted by things that don't have anything to do with your shooting. In extreme awareness, your observation could show you dirt flying up behind the targets, brass flying, or any number of other things that are happening while you're shooting. The solution is to become so focused on what you're doing that the distractions aren't there anymore. You can't actually get rid of the distractions, but by focusing on one thing completely, then the others cease to exist. The point is to not think of blocking out all the other inputs your awareness and observation brings in; instead, bypass them through a more intense focus on what you need to do or to see to shoot the stage.

Expressing something that's entirely intuitive in purely intellectual terms (writing it down) is really contradictory to the way awareness and focus must ultimately be understood. And the fact is that they are never really understood, they are only experienced. When you are experiencing them, you understand; and when you understand, the experience is gone. Hopefully, though, through a careful explanation of what these concepts mean to me, through your future experiences with some of the exercises elsewhere in this book, and, most importantly, through your patience in stopping and reflecting on what I'm giving of my own descriptions of awareness and focus, you'll begin to understand the terms in your own way. And that's all that really matters—that it makes sense to you.

When shooting, concern yourself with only what is happening and how you are feeling. That will leave no room for what "might happen" or what "just happened."

THE SHOOTING TENSE

Awareness in shooting comes from observation without thought. Awareness leads to action without thought. Awareness exists only in the present tense, along with shooting. Although awareness happens actively, it's perceived passively. You don't stop and think about something that you may be aware of between, say, your first and second shots on *5 To Go*. In between strings, you may want to recall what you noticed so you can make an adjustment for the next string, but that process is removed from the shooting at hand.

The present tense is fluid; it exists only for an instant. But the present tense also exists continuously. Conscious thought cannot exist in the present tense; only *action* exists in the present tense. By the time you read this sentence, the present tense experience of reading it has passed. Just as you're reading it, the present tense is engaged. The instant you stop to consider what you've just read, the present tense is shifted by conscious thought, removing you from the experience. You won't be focused in the present tense until you start reading again. What causes you to move your eyes or turn the page? Your awareness of the progression of words as you read them; your observation of their relationship to the page; a focus on your desire to read. But with one simple thought, you go immediately away from the experience.

The only shot that matters is the one you're firing *right now*. Make sure that it's the one in which your awareness and focus are peaked. *Right now* is the shooting tense.

What you read won't be knowledge until you've left the present tense and engaged your conscious mind. When you're facing a bank of plates, what you do on them won't be knowledge until you're through shooting, so "knowing" all there is about shooting plates is not what puts them down. In the present tense, there is only the act of firing this shot, then it's over. And the next shot, and next shot, and next shot are all over. Results don't exist in the present tense. It's not "I don't care about the shooting" (which would be the same as caring...). In the present tense there is no room for any such idea (or for any ideas). You can neither care nor not care—you can only shoot. Only the shooting exists in the present tense. If you want to engage in the shooting, the present tense is where you'll find it.

An awareness of the present tense is a very fleeting, delicate thing. The only way to achieve it is to not think about it. We all, if only for an instant, actually *fire* the gun in the present tense. For maximum performance you have to stay focused entirely in the present tense all the time that you're shooting. This takes ambition, and especially so since no amount of actual work or thought on the matter can accomplish it for you. Present tense shooting must simply happen. All through this book, and especially in the *Development* section, I'll show you ways you can bring awareness into your shooting. It takes time and dedication to achieve a level of awareness that will allow you to focus entirely in the present tense as you shoot. But since this is a very nondescript thing, it mostly takes your understanding and belief in its importance. At some time after firing a stage, you will "think" back and realize that you were focused entirely in the present tense. It most likely will have been a very fulfilling performance.

If you'd like to reflect on how much good your conscious thought has done for you, think back to a time in a steel match when your gun swung toward a full silhouette at close range that you needed to fire two shots on and a little input from your brain said, *boy this one's easy,* or *no way can I miss this,* and you didn't really even point the gun at the target, you just aimed in the general area and hit the trigger twice, usually missing one or both shots. When you look back on it you can't believe that you missed a target that large at that distance. It's a perfect example of what your conscious mind will do when it turns from a state of awareness to a state of thought.

If I took my wallet out of my pocket and threw it at your face, you would instantly protect yourself—catch the wallet, move your head—you would act. After it happened, you might wonder why you acted as you did, but the simple act—the fact that you acted—is what matters. Through observing yourself in that simple process, you can see what we're after here. That's the tense we need to learn to shoot in, not the tense of how or why this does that.

I analyze and interpret each match I shoot and every practice session I have. I am as technically-oriented as any shooter I know. There's no telling the hours I spend weekly thinking about shooting, consciously trying different things and applying different ideas away from the range. But when I actually shoot—even in practice where I might want to try out a new idea—I drop all my technical, conscious thoughts away. I open up to my experiences. My awareness shows me everything I need to see. After the shooting, I can look back and realize whether or not my idea had any merit. Without conscious analysis, there's no other way for me to develop the knowledge I'll use in the future. But I don't consciously carry that knowledge with me to the line—it's already processed, organized, and stored in my mind. At the match, I'll trust myself to use what I know at the time I need to use it. If I have to consciously search for the knowledge and ask myself what I should do and wait to remember it, the shooting's over before that search even begins.

It's important at this point for me give some description to my use of words like "strategy" or "plan" since I don't want you to think I'm contradicting myself later when I say to follow a plan and to not think at the same time. I might program a target sequence, for instance, into my mind through conscious thought and visualization, but that is done so I *don't* have to think about it while I'm shooting. Once you've studied a road map and know all your exits and turns, you don't have to stare at the map while you're driving. When you know exactly where you want to go and exactly how to get there, all you have to do is keep your eyes open and go. My "programs" are visual references rather than thoughts composed of words. Therefore, I am able to follow my plan or program by simply seeing it as I shoot—not by thinking about it. And I don't *try* to see my visualization. I just keep my eyes open and go.

THE CONCENTRATION FALLACY

This is a chapter heading in a famous old book, *On Learning Golf,* and that's a pretty good summation of my feelings about classical concentration. To help you better understand awareness and focus, know that they have nothing to do with concentration. The terms are, in fact, diametrically opposed.

Concentration, in its classical meaning, and as I refer to it in this book, is a narrowing down of the mind to one specific, predetermined focal point. Awareness is an opening up of the mind to all available focal points that have some bearing on your shooting performance. Concentration is outgoing; awareness is incoming. Concentration is limiting; awareness is limitless.

Concentration is conscious thought and is, therefore, a means of exclusion from the present tense. It is a state of contradiction in that thinking about an action means that the action becomes a thought. Conscious thought precludes action. You can either think or do, but you can't actually think *and* do at the same time.

There is action and there is the *idea* of what that action should be. The space that exists between the contradiction of pure action and the idea of action is the thought itself. The larger the contradiction between the action and the idea of action, the larger the space, and the more contradictory thought intervenes. If you wipe out the *idea* of action, you have also wiped out the contradiction completely because you have removed the need for thought. Only then can you be choicelessly aware of the pure action. However, this wiping out of the idea can only come about through a complete understanding of why the idea comes into being. Then the idea will disappear on its own, without any effort. To remove all the thoughts and ideas and controls from your shooting, focus yourself in the present

An idea is merely the formation of thought as a symbol; and the effort to live up to that symbol brings about a contradiction.

tense; all your thoughts and ideas and controls do not exist there.

Concentration, to me, means having a dogged determination to do one thing and one thing only when the gun comes out of the holster. Concentration, then, makes creative action and adaptation impossible. Concentration requires searching, comparing, confirming. When a shooter's concentration is "broken," he's caught without an alternative. He'll fire a shot in a state of mental limbo. Shooting then becomes a very fragmented process. Concentration can start a chain reaction of tense shifting while the present tense act of shooting goes unattended. Concentration is a barrier which prohibits learning because learning to concentrate is learning to limit yourself only to the techniques you already know. Concentration can be better than having no focal point at all, but it definitely is not the answer.

There's too much going on when you're shooting at high speed to concentrate on any one thing. Just observe what is happening.

Even though I don't believe it's possible to concentrate and realize any great results from it, I don't want to shut a person's mind off who may be quite good at his level and may believe that it's his concentration that allows him to shoot well. But let's take a look at the *experience* of concentration and relate it to focus. In a state of awareness, the actual focus at the instant it's happening may be very concentrated. A good analogy is that of a cat stalking a bird. If you watch the cat, he's so intensely focused on the bird's every movement that he can move to the left or to the right or straight ahead or jump into the air all seemingly instantaneously. But at the same time, when the cat's in that mode he could be easily caught with a net. And there's nothing wrong with being in that mode. You might have your focus tuned in, just like the cat's—not calculating, not thinking, just totally responding to the environment. The one specific thing the cat is focused on is the whole of the thing that matters to him. He's not planning or anticipating—he's decided to catch the bird and is now just doing that. You just need to understand what you'd like to do and what you'd like to see when you're shooting; that will help you discover your focus.

A lot of shooters think that blocking out everything that

doesn't deal with the shooting at hand is a form of concentration. To me, that's an incredibly attentive focus. In a state of awareness it's very possible to have a sense of classical concentration where the mind is very focused and fixed on one single thing, like the sight or center of the target. But it's not possible from a state of classical concentration to enter into a state of awareness. That's a much different level of functioning. From a state of awareness, when you look back on having that sense of concentration though some strings of fire, you may have been extremely concentrated on one particular point. And that may be all that was needed; concentration can be all that's needed in some instances, but it's not the only thing you should strive for.

The major point to the distinction between focus and concentration is that focus is not directed by your conscious mind, while concentration is. Even when shooting with a tremendously narrow, concentrated focus, you retain the ability to instantly shift to another equally narrow focus that's directed toward another point. Even in a perfect state of concentration—which is the experience instead of the ambition—the thought process has stopped. When you're getting ready to shoot, instead of telling yourself "front sight, front sight, front sight," or using a phrase over and over, what that could be replaced with is a dead calm mind that is holding a perfect image of what you want to see. If you can create an image of what you want to see, then having that image there could be defined as fairly classical concentration. But even in classical concentration, you want to be aware of turning away from thought; you want to turn everything you want to accomplish into either a feeling or a visualization. You turn away from thought by removing any and all words from your mind.

If you'll start tuning in to what you see *as* you are shooting instead of tuning out everything but what you decide to see *before* you shoot, you'll be on your way to experiencing the distinction between concentration and awareness and focus for yourself. I think that most shooters who have been playing this game for a while will now understand the distinction between these states. The real importance of the understanding is for you to eliminate the *pursuit* of concentration. Because even among shooters who, as is evident by their performances, obviously don't think their way through their shooting still maintain that concentration is what allows them to perform well. That's apparent to me from hearing their common excuse of "losing their concentration" following a poor performance on a stage. Hopefully by just understanding the distinction,

Concentration can exist through awareness; but awareness cannot exist through concentration.

these shooters will be able to understand what it *really* is that allows them to shoot their best.

I rehearse everything I will do on a particular stage before I get to the line—I concentrate on it. But when I raise my hands, I also raise my awareness. I shift my control to automatic and shift my focus to the correct point to successfully shoot the stage. Then I quiet my mind by focusing in the present tense as I immediately prepare to shoot. I no longer follow any plan. I stop thinking. I start shooting. And I act on what I *actually see,* not on what I planned on seeing.

MEDITATION

I once overheard a shooter say that he meditated before he shot. When you understand meditation, hopefully you'll see why you would, instead, want to meditate *as* you shoot. Meditation is simply a state of total awareness of your own function as your senses perceive it.

Your *perception of your functioning* is your awareness at any given instant. Perception is a present tense perspective; it's a constant state of inquiry without comparison and without conclusion. Perception is an ongoing monitor on what you're seeing and what you're feeling. Your perception is controlling what you're doing when you're shooting like you should. And perception is always going to be your limiting factor. Perception never stops. If it stops, then you're starting to function from a conclusion. If you stop and draw a conclusion that, "This is the way it works," now you're a habit shooter. That's a process I trap myself in continually and I guess everyone else does too.

The tricky part of this whole thing becomes the question of if you can't tell yourself or show yourself how to achieve awareness—an active state of meditation—then how do you achieve it? And there isn't a simple answer. By understanding what meditation is *not,* you will recognize when it's there. Any time you attempt to put some control over your thought, then *that's* not meditation. If you have a fixed focus for your mind before you shoot, then *that's* not mediation—that's just another form of a conscious thought (concentration) that you force into your mind. Shooting well requires razor-sharp attention. If a shooter tries to fall into some sort of directed trance, he won't be attentive to his environment—perception becomes limited by equally limited attention.

Anytime you consciously *try* to do something to achieve something else, there's no creativity in your actions. Forcing a thought into your mind in the belief that it will control your actions removes you from the experience. If that one thought is the only input you allow into your mind, then there's no room left there for your subconscious to intuit and control your shooting—as it is perfectly able to do. Thinking short circuits your perception. Anytime you're trying to do something to achieve something else, that would fall under the heading of concentration, not meditation. Concentration is a form of control. But who's the controller? The whole idea of control is just really an abstraction of the thought process. Your words and thoughts may have tricked you into thinking you have control. But control as such—conscious control over the outcome of your shooting—you have no control.

The quieting down of the mind through mediation results in an opening up of the mind to allow all inputs from your environment to come in. A quiet, open mind will perceive everything that's happening and send automatic controls to your body in an endless flow. A mind that's fixed with only one glaring thought in it cannot perceive what's happening beyond that thought. Meditation does not result in a barrier between you and reality. Meditation exposes reality—the truth of what's happening and what you're doing.

A perfect example is in the book, *The Warrior Athlete:* pull your car keys out of your pocket, toss them up into the air, and catch them. In that brief moment when the keys were in the air and your eyes were focused on the keys and you caught the keys, you were experiencing a state of meditation. Your mind was totally free from all thoughts and you had no anxiety over what you were about to do. You were totally focused on the simple act of what you were doing. If you are able to enter into a state of meditation before you shoot, that can help because it will quiet your mind, slow down the chatter, and remove you from the feelings of anxiety. But to fully realize the effects of meditation, you need to be able to meditate *while you're actually shooting*. You must have that state of total open-minded awareness that doesn't reject anything. It totally intuits and processes everything as it's happening. That's what will allow you to have a total "out of body" experience, and you'll find yourself going way beyond what you normally "thought" you could do.

To not risk confusing a shooter from a more regimented sport, such as Action Pistol or PPC, who may be wondering why he would even want to experience a state of meditation—one who may have only ever functioned at a level of concentration and who has done quite well in

**The truth—that which is actually happening—cannot be written down or spoken about.
Once it becomes spoken or written down, it is knowledge. And knowledge is not truth, because knowledge is fixed in time.
And the truth is ever moving and changing, without regard to time.
Truth is outside of all knowledge, of all thought.
As soon as you pause to reflect, it is not truth.**

that state—I want to clarify that the "need" for meditation or awareness is greatest in extremely high-speed shooting, and the higher the speed, the more necessary this level of functioning becomes. In Action or PPC, it's possible to rely on some form of concentration because these sports are much slower, much more mechanical and repetitious disciplines than extremely high-speed IPSC or Steel Challenge-type shooting, and, for the most part, there are very few high-speed decisions and corrections being made during a string of fire in Action or PPC. So since Action and PPC are not as dynamic as IPSC-style shooting, concentration can work well in them, even though, if they really look at it objectively, at the higher skill levels I believe that most "concentrated" shooters will recognize a point where the concentration gives over to meditation or observation.

But the distinction between functioning from classical concentration and functioning through meditation becomes extremely important in high-speed shooting. IPSC shooters must go beyond concentration and learn to function in a state of meditation or awareness—a state of total observation. And the reason that is so important and so necessary is because of the high-speed gun manipulations and the tremendous amount of eye-hand coordination and timing involved. Functioning through awareness and observation is mandatory to be able to instantly adapt to the ever-changing conditions in IPSC. Shooting IPSC in a state of concentration is like trying to play basketball in a state of concentration: there's just too much happening and too much involved to try to focus on only one particular thought or thing.

MINDFUL, NOT THOUGHTFUL

This is a wonderful summary of the distinction between classical concentration and awareness found in *On Learning Golf*. The author's advice on managing a golf swing is that a player should be "mindful, not thoughtful." This is a major point.

The distinction between mindful and thoughtful can be similar to a child learning to walk. The child is just attentive to his own body. He's not thoughtful because he hasn't really learned how to think. Only thoughts can be in memory, so a small child doesn't have a conscious memory of learning to walk. Most people can probably relate to when they learned to ride a bicycle because they had a conscious memory when that happened. You were just attentive to your own body and sensed what you had to do to keep peddling. You didn't learn to ride a bike mechanically, step-by-step. But that's how we learn to shoot and that's why we have so many problems.

People *want* shooting to be technical. They avoid this whole "mental" issue. The reason they are scared of their minds is because they haven't learned to make the distinction between how they learned to ride a bicycle and how they learned to shoot a gun. They try to say that shooting a pistol is something that they should be more proud of or have more control over, whereas riding a bicycle for fun is something that they don't have a big ego attachment about. If shooting a pistol is something you want to have a big ego attachment about and be proud of and have your friends pat you on the back over, if that's your motivation, then this "mental stuff" will scare you. Your ego constructs a barrier between you and the shooting as being separate "things." Total observation and attention removes the barrier between you and the shooting. When you are engaged in just the simple act of watching yourself shoot the targets, then that's all that matters because that's all that's happening. There is no room left for your ego to interject its illusions. Finally when that day comes when you're totally free, when you shoot totally free and creatively, then you shoot beyond any self-imposed limitations that you've ever imagined. And you stop and look at that and you realize that you, and your bundle of words and ideas, can't take credit for it. If you want to avoid that experience, keep plugging on mechanically. Accept the fact that there is a level of shooting that's like this; don't avoid it.

It's only through ego that you ever worry about how you do, how you look, and even how you think. It could be that ego is the source for just about all our problems, but in shooting it's a major point. It's ego that makes us attach ourselves to ideas. It's also ego that forces us to reject ideas and makes us afraid to try things that we may not understand. Don't look at shooting, yourself as a shooter—or the ideas in this book—through your ego. Your ego can draw a line and won't allow anything to cross it that doesn't agree with what it has already decided for you. Don't let your ego make your decisions; don't give it control. Let your choiceless perception of your experiences guide your shooting. But it's your ego that says, "Prove it..." Don't operate in the mode of *prove it—just experience* it. The proof will be in the experience.

If the experience is there, there may be no need for an explanation. Before you go searching for a right answer, consider first that perhaps you've asked a wrong question.

How much of shooting is mental? To me, there is no such question. It's all mental and it's all physical at the same time. We like to categorize things because that's how our brains like to work. Approaching something as precise a motor act as shooting and trying to break it down like that is a wrong question. You can talk about it, but that's not the way it happens. When a shooter can achieve a state of total awareness and gets to the point where he'll ask himself *how much is mental and how much is physical?,* he'll see that there's no need for an answer. I've never had any use for that question, but I've learned that the value of the question can be more important than the answer.

The uselessness of thought. We've become so entrapped with our ideas and thoughts that we believe that everything we think of must have some value or must in some way be real, so our conscious mind invents questions. Just because of the simple fact that it can invent a question, it never stops to think that the question maybe should never even be a question. Since your brain can string words together in sentences, and since you can put a question mark at the end of a sentence, the question is now possible and you believe that it must have some value and that it must be answered. And if you can't come up with the answer, you're left in a state of confusion, when the actual fact of the matter is that there's no place for the question. A perfect example is the age-old question of *which came first, the chicken or the egg?* That question is ridiculous. There's no such question possible because the chicken and the egg are the same thing.

REACTION AND HABIT

Consistency in shooting comes from being able to instantly and intuitively act on what your awareness shows you is happening. Consistency does not come from doing one thing the same way over and over. If you can function in the present tense and, thereby, allow focus and awareness to control your shooting, each performance will be consistent with your current skill level. To me, that's the most valuable property you can have as a shooter.

Conscious thought is the greatest hindrance to the proper execution of all physical action.
—Bruce Lee

There should be little tolerance for habit in shooting. Habit is the unaware, mechanical repetition of action. Habit can be either physical or mental. Habit, according to my definition, has its roots in the past, as memory; therefore, anything done as a habit will be lacking spontaneity and creativity. Habits are a better cage for a lot of actions than having no focus at all, but habit can be a very limiting cage to try to break out of. Some shooters feel that it's worthwhile to ingrain reactions to certain situations or signals and they will practice the same things over and over again until they become reflexive. You must continue to learn with every shot you fire, practice or match. No matter how practiced, any idea from previous conditioning must not affect the shooting as it is about to happen or is happening. Avoid habit by focusing in the present tense on what is happening—calling the shots as you shoot them—without a thought in your head.

Don't react, just *act*. When I hear "reaction," right away my mind goes to the word "habit." As long as we can keep reaction down to its pure form, we can relate it to awareness and focus. Pure reaction comes from the subconscious. The conscious mind processes information like a computer: it searches its memory until it matches a known response to handle the situation. If you can allow the subconscious to direct your shooting, the physical reaction to meet the demands of the shooting is able to bypass the searching—it takes a shortcut straight to the gun. And "allow" is the operative word.

A perfect example of pure reaction is when you shoot a miss on a steel target and make the shot up before your gun ever starts to move away from the target. You can do that because you were aware and you read the sights at the time they lifted before you ever moved the gun away. Your vision called the shot a miss, and by having the desire to hit the target, you shot it again. In retrospect, you realize that it all happened before your brain noticed that you didn't hear the sound of no sound. You reacted off your visual inputs as opposed to your hearing. Your awareness may bring in inputs from sound, but they are way behind light speed. Therefore, reacting off hearing is a habit. You see the sights and you see the target—your focus is visual—and hearing has nothing to do with that. If you catch yourself shooting a miss on a steel target and have your gun start swinging to the next target, you know you were reacting from hearing. Your gun leaves the target because your vision didn't call the shot a hit. When the sound of no sound finally registers, you'll swing back to shoot the target again.

When you're in a state of meditation, your mind is in a state of undirected total awareness. And when you're visually aware in that state, your body short circuits its normal reactionary process. If you're visually aware of the miss, you can shoot that makeup shot much faster than you could have ever thought possible. It's so fast that it's noticeable to an observer, and they ask, "How did you make it up so fast?" The reason they don't understand how is because they're stuck in the habit of hearing; they're confirming their hits on steel by waiting on sound. And that is too slow. Visual awareness is definitely the way to process information about your hits on steel, but because the steel goes "ding," it's easy to be lulled into the habit of listening for the hits.

A very good example of this happened to me years ago at the Steel Challenge on *5 To Go*. It was the first time I won that stage. I was shooting along on my first run and in my mind I called a perfect shot on the third plate. I had no reason to believe that the shot was a miss, but I didn't hear a single sound come back from the plate. My gun was already to the fourth plate so I shot it, and as I came back to make up the shot on the third plate, I saw a bullet splatter dead in the center of the third plate.

I stopped to think about that a little bit before I shot the next strings. It scared me. I thought, "I'm really in trouble because I shot that plate dead center and I didn't hear it." It caused an immediate anxiety attack to learn that I couldn't rely on my hearing. I decided that the only way to beat this was to just say that if I call the shot a hit then I'm not going back. I'm going to stick strictly to my basic strategy—visualizing the plates as being made of paper and then going down to score the hits when I'm done. So I did that, I focused. That fear, in retrospect, just caused me to call each shot on each plate in real detail. I never had a single miss.

Sometimes habit can work fine for a beginning shooter who's trying to learn a mechanic or something in a technical sense. Certain mechanical habits are ingrained. You can decide which things you need to routinely perform in the course of shooting that are essentially unvaried from stage to stage. If you're going to stand and make a normal draw, your habitual, ingrained draw is going to work well for you. But if you've got to make that same draw from leaning around the side of a barricade or in some other circumstance like kneeling or sitting, then the habit is not going to do you any good.

But it's important that actual *shooting* fundamentals don't become habits. For instance, if you've made following the front sight a habit, you'll have to discard that to take advantage of the different focus types that are available to you. Even a habit of automatically shooting when your sight focus is clear will get you into trouble when you may have to wait for a target to get out of the way before you can hit it. Anytime a scenario can best be negotiated in a different manner than what you're used to, then awareness and focus will serve you better than habit.

When you're beginning, you will develop some habits to help you build your basic shooting platform—you have to have a place to start in developing your skills—but realize that the habits will end someday. This is the same thing

I was talking about in the *Introduction* when I said that the mechanics only exist so that you can go beyond them. Something that really distinguishes a top shooter is that it doesn't really matter to him if he has to roll over on his back for every shot. The weirder it gets and the harder it gets, the more separation you'll see between a top shooter and the guy who's a few percent behind him. The top shooter can deal with those problems because he's not having to rely on habit to do his shooting for him. The person who shoots out of habit is stuck—he can't adapt to anything; he can't break free of his program. You just need to understand how habit works for you and when habit works against you.

YOU ALREADY HAVE THE SKILLS

The things I've been talking about in this section aren't difficult to do and they are not things that you don't already understand and experience perhaps hundreds of times each day. You just need to see how they apply in your shooting. Most competitive shooters have built shooting up in their minds as somehow being something that's complex and difficult to the point that they don't believe it's possible to shoot in the same way they do other complex things. Take just about anything you do that requires some motor skill and break it down into an exact, step-by-step description. Really go into perfect detail about some process—putting on your gear at the range, making a left-hand turn in your car—and think each miniscule detail through as if you were trying to program a computer to perform the task. Prove it to yourself that you can approach just about everything you do in a day in the same fashion most people approach shooting. But you don't need to do that; you just strap on your holster or make the left-hand turn. *And you just shoot the targets...*

This may be all you ever have to be aware of on some stages, but there's usually a lot more going on beyond it that you can open yourself up to.

A comparison of using awareness and focus in place of concentration is riding a motorcycle on a busy street. Concentration would be only looking for cars that are making left-hand turns in front of you. But through awareness, you can peripherally see all that's happening. If you see a car make a right turn in front of you, that's what you'd focus on. In that sense you'll be very concentrated on that car where the concentration is a narrowing of the focus. When that car was out of the picture, you'd again open up to perceive everything that's happening around you. When something else threatened your ride—say a ball rolling into the street—you instantly narrow your focus to making all efforts to avoid hitting it. From your experience in riding the motorcycle, you know how quickly you can swerve and how hard you can apply the brakes. And you simply do it.

Operating any vehicle is definitely an awareness, focus, feedback process. You're open to and aware of all inputs that are coming into your mind as you're driving—your speed, direction, traffic lights, oncoming traffic, traffic that's behind and to the side of you, maybe a conversation you're having with your passenger. You're constantly monitoring all these things by shifting your focus to the rearview mirror, the dashboard, the road, and so on. You don't concentrate on any one thing. When something requires your attention or action, such as a car cutting you off your lane, your focus shifts away from everything that doesn't have to do with avoiding that situation—it narrows down and becomes very concentrated. And in the middle of that narrow focus, you're receiving feedback as to how you're handling the situation. You'll act on your perception of what that feedback tells you to the best of your ability. And that's how you should shoot. Further along in the book, I'll talk a lot more about feedback and how to use and intuit what it brings you as you shoot.

Being totally aware of all inputs possible is a really different game you have to play in IPSC or any type of high-speed shooting. For instance, in the Masters *Speed Event,* you sometimes have to gauge how far a plate has fallen before you can shoot the next one. Your eye has to look at so many things during the course of fire. It's not like a static type of shooting, like bullseye, where that shooter can be fairly comfortable knowing that the only thing he has to be aware of is his front sight on the target. That may be the only thing he ever needs to see. On some IPSC courses, that may be the only thing you ever have to see, but in many of them there are a lot of areas you can open up your awareness to. Instead of just watching the front sight, you have to notice targets that may be moving, areas to place your feet, angles to engage no-shoots: *paying attention to anything and everything that can have an effect on your shooting is what I mean by awareness.*

Don't concentrate on your shooting —get interested in it.

Section 2: THE TOOLS OF SHOOTING

Techniques do not make the shooter. The shooter *is* the technique. These are the tools you'll need to fire a gun accurately at a high rate of speed, and that's all they are.

This section will give you some creative ideas you can use to help you develop your own freestyle technique. The first thing you should understand is that no technique, no matter how worthy or desirable, is ever an end in itself. Even when shooting 100 *El Presidentes* in a row, the elements of your shooting technique—grip, sight tracking, muscle tension, eye focus, and so on—are all constantly changing. Each requires continuous monitoring for the technique to be effective as a whole. Names that denote "styles" such as *Isosceles, Chapman,* and *Weaver* really only cause confusion about the actual technique being used. Some people say that I shoot from an Isosceles position, and without close analysis it would appear that I do. Actually there are quite a few differences between my overall technique and a pure Isosceles. When you isolate and define a technique by giving it a name, you turn an alive, ever-changing action into a static and lifeless pose.

Your technique as a whole is only a summary of all the separate components of your technique, and the quality of the overall technique depends on the shooter having a complete awareness of all its individual components. All those individual components should be tailored to fit your needs and the needs of the shooting. Think of each mechanic as being a means to realizing a result in your performance. It's important that you are aware of the effects each of these mechanics should have on your performance, and if you retain that awareness as you begin to experience the results for yourself, your best shooting style will surface.

The mechanics exist only to prepare the shooter to rise above them.

The only function of good form is that it affords maximum shooting efficiency; the mechanics I believe work the best give the shooter physical control in the least compensating manner. Good mechanics give you the physical means to open up and experience the shooting by not restricting the shooting. Good mechanics enhance awareness and focus. But always keep in mind that good mechanics won't, by themselves, make you a good shooter. What you actually do, technique-wise, is not nearly as important as your understanding and being aware of *what* you're doing *when* you're doing it. Many people have achieved great successes in their shooting without having "perfect" form. Dedication and determination are two often overlooked, but very important, aspects of realizing your potential. Confidence in shooting does not come from "knowing how." It comes from learning continually on every shot. You can never learn to shoot. You can only learn *as* you shoot if you want to reach your potential.

This section will give you the means to develop a fundamental base to shoot from. I refer to this position as the *freestyle platform*. To detail what I mean by that, it's the overall shooting posture you'll use by preference. When you're just going to stand and shoot, the freestyle platform is what you assume when you draw and mount the gun.

ACCURACY: THE FIRST FUNDAMENTAL

Before you even start with the goal of acquiring a freestyle platform and learning the fundamentals of IPSC shooting, you need to have the objective of learning how to shoot a gun accurately. That's something I was forced into since my first competitive shooting was in PPC; if you don't shoot accurately there, you're not even going to play that game. *I cannot stress the importance of accuracy enough*. Although it might be difficult for you to make the connections initially, learning to shoot accurately is directly related to most everything you'll need to do to become a successful practical shooter. I execute the same fundamentals of precision shooting as do shooters in other sports—the time limits are just radically shortened. Trust me: at the Steel Challenge, Bianchi Cup, and on any number of IPSC stages, my ability to fire with precision can be taxed tremendously.

Learning to shoot accurately is the most important time you'll spend in developing yourself as a practical shooter.

When shooters start up through IPSC, and all they shoot is IPSC, this "accuracy-incidental" background really shows when they reach a certain level. Most every club has several shooters who fit this category exactly—those who have broken through into Master class, but are stuck at the lower level of Masters. They never really learned the fundamentals of accuracy and what it takes to make an accurate shot. They never spent time at the range shooting off a rest and shooting prone and freestyle and seeing how tightly they can group their shots. They've got the gun handling down—they can run fast and reload fast and maneuver the gun quickly on the targets—but they just don't have the experience to back them up on any shot that's of any difficulty level at all. Sometimes they can burn through a stage, but the next time they're going to be erratic, and this is a main reason why.

And it's pointless to impose a limitation by defining what "acceptable" accuracy is. There's no point to saying that you need to be able to shoot, for instance, a 3-inch group off a rest at 50 yards. You need to have the skill to do that, certainly, but your gun and loads may not do it. *You just want to see an improvement.* If you stick with a program of learning to shoot accurately and shooting groups standing and from a supported position, you're just looking for an improvement. You want to see the groups getting smaller and smaller and you want to see the flyers go away.

You can get to where you can shoot to the gun's ability at 50 yards. I've shot 10-shot 1.5 inch groups with my .38 Super using major loads. There's no limit to how good you can get; the only limit is your equipment. There's no doubt that your eye and your body have the ability to shoot the gun from a stable, rested position to the gun's ability. And there's no reason to ever think you've reached any point in your ability to shoot accurately until you can shoot to your gun's ability. If you can do that from a rest, you can then attempt the same thing standing. But there's never any time to stop and say, "There, now I've mastered the fundamentals of shooting a gun accurately..." I've been shooting groups all the time I've been shooting. It's amazing, but I still find that every time I shoot groups I learn *something*. Even if I feel like I can shoot a gun to its potential, I still learn. I'm still aware of things. I see new visual inputs; I'm aware of very subtle things—things I see in breathing, pressures, heartbeats.

Working on accuracy has a major effect on learning the other aspects of shooting too: developing and refining positions, relaxation, pressures, stability. When you're shooting a group you're more sensitive to what's going on. You can get all kinds of inputs by just watching the exact angle the sight lifts. You might notice that you didn't catch the sight lift on your first shot and it didn't return to where it started, or maybe it returned too low because you were holding the gun down on the bags too much. Eventually you'd like to get to the point where the gun tracks exactly the same on every shot so you don't have to shift the gun's position each time to line it up. When I shoot my best groups, the sight tracks in exactly the same way each shot and returns to the same spot each time. Your body position has got to be neutral and relaxed to do that. You can almost shoot groups blindfolded if your body is aware.

When you move to shooting groups from your freestyle platform, you'll find that it's a good way to work out bugs in your grip and position. You have to be in a very relaxed, neutral position to shoot good groups and to experience consistent shot-to-shot gun movement and sight tracking. Learn from what you experience. How do you need to stand, how do your hands and arms have to be, how do you feel, overall, when you're able to find that consistency? I'll talk more about this later, but realize up front that accuracy work will be a central focus in your full development as a practical shooter.

Later in the book I'll also make the point that you must practice what you don't like to do if you want to become a well-rounded shooter, but I'll initiate that advice here because it really relates to how a lot of IPSC-bred shooters feel about the whole subject of group shooting. If you don't like to shoot groups, then don't ever expect to be a top-level shooter—because you never will be. If you haven't mastered the fundamental of accuracy and haven't learned to do exactly what it takes to produce an accurate shot and you can't do it on demand, then you can never expect to beat whoever is at the top. I can confidently say that there isn't a top shooter who can't shoot extremely accurately.

Although I'll talk more about this in the *Group Shooting* appendix, there are a few things you should pay attention to that will help you shoot more accurately. The first is understanding sight alignment and sight picture. The sights are correctly aligned when the front sight is exactly centered in the rear notch and the top of the front sight is exactly level with the top line of the rear sight. Sight picture describes how the sights appear relative to each other and to the target.

You can never learn to shoot; you can only learn *as* you shoot. Never limit yourself to what you know.

A real "textbook" focus on the front sight will give you the best results when you're shooting for extreme precision. In order from sharpest to fuzziest as you perceive them are front sight, rear sight, target. I focus exactly on the top center of the front sight, not just on the sight itself. Let that focus shoot the shot for you.

Experiment with shifting your focus from the sight to the target to center the gun in the correct place. Don't put *any* pressure on the trigger until the gun is centered and aligned in the area where you'd like to release the shot. Then notice any shifting of the gun's position as you start to put pressure on the trigger. That will help you to be more neutral on the gun.

Followthrough is one of the most important fundamentals of accurate shooting. Followthrough, essentially, means that you are able to fire the gun when the sights are exactly where you want them without causing the sights to move. Followthrough comes from having the visual attention and acuity to monitor the exact placement of the sights every millisecond until the gun fires, and most importantly, at the exact instant that the gun actually fires. You don't sight the gun and pull the trigger as two distinct operations; it's all one operation. Your sighting awareness controls the trigger pressure, and it's all happening at the same time. This is the main understanding you must have about followthrough. Even though you're stable and happen to be rested on a bench, you cannot separate visual awareness and trigger pull into two processes. Followthrough is a visual process that your body follows. Pulling the trigger is just coinciding with attempting to keep the sights aligned as still as possible. And there's never any time pressure; there's never any feeling toward trying to hurry up and get the job done sooner.

Followthrough is visually staying with the shot so that you can call it exactly. Visual attention and trigger pull are not separate things. There should never be a sensation of seeing and then shooting. You see all the time you shoot.

LEARNING THE MECHANICS

Even though the importance of the mechanics is in that you learn them so that you can go beyond them, unless you put forth some effort to improve your technique by improving individual aspects of it, you may actually limit yourself to staying in the rut of mechanics. Without developing a relaxed, neutral shooting platform to work from, for example, it will be very difficult for you to get your attention away from your technique and onto your shooting.

I've broken down and analyzed each of the components of technique because that's the only way they can be understood. But you can't think about the pieces while you're actually shooting. It sounds like a contradiction to say that you should do this and do that, and then, in the same breath, say that you can't think about it while you're doing it. But it's really not. Learning though awareness is an endless, full-circle experience. When you know what you want to see, your awareness will show you what you need to *do* to see it. Through awareness, there is no distinction between learning and application, even though intellect and instinct are generally thought of separately. Maintaining awareness as you're experimenting with your technique will allow you to almost immediately change, add, or discard any variation on a particular component of your shooting style as you intuit your experience.

As you're experimenting with different components, don't discard something you feel is important just because you realize that you're not doing it the way you want in all your practice runs. Frustration can set in if you attempt to experience shooting as I advocate before the new way is physically there on demand. If the change is something major, such as moving from a Weaver to a neutral-type stance, remove yourself from actually shooting until the basic physical change is more spontaneous. Dry-firing and just thinking through and visualizing the change, over and over again in detail, will get you where the stance you want is what you'll have when you draw and mount the gun. There is no such thing as "muscle memory" because your muscles don't think. When you're making a fundamental change in some component of your technique, you often have to pay full, conscious attention to it.

If you're a beginning shooter, slowing down your study of the mechanics may speed up your progress. For some things, you may accelerate your improvement by learning each component piece-by-piece. When you're learning the draw, for instance, you might want to first work on getting both hands to the right spot until you have the fundamental of your hands going straight to where they should. When you can do that, then move on to getting the gun up and to the target. If you want to reach your potential, it's important that you develop the skills that a good application of the mechanics will give you. Even if it takes you several months to get to where your freestyle platform is what you want, that just means that from that time forward you can devote your time to experiencing the shooting instead of working on your mechanics.

Be aware of what you're actually doing at the time you're actually doing it. Keep yourself open to your experiences.

And don't ever be afraid to make a change in your shooting technique. As you progress beyond the point where you feel the basic motions, positions, and sequences are correct, then any minor variances will show their values very quickly. Once you have the confidence and experience to realize that your intuitive sense will allow you to either change or not change something, that will remove the fear of experimentation. With the correct focus, you don't have to worry about learning bad habits. Maintaining awareness as you are shooting won't allow anything that doesn't serve you to remain active as you shoot. Through awareness, you no longer fight the dogmas of prior limitations and limiting beliefs. You can adopt whatever your observations show you is working best. You'll be able to try different things without worrying that trying something that turns out not to work will "mess up" your shooting. If you keep yourself open to your experiences, and let them guide you, that won't happen. Trust that, and trust yourself.

CAUSE & EFFECT

As I mentioned earlier, mechanics should be thought of as results you'd like to see in your performance. Don't ever get concerned with trying to just clone positions because there are a lot of different ways to get where you want to go. Instead of thinking of the mechanics of a good grip as being just ways to place your hands on the gun, think of them as a way to help you achieve neutrality and consistency. When you're working on your grip, keep clear what the grip means to your performance. "Knowing" the better grip is only the most limiting prerequisite to improved performance.

The relationship between mechanics and results isn't something as simple as "cause and effect." That phrase is, in itself, limiting because it alludes to an idea that if you do one thing then everything else will be affected in some predestined way. And that's not true. Causes and effects can be the same things; therefore, it's impossible to separate them. At the very least, it's obvious that as long as we all perceive the same things differently, then causes and effects won't "work" the same way for everyone. Your perception is your internal cause and effect monitor. Cause and effect is too delicate and complex of an actual process to try to discover black and white relationships in. The truth about cause and effect is that the whole area is gray.

Free yourself from the "do this to get that" syndrome.

Through experiencing awareness in your shooting, the causes and effects are no longer even important. Being aware of what you, and the gun, are doing on each shot will quickly show you how well you're exercising your technique—whatever that may be at the time. Don't analyze what you're doing as you're experiencing the shooting, because that would immediately take you away from the experience. After the shooting, you can think back on your internal sensations and what you saw and find a direction to take your experiments. But with a high level of awareness as you are shooting, the internal sensations and external results will be very close to the same.

NO LIMITATIONS

When I began practical pistol shooting I had only very basic ideas about technique. So I did what I felt was the logical thing. I found the best local shooter (who was also competitive nationally) and asked him how I should shoot. He told me without hesitation: left index finger on the trigger guard, left elbow bent and pulling back, classic boxer stance, etcetera, etcetera. I adopted this system blindly for a year or two before wondering whether there might be a system that better suited my structure and attitude, and one that better suited the shooting. This first style that I adopted didn't seem to fit me because it felt as though I was having to struggle to control the gun; I was never actually flowing with the gun as I feel I do now. My experimentation led me to pull ideas from all types of shooting styles: Isosceles, Modified Weaver, Bullseye, and from people such as Bill Blankenship, shotgunner John Satterwhite, and martial artist Bruce Lee.

But ideas coming from your environment only steer you in the right direction. These ideas can limit your thinking by their very nature, whereas all truly great ideas will arise from a feeling within yourself. This intuitive awareness will allow you to accept anything that works for you and discard anything that doesn't. Ideas from within yourself are limitless and can expand to meet any situation. Using feelings and ideas from within your mind you create your own total style. This total style has no name because it is constantly changing to fit into any environment or to meet any situation. The more I shoot, the more I'm convinced that my "style" becomes more flexible, not more fixed. My "style" changes every time I draw and fire.

THE COMPONENTS OF TECHNIQUE

Following is an analysis of what I believe each component of an efficient shooting technique should accomplish, as well as how I perform them specifically. None of this is cut-checkered into metal anywhere. The advice in this section comes from experiencing my own evolution as a shooter. Keep what works; modify what doesn't; discard the rest. Regardless of how you might gravitate from any specific form I suggest as you experience your own unique evolution of technique (which will be continuous), I do think that what's coming is a good place for you to start.

GRIP

Consistency and *neutrality* are the goals. You should have a totally neutral feeling in each hand. Achieving neutrality allows the grip and stance technique to perform its most important function: allowing the gun to recoil in the same direction, to the same level, and on the same path—both in lift off the target and return to the target—on each shot. The grip and stance cannot control recoil in the sense of *stopping* recoil. That's not possible. What is possible is control of the sight and gun, and that's what a neutral grip helps you realize.

If the recoil you experience is consistent, it really does not matter how high the muzzle actually lifts.

I define "neutrality" by both position and tension. If you were pressing your palms together in a "praying" position about 8 inches from your chest, an observer couldn't tell how hard you were pressing. You may be pushing hard or your hands may just be barely touching. Your hands aren't moving, so it appears, in positioning, to be a neutral grip, but that's not what you want. If you were to place your hands in that position and leave one-half-inch of space between them, that would much more accurately describe a neutral grip. You want to have that same feeling with your arms extended into a normal position. Practice that by dry-drawing without the gun and just running both fists out, leaving about one-half-inch space between them. You don't want to force your hands against each other. You'll also immediately realize that there's no pushing/pulling with either arm.

This accurately describes neutrality in the grip. Practice this until you get the feel for equal pressure in the hands.

Something that seems so simple but is actually an important point to understand is that the only reason both hands grip the pistol in the same place is because the pistol only has one grip. If a pistol had two vertical grips, then you could easily see the importance of not gripping the pistol with any side pressure from either hand. If you used side pressure you'd never be able to hold the muzzle pointing in any steady direction. Even while both hands are gripping one grip as one grip, neither hand is exerting any pressure toward the other. A good test is to set up a target at 7 yards and put two shots into the A-box freestyle and then take away your support hand and immediately shoot two more shots into the A-box strong-hand. And when you take the support hand away to fire those shots, pay attention to how the gun's muzzle moves. If the muzzle tracks to one side, then you can see that your grip isn't neutral.

A neutral grip requires sensitivity of touch. A death grip not only takes away your feel to the point where you can no longer discern variances in the levels of pressure you're holding the gun with, but it also means that you're not able to return the sight to the target as consistently. If your hands are positioned well, and if your stance supports the neutrality of your grip, then there will be very little pressure required to stabilize the gun. Of course, there is some amount pressure involved in firing a gun. This pressure, however, should never exceed what's necessary to just suspend the pistol in a level position and keep it from dropping down. Experiment with this feeling.

Natural tension progresses outward from the draw as the gun goes toward target. You have to trust that. If you start out with only the necessary amount of pressure necessary to suspend the pistol, any additional pressure required to control the gun will come naturally and instinctively. It's like driving a car: when you're idling along at 20 mph, you're gripping the steering wheel very lightly because that's all that's necessary to control the car. But when the speed increases to 40 and then to 60 mph, or when you turn the wheel to negotiate a curve, your pressure on the wheel increases from the feedback you're getting from the road. You don't consciously increase your gripping tension; your gripping tension increases from your desire to control the car. If the speed became increasingly faster and faster, the feedback from the steering wheel would automatically increase the pressure in your grip to what's necessary to keep the car in control.

The same goes for shooting. You cannot maintain a death grip as recoil moves through your hands. And it really does not take much pressure to control a pistol; so little, in fact, that only a trust in the fact that you know the amount of pressure needed is all that's necessary. You are using only the force needed. It is a similar idea when you push the gas pedal to the floor in your car. Any effort beyond simply overcoming the spring pressure on the pedal is wasted. For a reference to the amount of gripping tension you should start with, hold the gun with about the same pressure in your hands as if you were going to drive a nail into a wall with a hammer. It's a firm, relaxed grip that allows you to maintain flexibility in your wrist.

The support hand should touch the pistol frame, not just the grip panel. You should be able to hold the gun with only your support hand.

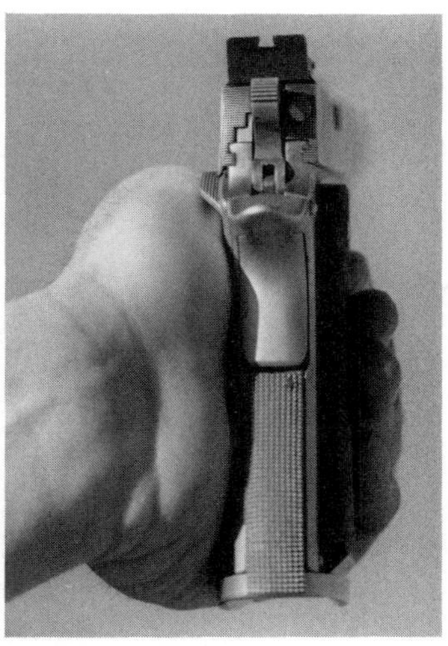

Hand Positions

The shooting hand should be positioned as high on the gun as is comfortable, and should be securely and firmly up into the grip safety. The closer the line of the bore of the gun is to your hands, the less mechanical advantage the muzzle has to lift in recoil. I'll talk more about this subject in *Appendix A* regarding grip safeties.

Part of achieving neutrality in the grip means that the support hand must be directly and equally involved with holding the gun. The support hand doesn't just contact the shooting hand, it also touches the pistol itself. The heel-portion below the thumb of the support hand makes full contact with the grip panel. I work my support hand into the pistol so that the heel of my shooting hand is locked together with the heel of my support hand. I'm not pressing my hands together; they're just butted against each other. The result is a "locked" grip, but one without excess tension. You should be able to take away your shooting hand once you've gripped the gun and easily hold the gun level using only your support hand. This grip positions the support hand so it can provide exactly the same gripping force as the shooting hand.

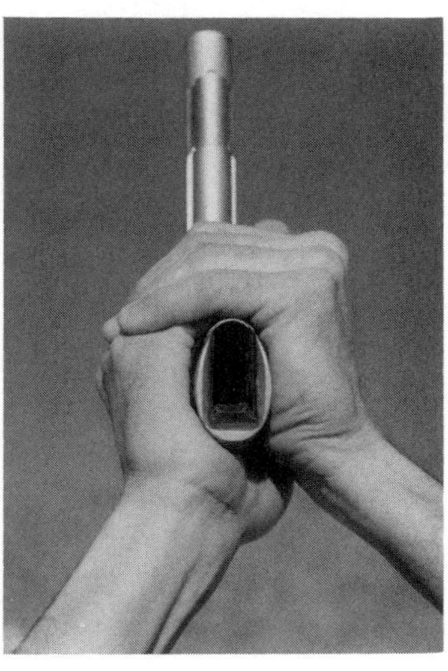

The heels of my hands are butted solidly against each other, but there is no inward pressure from hand -to-hand.

With this grip, the support hand is positioned slightly forward on the gun so that the support-hand fingers can just engulf the shooting hand. The support hand should also be placed as high up on the gun as is comfortably possible, with the index finger firmly up against the bottom of the trigger guard. There should be no gaps in the fingers of either hand, and while some shooters like to extend the support hand's index finger to wrap around the front of the trigger guard, I don't think this technique offers as strong a grip. The thumb and index finger are the strongest part of your grip, and when you put one of them up on the trigger guard you've split them apart. You lose not only your strength but also some of your consistency because the index finger is now having to grip independently and is introducing another pressure point that can change in different shooting situations. If you have some type of hook device on your trigger guard, this type of grip is a possibility, but it still requires exerting what I think is inconsistent and excessive pressure.

Top: Both thumbs are pointed at the target, but neither touches the gun. Doing so can steer the muzzle.

Bottom: Both hands are as high on the gun as is comfortable. Notice the slight arch in the support wrist. This adds a downward camming action.

When the safety lever is depressed, the shooting-hand thumb can stay atop the lever. A lot of top shooters do this to gain a little leverage to help hold the muzzle down. I can't use that technique because the heel of my support hand is placed up high enough on the gun that my thumb presses on that instead of the safety. My thumbs just fit together naturally with the grip I use, and neither thumb touches the gun. So I don't really feel like there's any benefit to pressing on the safety; I'd rather let the pistol recoil freely. But I don't really want to recommend that you not try that. I do recommend, however, that you don't press down really hard on the lever. Anytime you introduce more pressure than is needed to just hold the gun, there's the chance that different shooting circumstances may cause you to use inconsistent pressure. If you do rest your thumb on the lever, look for wear marks on the slide and install a thumb shield on your gun if you see them.

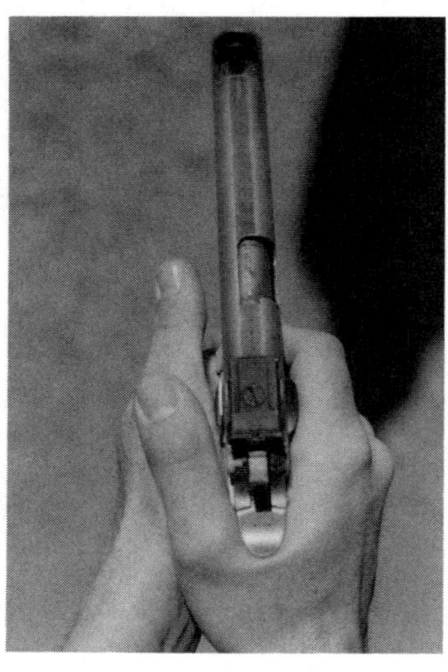

I extend my left thumb and point it pretty forcefully at the target, alongside the frame of the gun and on the same line as the slide release. A lot of people using this high grip force their support thumbs inward against the slide or frame, and I don't really have any use for that at all. Again, I prefer to just let the gun recoil freely. Pressing the thumb inward against the gun will steer the muzzle, and that pressure is just one more thing that will change from day to day and from string to string.

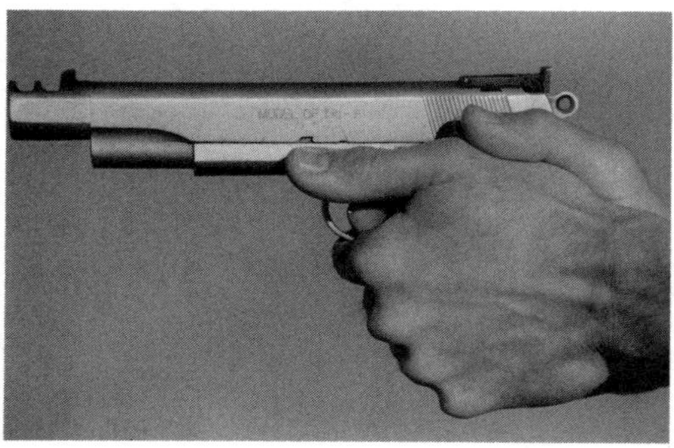

When viewed from the side, the support hand is cammed down slightly over wrist center; there is a slight arch in the upper wrist bone. The action of the wrists only having to break back up to their center helps return the muzzle more quickly after recoil lifts it. This action is similar to what you experience if you were to shake your finger to scold someone. To discover this position, bring the gun up in front of you to where it's about one foot from your face and at eye level. Now level the muzzle so it's parallel to the ground and notice how your support wrist cams downward. That's how things should be at the finish of a normal draw. Incorporating this camming action into your grip is a reliable way to help reduce some muzzle flip without penalty because it achieves the effect through position instead of pressure.

Your finger will fall on the trigger where it will. There is no perfect position. The position that will work best for you depends partially on your grip and the length of your finger. I've noticed that my finger is positioned on the trigger in different places depending on the speed with which I'm manipulating the trigger and on shooting conditions.

The most important goal of a good grip is that it gives consistent muzzle control so that the sight is always coming up and down in exactly the same pattern. It's that consistency that offers the possibility of high-speed shooting. You want the gun to recoil as if it were in a machine, and, as I mentioned earlier, I've proven it to myself that it doesn't really matter how high the sight tracks in recoil as long as it returns to the exact same place and that it travels on the exact same path to get there. Watch how the sight tracks in recoil and make sure it's moving consistently, regardless of the shooting situation.

The grip is solid, relaxed, and neutral. Hold the gun with about the same tension you'd use to hammer a nail.

Neutrality is both pressure and position in your hands. Pressure should be absolutely equal in each hand, and through your relaxed group shooting you'll be able to sense the best positions for each hand to be in to achieve neutral gun movement. It's an even better idea to not even fire at a target. Just direct the gun to the berm and pay attention to the gun and sight movement.

STANCE

Control

There is no effective way to actually stop recoil from happening. All we can do is recover from it as precisely, consistently, and quickly as possible. A technique that results in consistent control can be accomplished only by keeping your mind and body relaxed and your *antagonistic* muscle tension to a minimum. *Antagonistic muscles* are those that aren't directly involved in supporting the gun. Any tension in these muscles threatens the neutrality of your stance and will cause the muzzle to track inconsistently during recoil.

Muscle tension does *not* provide recoil control. Prove this to yourself by a test: the next time you're at the range, grip the pistol with as much muscle tension as possible using your hands, arms, and shoulders. Have a friend gently pull the trigger so that the gun fires unexpectedly. Watch the muzzle. You will see plenty of recoil or muzzle flip, and you'll also notice that the muzzle tends to stay elevated.

Recoil recovery is only possible through exercising the fundamentals of position, timing, and relaxation. If you're not too tense, rigid, or locked up, a lot of the gun's energy can be absorbed into your body and through your arms. Then the gun won't appear to batter you around as it will in a shooter who's so "locked in" that the gun's energy can only serve to destabilize his stance on each shot.

And it's important to understand that I apply the very same ideas whether I'm shooting my practical race gun, my .22, my .44 Magnums, or a 5-inch gun with bowling pin loads. No gun can be consistently controlled through muscular tension or effort.

Arms

The shooting and support arms are relatively straight. Some shooters may find it works better if their arms are locked, straight, or slightly unlocked, and in varying degrees with each arm. From looking at a lot of top shooters, I've found that this is a totally different position for everyone. Some people's arms hyper-extend naturally straight and long; other's arms are several degrees back off of locked. It doesn't really matter whether your arms are straight or bent as long as they're relaxed and you don't have to use any unequal muscle tension to hold the gun. Tension in the bicep of the shooting arm seems to be especially detrimental. Wherever your arms naturally extend without having to be forced into any position is where they should be. Just be alert to feeling any excess tension.

I've found that relaxing my arms and positioning them so they're just shy of being locked gives me better control because I'm visually able to react faster to recoil. The more relaxed state reduces tension to the point where my timing becomes extremely precise. In other words, I control recoil just through my visual awareness of where the gun is at all times. I believe that a more relaxed, neutral position is what allows this extremely precise high-speed seeing to control the gun. For shooters who feel they do their best by having their arms locked, it's important that they understand that "locked" does not have to mean "tense." When

Whether straight or bent, the arms must be relaxed. Be especially alert to any tension in the bicep of the shooting arm.

the elbow is in a locked position for shooting, it's the same natural locking that accompanies things you do every day: picking up a toolbox, reaching up to a shelf, etc. A correct, tension-free lockup actually takes stress off the arm muscles; it's a gentle stopping place when the arms extend. Avoid stretching them out too far forward and forcing your arms to lock up beyond that natural stopping place. Doing so—plus "unplugging" your arms from your shoulders by stretching too far forward—causes too much tension in the antagonistic muscles. If your arms are locked straight through tension, or if your arms are bent because there's so much tension that they can't extend any farther, neither position is correct for you. The main thing is that your arms are in a relaxed, natural position and are not forced there.

The overall shooting stance should be relaxed and neutral. I keep my back straight, flex my knees, and lean forward slightly from my waist—just enough to feel balanced. The knee flex is crucial.

Posture

I shoot from an essentially upright stance in that my spine is straight. I bend my knees down somewhat because my legs move my upper body and pistol from target to target. I don't twist from my waist to move the gun. I stay still from the waist up to keep the gun centered in my upper body triangle. The knees must be kept flexible to allow this type of gun movement. The faster I need to shoot, the more my knees bend down.

There should be a certain amount of weight placed forward to counter recoil, but avoid any sort exaggerated forward-leaning stance as that can lead to tension in different antagonistic muscles. I don't really lean forward so much as I just flex my knees to give me a balanced, stable position; the knee flex moves my center of gravity down and slightly forward. My weight slightly favors the balls of my feet and I bend forward slightly from my waist—just enough to counteract the recoil of the gun and to feel slightly aggressive. Bending from the waist allows my spine to stay straight.

I feel that it's very important to allow your shoulders to stay naturally down and back and into their sockets as they

In a neutral stance, recoil is directed straight back, not laterally. The farther the centerline of the gun shifts from body center, the more recoil will destabilize the stance.

are when you're standing at rest. Having relaxed stability is important when you must face multiple targets or multiple shots on one target. For a physical key, don't allow your shoulders to extend beyond your chest. Another key is keeping your spine straight; overextending your arms will round your shoulders and cause your spine to bow.

The head should be positioned so that the eye can look directly out of its socket and straight through the sights. Avoid extreme head positions such as canting to one side. The more naturally upright and centered your head can be, the better. Tilting your head too much can impair visual perception and peripheral vision, and, in an extreme case, even your balance. And bring the pistol up to your eye level, not the other way around.

Alignment

You should stand, essentially, directly facing the target. I say "essentially" because most shooters position their weak sides slightly forward; I stand with my right foot a little bit farther back than my left for reasons I'll go into shortly. Avoid any extremes as you don't want to pull the gun away from your body's centerline. Ideally, if you drew a straight line back from the target and through the pistol's front and rear sights, it would intersect the shooter's spine. This alignment gives the pistol the smallest angle to laterally pivot the stance, and muzzle, in recoil. Conversely, if the line ran down the shooter's strong arm and intersected his body at the shoulder, the pistol would then have the maximum angle to destabilize the consistency of muzzle control. The farther that line shifts away from body center, the greater the lateral shifting of the stance will be in recoil.

Natural Point of Aim

Your feet and body must be positioned so the sights align naturally with the target when the pistol is raised to eye level. This automatic alignment is called *natural point of aim* ("npa" for short). One important thing to understand about npa is that it's possible to get your gun on target almost no matter what sort of stance position you're in. But that's not necessarily your natural point of aim. There should never be any excess tension in your upper body in keeping the gun suspended in the center of the target.

Another important thing to understand about npa is that it's not the same for everyone. When my stance changed from being sharply quartered away from the target to almost directly facing it, I didn't just go out one day and make the conscious decision that I was going to experiment with facing the target. I noticed over a period of time that my stance was opening up to where I started naturally facing the target more and more.

If I let my stance be totally neutral all through my body, for me to have a natural point of aim, my right foot will be forward of my left foot. On some days it will be several inches forward of my left foot where I'll actually have a "reverse" stance. I noticed that phenomenon when I first started to shoot. At that time my mind was so attached to how things should be done that it immediately rejected the idea of the possibility of having a stance with my right foot forward because nobody did that. It didn't look IPSC, it didn't look "combat."

As my mind has changed and my way of thinking about that sort of thing has changed over the years, my body has opened up more and more and my natural point of aim is still with my right foot forward. I may stand that way in a scenario where I only have to put a shot or two on an easy target, but the reason I don't do that in all but the most simple shooting scenarios is that I still feel more comfortable with my right foot pulled back. When I stand with my right foot forward, I have a feeling that my weight isn't distributed so that my body can absorb the gun's recoil. When I stand that way, it feels great as long as the gun isn't actually firing.

I stand with my right foot slightly farther back because that's comfortable for me. My actual natural point of aim is with my left foot forward. Notice how my right leg flexes somewhat so that I can hold my upper body square to the target and still maintain a relaxed, neutral index.

But when the gun is actually firing, I feel more stable and balanced when my left foot is forward, but now my npa is off. If I just stand naturally, right foot forward, line the gun up, and relax all my muscles, I'm pointing dead on. When I move my right foot back to get the balanced feeling, it takes some tension in my leg muscles to twist my torso back to the left so that my npa is straight away with the gun centered. To hold myself straight, I end up in a position where my right leg is bent in, and my left leg is really relaxed. Bending my right knee slightly more than the left knee swivels my body from the hips to make them and my upper body square with the target. I'm actually holding my waist turned slightly to the left with the more bent right knee. My upper body tension is totally neutral.

I mention this because I know that I'm not the only shooter who may experience a contradiction in stance and npa. What you should learn from this is that, first, you must find your true npa. Second, if your true npa doesn't match the stance you'd like, there will be a way to balance the two so that your upper body can stay neutral and so the gun can stay centered. But whatever it might take for you to equalize the relationship, don't do it through tension or accept anything but a relaxed, neutral upper body position.

So as to not cause any confusion in the next sections, I should make the distinction here between index and natural point of aim. I use the term "index" to denote the shooter's position or "point." Once you've confirmed body and sight alignment on a target, then that's your index. You can have only one npa on a stage; however, you're indexing to all the other targets. For example, on *5 To Go* I may line up on the third target, which is about in the center of the stage, and then to shoot on the first target, I shift my index to the first target and holster the gun, keeping my body indexed on the first target. My natural point of aim is on the third target, but my index—my body's point—is on the first target.

Stance Width

Stance width is largely a matter of comfort. Your stance should be wide enough to give you stability, but you shouldn't spread your feet apart to the point where your knees might straighten as you move from target to target, or where you have difficulty moving if the stage requires it. On the other hand, the feet should not be placed together so closely that you could lose your balance when you must swing through your full range of movement to hit widely-spaced targets.

In getting together the material for this book, I decided to measure my stance width when I'm in my most normal shooting position and found that I stand with my feet 23 inches apart, measured from little toe to little toe. My stance width will change depending on the shooting. I find that I use a slightly narrower stance when the shooting is slower and requires more precision; when the shooting is close and fast, I tend to step into a slightly wider, more aggressive stance.

BUILDING A POSITION

To help you discover your best stance, start noticing the differences between your overall body feels when you're shooting groups as opposed to firing one-shot draws or shooting close, fast targets. The tendency is to grip more tightly with the hands and arms, to lower the head, and tense the neck and shoulders when more and more speed is necessary. Awareness, focus, and timing are your controls for shooting. Tension makes those three things nearly impossible. Chances are that you're more relaxed when you're shooting groups. From your group shooting posture, turn up the speed. Turn it up faster and faster. Then slow it back down and notice the differences you felt in your tension, positions, and pressures. Notice, especially, different sensations in your arms, shoulders, neck, and hands. Learn from it. Strive to experience your body's group shooting attitude and sensations while firing at high speed.

You also may benefit from practicing your draw by first beginning with the gun mounted in your group shooting posture. Reholster the pistol and then draw "back" to that group shooting stance. At first you may find you're overextending or changing your arm positions or grip pressure. Also practice this by starting with your arms extended as if you were shooting a group, pistol holstered. Slowly bring your arms and hands into your starting position. Then draw back to that spot where your hands just were, paying attention to the body feel necessary to duplicate the position after the draw. Working with these exercises will really pay off in developing your body feel.

SIGHT TRACKING

As I described earlier, watching the movement of the sight tells you how effectively you're achieving neutrality and consistency in your shooting technique. What you actually see is pretty much all you need to know to understand how you're doing. Now that you have some ideas that will help you achieve a neutral grip and stance, it will help if you understand sight tracking in more detail.

I'd like to share an observation I've had about sight movement. And when I mention sight movement, I'm talking about lifting, tracking, and returning. When I'm totally relaxed and totally focused on the sight, I'm aware of all types of movements and recoil surges that I'm not normally aware of. And when I'm in this totally relaxed state, often firing at no target at all, the sight does not move straight up and down in the rear notch in recoil. I see the sight lift out of the rear notch on a path that goes up and to the right. The angle is about 45 degrees, and the reason, as best as I can diagnose, is from torque caused by the twist of the rifling. The more relaxed I am, the more my sight tracks to the right; it's a signal to me that I'm relaxed and neutral and not trying to muscle the gun. The more tense I get and the faster I go, the more the sight tracks out of the notch approaching just straight up and down.

Likewise, when I'm relaxed, the sight doesn't track

Carefully observe the sight's movement. It will tell you what you need to know about your technique. You should see it lift, track, and return exactly the same on each shot. If you don't, watch closely, and you'll see where you need to place your attention.

directly back to where it started, although it ends up there. I see a two-step return: the sight starts back, then pauses, raises just slightly again, and then tracks back to rest in the rear notch exactly where it was when I pressed the trigger. This most likely is due to the slide's cycling causing a jiggle in the tracking, but the point is that I can see that when I'm relaxed and totally focused on the sight's movement.

Your sight doesn't have to track straight up and down out of the notch. It can track any way just as long as it's consistent. And consistency is the whole point. What you may see might not exactly match what I see; however, pay attention to what you *do* see. There is only one thing that you absolutely should see and that is the front sight returning to exactly the same place—on its own—where it was when you fired the gun. My sight lifts and returns like it's spring-loaded when I'm shooting my best. Again, where the sight goes doesn't matter as long as it comes back. It doesn't really matter if the sight lifts and makes two figure-8s as long as it comes back to rest where it started. If you can't see that, or if the sight returns to different points every shot, relax. Don't force anything; just keep shooting and keep watching. Through relaxation and observation you'll be able to intuit how to achieve the neutrality that allows the sight to track consistently.

DRAW

Your draw completes your stance. It's important to understand that the grip, stance, and draw are all interrelated, and they ultimately result in allowing you to flow into the shooting. But some shooters think of the draw as being something totally removed from the shooting. And some think that it's the most important thing in practical shooting. It's far from being unimportant, but don't forget its purpose: the draw gets you to the shooting.

To the Gun

From a surrender start, both hands get down at the same time and as quickly as possible. You've got to get your support hand down just as quickly as your strong hand so you can get both hands on the gun as soon as possible. Don't leave your support hand up high and waiting on the strong hand to bring the gun up to it. For an exercise, practice slapping your belly just above your belt buckle with your support hand until you can do that before your strong hand can grip the pistol. From a hands-down start, the support hand goes immediately to the same place.

You want the support hand on the pistol and into the

shooting grip as soon as possible. As soon as your support hand reaches your belly, the strong hand should be bringing the gun by that area. As soon as the pistol is in front of your body and you can get your support hand on the pistol, that's where you want to make your grip. From that point on to your final position, the pistol is then being pushed out uniformly all the way. Getting both hands on the gun as soon as you can also gives you just a little more time to adjust your hands into a good grip if necessary.

Both hands go down at the same time and as quickly as possible. For practice, try slapping your belly just above your belt buckle before your shooting hand can grip the gun. And don't waste any time getting the gun out of the holster!

The strong hand moves directly to the gun as fast as it can and on as straight a line as possible. When my hand touches the gun, the web between my thumb and forefinger is all the way up into the grip safety and my fingers just lift the gun straight up. I'm not aware of any process here, just the objective of getting my hand down and the gun out as quickly as I can. As my hand reaches the gun, my index finger extends naturally along the outside of the holster, in position to find the trigger. But my finger doesn't actually touch the trigger and the thumb safety isn't released until both hands are on the gun and the gun is well in front of my body. Where each shooter actually releases the safety and touches the trigger can vary, but for safety's sake later is better than earlier. There is no difference in speed if those operations don't occur until the gun is nearly in its final position. If you're just beginning, I would advise you to wait until the gun is at least at chest height before you perform either action.

My safety goes off when the gun is safely pointed away from my body and happens as part of assuming my shooting grip. Assuming that the mounted gun is at 90 degrees, my safety goes off at about 30 degrees. My finger doesn't go on the trigger until the gun is fairly close to the direction of the target; and in the last 6-8 inches of movement toward the target, my finger pre-loads the trigger by pulling through its takeup, or free movement, so it's only holding against the sear. And no matter how fast or slow the draw is, those things *never* change. I don't get off the safety and on the trigger any sooner if I'm drawing and shooting my fastest possible. By waiting until the gun is almost at eye

level before I get on the trigger, if I ever shoot a little bit before I planned, it's always a safe shot that's real close to the target. Pre-loading the trigger is definitely a Master-class technique; until you're at that level, don't put any pressure on the trigger until the gun is *on* the target.

I hold both hands very relaxed in my starting position, and while I do hold my strong hand in a "pre-fitted" form to the pistol grip, I do so with no tension. Your hands and wrists must be relaxed to move quickly, also, a "stiff" hand can't naturally conform to the pistol. Your best starting position is the one that lets your hands move the straightest and shortest distance to their first positions. You only want to feel motion in your forearms and hands in going to the gun; the elbow should stay relatively on the same level, although it will move to the rear somewhat as your hand goes to the gun. I keep my shoulders down as they are naturally when I'm at rest so they don't lift up out of their sockets as I draw. The shoulders, and especially the right shoulder, should not move; I feel the motion to the gun and then out to the target only in my arms. Of course, my arm will swivel in my shoulder joint, but I just don't want to feel any change in the shoulder's position. You'll find your own best starting position if you'll just remember that the first motion is your strong hand going straight to the gun and the weak hand going straight to your belly, both as fast as possible. And look at your target when you draw; don't watch the gun.

To the Target

After I place my hands on the gun, I bring it almost straight to final position along a diagonal line that ends at eye level. I say "almost" because I want to bring the gun up in such a way that my eyes can be aware of the gun and sights as quickly as possible. Getting the gun up into your sight line more quickly gives you a split second longer to adjust the gun's direction prior to reaching your final position; that helps you get the first shot off more accurately and quickly. For me, that means that the gun needs to be level with my eyes and target 3-6 inches before my

arms are fully extended. So the path the gun follows is basically straight but with a little 3-6 inch curve right at the end. It's amazing how your body can make use of this little bit of extra time. I've noticed that my eye just *drives* the gun into the center of the target. If a sight focus isn't central to the type of shooting I'm doing, such as on a close, fast stage, getting the gun to eye level quicker also serves to orient the gun and the target sooner. In this type of scenario, it's possible to get a head start on the shooting before the gun is fully mounted. You may find that this also helps you reach a better final position. Having this slight amount of straight motion outward prior to reaching final position seems to help the support wrist position itself to achieve the downward camming action I described earlier.

Getting the gun between my eye and the target sooner allows me to shoot at the instant the gun stops moving.

Opposite page: My shooting hand goes straight to the gun, both hands go down together as quickly as possible. Only the arms and hands should be moving during the draw. Both hands form the grip as soon as possible. My safety comes off at the point shown in the third picture. I get the gun between my eye and the sights 3-6 inches before my final position and preload the trigger. Once the gun is mounted, the stance is complete.

An exercise you can work on at home is to tack a string across an open door frame and practice bringing the gun over the string and onto target. Place the string about solar plexus height and stand close enough to it so that it's at least 3 inches behind where your hands will be when the gun is mounted. Experiment by seeing how close to the string you can stand without feeling that you're cramping your motion or slowing it down too much. Make sure that the string is attached loosely enough so that it won't pull the gun out of your hands if you don't make it.

When you're working on your draw, just make sure that there is no point where the pistol is lower than it just was. It's constantly rising until it gets to that point 3-6 inches from its finish point where it pushes straight out to the target. There are just about equal amounts of "up" and "out" in my draw, and I wouldn't recommend unbalancing your drawing motion by using too much of either. If you were to raise the gun almost straight up to your eye level and then push it out, or if you pushed the gun nearly straight out in front of you and then raised it up, neither way is as efficient as a more diagonal approach.

During the draw, the *only* things that should be moving are the shooter's hands, gun, and arms. The head, especially, must stay still. Here's an exercise that will help you keep your head still as you draw: sight your gun on a target downrange, then locate some object—a rock for instance—on the berm beyond the target and position the target between that object and your eye. Line up the object with one edge of the target so that you have an alignment plane you can reference to. Holding your gun out in shooting position, compare the alignment of the two images, then reholster and compare the line-up again. Hopefully it hasn't changed. And then while you're drawing, monitor the reference plane so you can see if your head moves as you're actually drawing the gun. You can also do this in front of a mirror by picking out a spot behind you or by placing a piece of tape on the mirror. By lining up, say, the top of your head with the spot, the reflection in the mirror can tell you the same thing.

Speed

A faster draw comes from eliminating wasted motions and smoothing out the motions that are necessary. The time from when your hand touches the gun to lifting it clear of the holster is a critical point in a fast draw. *Don't waste any time getting the gun up and out of the holster!* This is an area where you can increase speed without sacrifice. Make sure that your grip is *close* to correct before you pull the gun clear. It's perfectly okay to make some adjustments as the gun is coming up. Overall, there's extra speed in getting the gun out of the holster faster as opposed to waiting on a perfect grip before you lift the gun clear.

As your hand goes down to the gun, there should be neither the sensation of slowing down to grasp the pistol or of jamming the gun into the holster by hitting it too hard; once the hand starts the movement toward the gun, it never stops or slows. I feel my hand coming back up *just* as it touches the gun. There obviously is a stopping and a return to motion in that instant, but I feel that the sequence of my hand first touching the gun, to gripping it, to bringing it clear of the holster is all one motion rather than a procedure. I'm aware of a short, circular, rolling action in my wrist at the "bottom" of my draw that brings the gun straight up. The feeling is very subtle. If you'll just keep the idea in mind of getting the gun out of the holster and going toward the target as quickly as possible, you'll be able to discover what works best for you.

A fast draw, taking that to mean sheer speed in moving the gun, doesn't, in itself, lead to a fast first shot. And a fast first shot is only a portion of the measure of a good draw. What really matters are two things: a fast first hit, and equally fast successive hits. To achieve the fast first hit, the final position reached from the draw must have the gun mounted on target. You should be able to fire the millisecond after the gun stops. Fast subsequent hits are possible only if the final position reached from the draw is one you can shoot from without modification. Some shooters have an explosive first shot but cannot continue the pace beyond it. Remember that the draw completes your stance.

Holster Position

Holster positioning is really a personal thing. You'd like to find a position that will allow you to bring your hand straight to the gun with as little rearward or sideways motion in the elbow as possible, and where your shoulder doesn't have to move up or back to get your hand on the gun. I also believe that the ideal holster position places the gun in line with the first target. Ideally, I want to have the gun off the point where I can pick up my index. This will usually result in a pretty standard strong-side position for most people. If you can be comfortable using this formula, it serves to make the motion from holster to mount very straightforward.

My holster position is pretty standard strong-side. I think there are a lot of advantages to this position. Whenever possible, I like to line up so that my gun is straight away from the target.

I wear my holster pretty much right at my side and flat against my hip. The rake is basically straight up and down. Another popular placement is the "appendix" position where the holster is approximately in line with your front pants pocket. It's been argued that appendix is a faster position, but I've never been able to tell any difference. I don't give away speed to anyone using the strong-side placement. Using the strong-side arrangement, I'm never aware of any twisting action as I bring the gun out as I experience with the appendix position. And, although this may sound trivial, the appendix position is a constant irritation when you're picking up brass or making any other bending movements. Likewise, the appendix position puts the holster right in the way for kneeling and prone shooting. On the other hand, starting from a seated position is easier with the appendix.

There is no real reason that you should choose one over the other, because both work well as is evident by the amount of top shooters who use each. You should experiment with each position, and variations in between, to see which gives you the best result. And your holster position

Opposite page: (left to right) The free hand goes straight for the magazine. The gun is brought back as the arm just folds naturally. The arm is totally relaxed. The magazine is inserted by a simple pointing of my finger. The magazine is seated by my palm pushing firmly upward against the base pad. My free hand continues upward naturally back into the shooting grip. All through the procedure, it's critical that your arms and hands stay very relaxed.

can change from day to day. Although it's against the rules to alter the holster's position once you begin the match, if you know beforehand that you're going to be making a lot of draws from a certain starting position, you can intuit your own compromises by adjusting the holster position and rake. For instance, if I know I'm going to do a lot of hands-down starts, I tilt the gun a little more muzzle forward. Also, your holster position may change from time to time just to accommodate subtle changes in your npa.

Don't fall in the trap of feeling like you always have to have the holster in exactly the same place so your hand will know where it is. Just put the holster where it feels comfortable to you for that day. Once you've been shooting for a few years you can make a slight holster change and with a few dry-draws or dry-grips you know where it is. That's why a really good shooter can make a smooth, fast draw from any starting position. Just being familiar and in the present tense is what allows that to happen.

RELOADING

A quick, dependable reload is definitely a fundamental of practical pistol shooting. You never want to have a blown reload put you out of a match. Once you understand it, the process is pretty simple. So with practice and a focus on the right thing, the reload will become a reflex.

The Process

The first step is getting the magazine out of the gun. Ideally, you'd like to release the empty magazine without having to shift your grip on the gun. Most race guns have some form of extended release button; however, I've taken that one step further by milling a groove across the left grip panel on my pistol to give my thumb some extra room. I don't necessarily recommend doing this; I only mention it to assert my belief in the importance of being able to reload without having to shift my grip.

Hold the gun as upright as possible when you hit the release to make sure the magazine drops freely. As the magazine clears the pistol, the free hand is already on the new magazine.

When the magazine comes out and the gun comes back for the reload, the shooting arm should fold so there's about a 90-degree angle, or slightly less, between the forearm and upper arm. Your arm should just fold naturally to that spot. You don't need to leave the gun way out away from your body or pull it into your stomach—it just folds right to that natural angle.

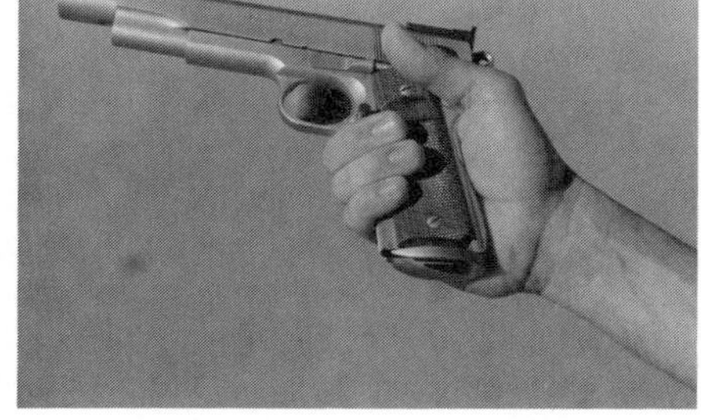

My hand tips the gun so I can see the line in the bottom of the mag well where the well joins the frame. When I can just see that line, the gun is tilted to the right angle.

The most important visual key for me is that I want to see the line in the mag well that's shown in the photo. When I see that line, I know that the gun is tilted exactly where it needs to be for me to insert the magazine. Your elbow should be positioned at about the side of your body so you can see that line. Likewise, the mag well should be positioned out just to the right of the body. So as you practice bringing your arm back to its position, combine that motion with tipping your hand so you can see that line. That should all just become one process.

As you're learning the reloading process, don't take your eyes off the magazine well. Your peripheral vision will show you that the spent magazine has cleared, and the

the fresh magazine can then be inserted without having to shift your focus. Focusing on that line in the mag well is a visual indicator that makes it very easy to just look the magazine into the gun. After you've mastered the process, reloading then becomes a totally reflexive movement that can be done by feel, like drawing.

Grasp the magazine so that it's supported by your palm and your index finger is touching the bullet.

Grasp the magazine so its base is supported by your hand; the index finger touches the tip of the bullet. Place the magazines in the pouches with the bullets facing forward so that your finger will be on the same side they're on. That way, the process becomes just pointing your finger into the magazine well and then seating the magazine with an upward push of your palm. And as your palm pushes upwards, it naturally goes right back into position on the gun to reform your shooting grip. As the magazine slides into position, make sure it seats by really pushing upwards with your palm against the base pad. The reason for the base pad is so you can seat the magazines better; it really has nothing to do with protecting them. Your base pads should be deep enough so you can seat the magazine fully without having your hand touch the mag well.

The Key

You can mechanically map it out, but when it's all said and done, the most important thing is that the arm is relaxed when the gun comes back for the reload. If the arm comes back tense, the magazine is never going to go in smoothly; it's only going to be luck if it does. If the arm just floats back there relaxed, it's amazing how the magazine goes right in. Get a focus on that feeling.

Relaxation is the key. Your arm should just fold naturally to this spot and your hand should tilt the gun all as a reflex.

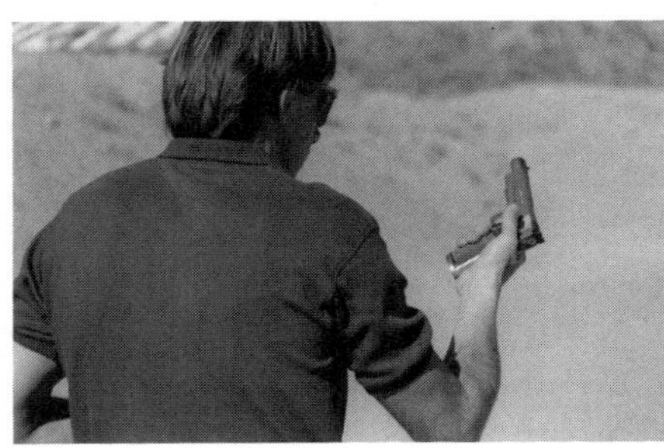

As you're doing dry-reloads at home, first of all, learn that spot—the combination of folding the arm and tipping the gun—without even reloading; just learn to pull your gun to that spot. Then when you put a reload into your practice, just learn the feeling of keeping the arm relaxed. That pretty much relaxes your whole body and lets the free hand do what it needs to do.

The whole thing can happen by feel, and once you've got the feeling down, you can do the same thing by visualization. When you've got the relaxation part of it down to where you're not tense and trying, you can visualize that line you want to see in the bottom of the mag well, and then just pull the gun back to the spot. The only thing you're aware of is your visualization of what the mag well is going to look like, and as your mind locks onto it, the magazine is in. There's no interference from anything. Eventually that will transfer into blind reloading where it all just happens routinely. Then when you reload in a stage where you have to move, if your focus is good you can have the reload in before taking your first step. The reload should be instantaneous. Along with keeping your arms relaxed, another key to the blind reload is maintaining uniform gripping pressure on the gun and the magazine.

When you're practicing dry-reloads, it's a good idea to make up some dummy rounds that you can load the magazines with. Just make sure that you identify them in some way so you can't get them mixed up with live rounds. You always want to practice reloading with a full magazine because it requires a greater force to seat a full magazine. Since you want to make the reload an afterthought, it's important to get the feel for the weight and seating force you'll actually experience in a match.

Magazine Positioning

You should position your magazines with as much care as you do for your gun. They have to just "be there" wherever you want to reach for them. I prefer the single, adjustable type of magazine pouches because they allow almost unlimited options; I can place them at any height and angle. I position each magazine independently so my free hand can just sweep back along the row of magazines and be able to grasp each one without forcing me to alter the arc my hand makes naturally. Pay attention to where your hand naturally goes, or wants to go, for each magazine, and then make sure there's one waiting there for it.

BUILDING CREATIVITY

In the so-called learning stage, many people work hard on their fundamentals until they feel confident in their technical ability to shoot. When they find that this intellectual process often fails them at the match, they begin to get interested in, sometimes obsessed with, the "mental" aspects of performance. Their mistake is in separating the physical from the mental. They cannot be treated separately. You are one person and, therefore, no matter what you're doing, both mind and body are performing at once.

Being able to transfer mechanics into results requires much more than knowing, rehearsing, and memorizing positions. Consider a baseball pitcher. A good fastball technique can, and has, been broken down into exact movements and positions. However, the exact moment the pitcher releases the ball cannot be defined by the pitcher.

The overall goal these components of your technique should achieve is that of making a relaxed, neutral position from which to shoot. The relationship between the pistol, the shooter's arms, neck, and head should be as comfortable as possible. This relaxed shooting position will allow the body feel and body action necessary for consistent high-speed shooting.

There is tremendous room for experimentation in all these relationships. You are trying to achieve a shooting technique that allows you to hold the gun on target and control the gun with the least amount of tension. You'll discover that the positions you put the various body parts into and the relationships they develop are what let you reach these goals, not muscle tension. You are always striving for a totally neutral position—one in which the gun will recoil the same amount and in the same direction, and then return on the same path and to the exact same spot each time. That consistency is the most important thing.

When you learned to write, you quit thinking about the mechanics of making the letters and moved on to what the letters mean—using them for creative expression. In shooting, you must also quit thinking about the mechanics and move on to using them for creative expression—the desire to hit the targets as quickly as possible.

As you're working with the mechanics, remember that they're all just different ways you can handle a gun and fire it to get different results. When your experience and experimentation have shown you results that most closely match your wishes, then you have discovered the *(Your Name Here) Stance.*

There is a level of shooting that towers over mechanics. We all work so hard in developing the skills we need that our minds get so into that cause and effect mode of, "If I can only do something else, then I'll get where I want to go..." You have got to free yourself of that mindset. You have got to free yourself of the limiting rut that a constant concern over the mechanics can stick you in. As long as you shoot, your technique will change, but once you have developed the technical skills, the changes come from within—not from more mechanical tricks. Accept the simple fact that after the mechanics there is *shooting.*

Never end your search—never limit yourself to your present knowledge of your technique. You can take a journey, right along with the bullet, on every shot you fire.

So relax, observe, *and let the shooting come to you...*

Section 3: CREATIVE SHOOTING

So far we've talked about focus and awareness and about the mechanics of firing a pistol at high speed. You've been exposed to the "two sides" of shooting and, hopefully, are starting to see how shooting isn't just a combination of awareness and mechanics, it's an integration to the point where they're inseparable.

The truth beyond the technique. The application beyond the analysis. The means beyond the methods. Here's where we stop thinking and start shooting.

The mechanics you will use in practical shooting—the grip, stance, draw, and so on—can be committed to memory as knowledge, as I explained in *Awareness & Focus,* just *knowing* about shooting is not what gets it done. You must open yourself up, and trust yourself, to apply that knowledge without thought and without limitation. I like to call this the *creative* level of shooting, and this level is only attainable through an awareness of what you are doing and what the gun is doing on every shot you fire.

In any sport, the successful competitor is the one who can play creatively. Concentration and conscious thought stifle creativity. When you hear that an athlete can "think on his feet," that is because that person can act on what he sees happening before him. He doesn't "think" in the classic sense. *After* a great play he can think about it; *before* the great play he can concentrate on it. But *during* that play there is only awareness, observation, and action. So it is with shooting.

Creative shooting requires relaxation, awareness, and focus. Those things aren't directly "applied" to the shooting; they make shooting possible. Your seeing—visual acuity and perception—must be razor-sharp. Your ability to meet the shooting is dependent on visual attention bringing in images to an open, dead-calm mind. Creative shooting is possible only in the present tense.

FULL CIRCLE

After 10 years of training, I came back full circle to the original things I was concerned about when I started.

When I first started competing, I had no knowledge of

mechanics, no knowledge of tricky, full-race positions, no knowledge of all the complexities of shooting. From seeing pictures of myself then, I looked totally unmechanical and I can't imagine how I could have been competitive because I had no idea of how I should do *anything*. All I did was try to *call each shot as I shot it*. I knew enough about accurate shooting from my PPC experience to know what the sights had to look like and how to read them. So that's all I tried to do. No matter what the course looked like, no matter how tricky it was, no matter if the targets were close or far, I let my body sort it out at its own speed and just tried to call the shots as I shot them.

I did really well and was very competitive right away. And then I started going through a phase of where, for years, I had to break everything down and technically understand it *all*. I had to understand the technical differences between the finger on the trigger guard and the finger off the trigger guard, and a thousand and one variations of the same meaningless technical stuff—things that your body will work out on its own if you'll let it. During all that time, the shooting wasn't just shooting anymore. I was no longer just trying to align the sights and pull the trigger. At this time I was trying to keep this arm straight, trying to keep this arm bent, trying to keep my head here, keep my eyes here, keep my feet here... I was trying to do all these things that *weren't* shooting. When I finally saw through all that and was able to put all the technical knowledge I learned aside and quit making it my main focus, then I was able to use that technical knowledge I had already learned to perfection without actually ever trying to do so.

Now, today, I'm back to just doing the same thing that I was doing 10 years ago—*calling the shots on the targets by whatever the scenario dictates*. I'm just able to do that a lot faster now than I was then. But the plan is the same. My improvement now comes from trying to learn how to see more than I thought I could see and intuit past my own experience. There's not much more in the way of external things to be found. Once you've settled into the basic mechanics you feel comfortable with, then it's all internal. The improvement comes from the mind's ability to open up, intuit the truth, and perceive what is actually happening, not from any more thoughts. That's what this section is all about.

The seer and the seen exist only in confusion. There is only the seeing.

SHOOTING FOCUS

In the first section we talked about focus. In this section, I'll go into much more detail about focus as it can affect your shooting.

When you're reading over what's to come, keep in mind that my description of the different shooting types and focal points is just a way for me to break down, in retrospect, the details of what I see when I shoot. These are the types of seeing that *come* to me; I don't go to a stage and insist on seeing anything. I know what I will likely need to see from looking at the stage, but I leave myself open to the experience of being aware of what I actually do see. As I made a point of in the first section, there can never be any great result from forcing or fixing a thought into your mind as you immediately prepare to shoot, and certainly not as you are shooting. Therefore, none of the ideas in this chapter should be taken so strictly as to give you the notion that one of these focal points is *absolutely* the only way to shoot a particular string or target. Again, they've been broken down and analyzed just to show you what's possible to see.

You can only shoot as fast as you can see, and you just see what you need to see to make your hit.

You want each shot to break no sooner or no later than it's possibly able to. If you can do that, then you'll be shooting as fast and accurately as you're presently capable of shooting. Each of these focal points shows me what I feel is necessary to see in each shooting circumstance. But what I need to see to hit a target can change from day to day and from string to string. I don't exclude the possibility of using any or all of these different focal points for most any target and most any circumstance. My experience may tell me, for example, that I most likely will see a certain focus on a stage I've shot many times, but when I start shooting, my awareness and observation may show a need to shift to another in order to get the targets. Freezing myself into an unalterable mindset, when the actual circumstances dictate a shift, would be a self-imposed limitation. When I defined focus as being a flexible preoccupation with something that has a bearing on your shooting, take that to mean that you must be able to shift your focus in reaction to what you see. Shooting in the flexible realm of awareness allows you to constantly monitor all the relationships that exist between you, your gun, and your target and to instantly modify components in those relationships to shoot your best. *What you see is more important to your shooting than anything else.*

I think that just being aware of these things may help you begin to experience these different focal points for yourself. Accept them and let yourself see them. Just know-

**I'm only aware of the front sight being my sole focal point for one type of shooting, and even then it may not be intentional—it may just be what the shooting requires.
You must first see your target before you can hit it.**

ing that you can use them with perfect success may get you to open up and see what you can get away with. You'll come to realize that what you can get away with will likely be exactly what you need.

Sights Or Targets

I did a test once on Bianchi targets with an 8-inch 10-ring. I put two of them at 50 yards and fired my automatic with iron sights. Just standing and taking my time, I fired 10 shots on each target. On the first target I used a very accurate and intense focus on the front sight to where I was "looking the gun off" without focusing at all on the trigger; the gun was going off on its own.

On the other target, I shot with a clear focus on the target itself and just kept the sights in my peripheral vision. The sights looked very fuzzy because I couldn't see exactly where they were. Since I didn't know exactly where the sights were aimed, on this target I found that I didn't really have the same feedback coming into my mind as I did on the first target. Trigger control was no longer automatic; I had to consciously squeeze the trigger on each shot.

On both targets, all the shots scored in the 10-ring. But on the target where I focused on the front sight and allowed the trigger pull to become automatic, they were just about all in the X-ring. On the one where I looked at the target and had to consciously control the trigger, the shots were still 10s, but they used up the entire 10-ring. You can definitely shoot 10s by looking at the target, but at 50 yards it's not the focus you'd want. But my biggest impression of the difference was not in the clarity of the visual focus, but in the way the entire firing process changed.

Focal Points & Shooting Types

Through my experience and experimentation, I have identified five separate shooting types that can require five separate focal points—points of attention—and depending on the targets and shooting requirements, I'll see one or more of them in each stage of fire. A very complex stage can conceivably require seeing all of them for different shots, and I won't always be aware of just one focal point for an entire stage. As I just mentioned, it's possible to shoot well on almost any stage by focusing on the target, front sight, or anything else that works for you. It's when you don't see *anything* that you get into trouble!

Since practical shooting courses vary tremendously in distances, target sizes, and the levels of accuracy needed, my ideas on shooting focus developed through an awareness of what is necessary at different times to hit the targets. By keeping only the desire to hit the targets as quickly and effectively as possible, I discovered what was necessary for me to see and to feel in order to get that done. I'll go into much more detail about how to "use" these focal points, but first I'll define the shooting types in general.

Type 1: Single target at extreme close range; extreme high-speed shooting.

Type 2: Multiple targets at close range; extreme high-speed shooting.

Type 3: "Standard" practical shooting: medium range, multiple targets; speed limited by the difficulty of the targets and the size of their scoring surfaces.

Type 4: Multiple, difficult, closely-spaced targets (plates or bowling pins); precise high-speed shots; shooting speed as high as possible.

Type 5: Very difficult shots; prone or long range or anytime a shot is considered extremely difficult. Accuracy more important than speed.

Here's the focus I usually encounter for each type:

Type 1 Focus. For the single target at extreme close range where I need an extremely fast hit, there is no *directed* focus on the sights or the target. There may be some focus on the sights or target, but it doesn't really matter. In other words, I may be seeing the target or I may be looking for the sights to come into my peripheral vision, but I may not wait to see them. Even though I may be aware of my sights when they get there, I shoot by feel. Any preparatory thoughts I use are those that help me relax and stay relaxed. That's the most critical thing in this type of shooting, and it's very hard to do.

Type 1: Arm's length, hyperdrive. There's no time to confirm anything here, it's total feel. Type 1 emphasizes relaxation.

This is definitely an advanced technique, and chances are that you would only encounter this focal opportunity in your own practice or in an extremely close and fast, "arm's length," single-target IPSC stage. Developing an awareness of where the gun is when you draw it and move it toward the target will help you to use this

Type 2: Once I confirm my index on the first target, I shoot the others by focusing on the targets.

focus. This shooting type requires total body feel for where the gun is pointed at every instant.

Type 2 Focus. When I'm faced with multiple targets at extreme close range and, as above, I need extreme speed, I first confirm correct body and gun alignment (my index) on the first target, then I simply focus to the scoring surface on each target. The sights may or may not be in my peripheral vision. Once I confirm my index, then the gun just appears wherever I look.

If I need to shoot two shots on each target, I may keep my focus on the target or shift my focus back to the sights, depending on the difficulty level of getting the shots onto the scoring surface. If I keep my focus on the targets, the sights are very clear in my peripheral vision and I have the sensation of looking *through* the sights to the targets. When you're moving to this focus type, be aware of the danger of shooting without focusing on anything. It's awfully easy to do, especially because your perception of this type of shooting often forces tension in your body, making it easy for your eyes to glaze over. The tension you feel from trying to force the speed usually causes this shooting without seeing.

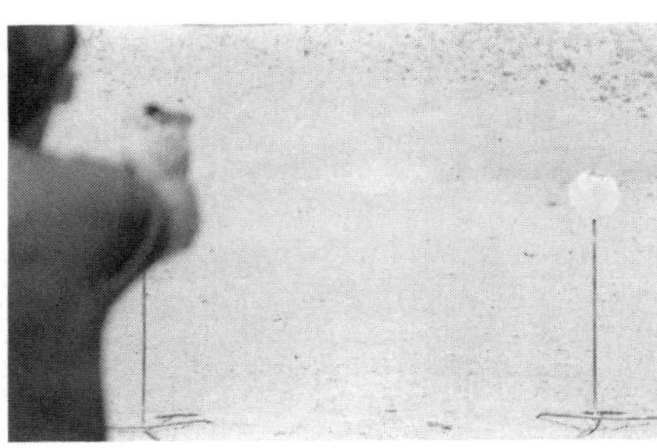

Type 3: Looking to the target acquires it quickly; looking to the sight creates the hesitation necessary to follow through.

Type 3 Focus. This is the focus I use for most targets. For what I call "standard" practical shooting, my focus goes from targets to sights on each shot. I draw, confirm my sight position, and break the shot. I then shift my focus to the next target, bringing my gun along with my vision. Then I focus from that target to the sights and break the shot. And so on.

This is a simple focus shifting, not a step-by-step procedure; the gun moves quickly and smoothly along with my eyes. You *have* to look to a target to acquire it smoothly, but your mind doesn't always remember focusing on it clearly, so it's not important to be aware of a distinct focus/shift/focus process. The focus back to the sight is necessary because of a higher shot difficulty.

This is the most common focus and the one that's used in virtually every type of shooting you'll encounter in freestyle pistol competition. It's the one that you need to be the most familiar with and the one that you need to be able to do on demand.

Most all the shooting at the Steel Challenge requires this focus. There you may not be aware of a conscious focus on some of the targets, but you'll almost always need to be aware of a front sight focus before the shot breaks so that you can call the shot. Almost all the targets in that match are difficult enough to require your being able to call the shot exactly each time you fire the gun. The pace I can shoot using Type 3 depends on how quickly I can be aware of my sight moving onto the target I'm currently seeing. When I can shift my focus from the target to the sight and be aware of the sight resting in an acceptable area, the shot breaks.

Type 4 Focus. Type 4 shooting is now where I more closely follow the "rule" of focusing on the front sight through the course. And I keep that focus to the point where I *see the sight lift when the gun recoils.* I see the targets only in the background, or peripherally. I actually consider this to be a more advanced type of shooting than Type 3 since it's really difficult to maintain *complete* focus on the front sight. When the distance between targets is very short, as soon as the shot breaks on the preceding target and you see the sight lift, the next target is already in your immediate peripheral vision. You may see toward the target slightly without ever acquiring a focus on it; your eye, therefore, has the *image* of retaining the front sight in clear focus because the focus shift to the target is so slight that it goes unnoticed. I think that if you'll really pay attention to what you're seeing, you'll find that you see at least a partial Type 3 focus in most situations where you might believe you're using strict Type 4.

Type 4: When the targets are close together, I have the sensation of staying with the front sight. But the main thing in Type 4 is that you stay with the sight until you see it lift. That allows the followthrough necessary to make a difficult shot.

Seeing the sight lift out of the rear notch is the most critical thing when using this focus. For that reason, Type 4 can be introduced into other types of shooting anytime a target is of a sufficient difficulty to require the followthrough of maintaining focus on the sight until you see it lift. So while you'd tend to need to see Type 4 all the way through a stage composed of closely-spaced, multiple targets, you may need to shift to a Type 4 if, for instance, a stage has one or more long-range targets or tight no-shoot situations. The intense Type 4 focus gives me the sensation of automatic firing that I mentioned in *Targets Or Sights.*

Type 5 Focus. When I'm faced with an extremely difficult shot—one that's either at extreme long range or one that offers an extremely small scoring surface—my focus may shift more to trigger control. I'm aware of where my sights are, but I know that keeping the gun on the target as it fires is the most important thing. The gun must be in a very stable position to use this focus; I'll usually only be able to shift to a trigger focus when I'm prone.

Type 5: For an extremely difficult shot, I'll focus on the relationship between trigger pressure and sight movement. This is total followthrough during the entire firing action. If the sights are made stable by my hold, I may focus on the actual mechanics of trigger pull.

From a freestyle position, I'll focus on the front sight for an extremely difficult shot; however, my focus there is actually on the *relationship* between trigger movement and sight movement. In other words, I am constantly monitoring the front sight position in relationship to increasing pressure on the trigger. Sight alignment is the most variable part of the shooting when faced with an extremely difficult shot, so I'll force a visual followthrough on the front sight until I see recoil lift it. Sometimes I feel that trigger control and front sight focus are the same thing: I'm forcing the sight to stay there until I *look the shot off* with my eye.

Many times a shooter will miss a shot at 50 yards, for instance, and say that the sights were "right there" when the shot broke. The reason he missed is because the sights didn't *stay* there. You should be able to reverse the statement and say that the shot broke when the sights were right there. Good trigger control keeps the gun still. I believe that trigger control is born of a desire to hold the sight on target. An intense focus on the sight for a very difficult shot leads to automatic firing for me. Even a slight movement can cause a miss at long range, and most of the movement will come from the anxiety of trying to break the shot while the sights are "still there."

MORE ABOUT FOCUS TYPES

For the reason-oriented shooters, I'll give a more detailed description as to the reasons these focus types actually work for you.

In Type 1, you don't really need that much visual input since it's totally a feel process. You may be seeing the target and seeing the sight recoil clearly, but Type 1 really just emphasizes relaxation. Using this focus in a match requires an extremely well-developed index that doesn't have to rely on visual confirmation of alignment. Extreme speed is the obvious reason for going to this focus in a match. There you're looking for a .60-zone first shot, and at that speed you're not going to be confirming *anything*.

Even on a stage that began with an arm's-length target, I would tend to follow Type 2 from the start. Beyond one shot on one target, Type 1 focus could essentially become shooting with no focus. Type 1 *can* carry on beyond the first target if the targets are extremely close; all you're usually seeing then is the targets and the gun just keeps up with them while your body points it. The only reason I include Type 1 as a potential match focus is because you could set up something where you'd probably do just as well with your eyes closed; I didn't want to leave anything out. You should use this focus occasionally in practice for both single and multiple target scenarios. Experiencing what's possible through just total body feel helps you find out where you are in your overall technique development.

But it's really not the "quick draw" that you learn from Type 1—experiencing what Type 1 shows you about your relaxation is its real function. Whatever you need to do to relax and stay relaxed is what will work for you in Type 1, and that's what you'll learn from it. I may shoot Bill Drills (see Section 6) using a Type 1 focus even though I'm trying to hit the A-box and it's a difficult shot. My focus there is occasionally just on being relaxed, so for me that would be Type 1. I might be seeing other things happening but my emphasis is on being relaxed and monitoring my ability to stay relaxed. A Type 1 focus is how you test how relaxed you can be when you're actually shooting.

And you have to see how well you're relaxed. It may sound silly, but you should fire six shots into the dirt just as fast as you can do it. It's really difficult to do that without getting tense. And that's what working with a Type 1 focus will help you overcome. Type 1 alerts you to your tension level and your body feel and lets you see how strongly you're muscling the gun. The harder you try to muscle the gun, the harder time you're going to have shooting just as fast as you possibly can. I can stand there feeling all nice and relaxed, but when the buzzer goes off and the target's only 3 yards away, to come out relaxed and stay relaxed is a very difficult thing. The whole thing in IPSC is to be able to stay relaxed when the stage is pressuring you.

In Type 2, when I say that you "confirm alignment" on the first shot, I mean that you confirm total body, gun, and sight alignment—a totally neutral, stopped alignment on the target—to where your body can pivot to anything and

**Type 1 is total body feel.
Type 2, you're looking through the sights to the targets.
Type 3, you're focusing from targets to sights.
Type 4, you're staying with the sight until you see it lift.
Type 5, you're aware of continual followthrough.**

retain that alignment. In other words, you're confirming your index. You're set, and now wherever you look, the gun goes—provided your upper body technique is sufficiently developed to allow you to do that.

I gave the caution of being alert to shooting without focusing on anything when moving to Type 2. What's going on when you shoot without seeing anything is that you've set up and lined up but then you shoot without any visual input. You can't really expect to hit the target reliably like that. The target focus in Type 2 must be just as clear as the sight focus in other shooting types.

But at the warp drive speed you're looking for on a close, fast Type 2 stage, what focusing on the target actually does for you is that the time it takes your eye to acquire the focus on the target gives your body the time to get the gun on the target to fire the shot. Just the visual act of bringing the target into focus creates the hesitation on the target for the gun to actually stop there and for your body to regain its alignment. And in that hesitation—the time it takes for your brain to realize that you've acquired the visual focus on the target—you may see the gun in alignment, and you may also pick up the sight alignment where you're looking *through* the sights to the target. It's really easy to do that once your vision becomes sharp and relaxed. Or you may not. You may just have the sensation of seeing the gun on the target—your gun pointing at the target like you were pointing your finger at something. The key thing to remember here is that just the visual acquisition of the target, bringing the target into focus, is all the hesitation and followthrough that's needed to acquire and shoot a target of that difficulty level. An inexperienced shooter may not be able to use Type 2 focus because his index is not yet perfect enough to materialize on target without him having to recheck sight alignment on each shot.

When you shift to a Type 3 focus, the shot difficulty level is higher now to where it takes more than just pointing your finger at the target to make the shot—it takes an actual visual awareness of sight alignment and sight placement. The focus back to the sight allows your body the time necessary to fire a more accurate shot. So the reason Type 3 works for you is again related to creating the hesitation necessary to followthrough. You've shifted your visual focus back from at least a general focus on the target to the front sight, and then you bring the front sight into focus. The time it takes you to visually bring that front sight into razor-sharp focus is the time your body needs to followthrough to fire an accurate shot. The visual inputs of shifting focus, and the refinement of those visual inputs, take a little bit longer so the hesitations on the targets are a little bit longer. However, if you're working well and your seeing is short circuiting your thinking, those hesitations are probably not even measurable.

Speed Option: I'll see Type 2 on the first three plates. I acquire the bonus plate by target focus, but since it's more difficult, I then focus to the sight, holding my attention there until I see it lift. I retain the image of the sight so that it "reappears" on the stop plate.

In Type 3 shooting, you may or may not see a Type 4 sight lift off the target. If it's a high-speed stage and fast target acquisition is important and the shot difficulty is not such that it requires that amount of followthrough, you may not see the sight lift at all. As soon as you've seen an acceptable focus, right at the time the shot breaks your eye has already moved to the next target so the gun can get there quickly. In Type 3 shooting, like on *5 To Go,* very seldom do I see the sight lift off the target. The instant my eye acquires an acceptable focus on the sight, my eye pops to the next target. That's what enables me to get the gun to each target quickly. And what gets the gun to stop quickly on that target is your eye getting a focus on the target before the gun gets there. (On *5 To Go,* you may not see the sight lift on the first 3 shots, but since the 4th shot is a little more difficult, you may see it lift off that plate and then see it reappear on the stop plate; you definitely don't want to leave the 4th plate without hitting it because it really slows you down to make the big swing back to it.)

When you shift into Type 4, you're now not only bringing the front sight into clear focus before you break the shot, but you're focused on watching the front sight lift out of the notch and off the target in recoil. So now you're at a shot difficulty level that's higher than Type 3 to where the extra followthrough of watching the sight lift allows you to hit the target. Wanting to actually see the sight lift off the target so that you can call the shot *exactly* gives your body the extra time it needs—seeing the sight lift is allowing you the hesitation necessary to follow through to make the more difficult shot.

So the main thing in Type 4 is not so much that you're seeing the sight in between the targets, but that you're seeing the sight *lift* off each target very clearly. That's what really defines a Type 4 focus, and you see that just because it's a more difficult shot and you need to be able to call the shot at the last instant.

As the photos show for what I might see on the *Speed Option,* the progressively longer targets usually require a shift from Type 2 to Type 4. For another example, On *Outer Limits,* the shots are sufficiently difficult to require a Type 4 focus where I may want to see the sight lift, but the movement to the next target may be a Type 3. Again, watching the front sight *lift* is really what defines Type 4. I used to see a Type 4 focus on *Outer Limits* where I would never be aware of anything but the front sight movement—onto the target, lifting off the target, through the air to the next target—but the more I shoot that stage, the more I see that I'm using a Type 3 focus and Type 4 followthrough.

Even on bowling pins, I'm leaning more towards that now. I used to be just totally aware of watching the sight bounce from pin to pin like those "follow the bouncing ball" sing-alongs on TV. But anymore I'm more conscious of a Type 3. I am not big on watching the sight go from target to target. Even when you're actually doing that it's very difficult to describe. You're seeing so many things when you're shooting that it's really impossible to set up a stage like *Outer Limits* and dry-fire and move your gun to the next target and actually keep a front sight focus all the way to the next target because *your gun just doesn't do that.* Your gun doesn't move to a place that your eye hasn't already directed it to go. It may move near it, but to stop the gun in the center of the target, *your eye has got to look that way.* Usually when a shooter overswings a target, he didn't let his eye look to where he wanted the gun to go. If you swing past a target, it's because you didn't see it. That usually happens when you're too fixed on your front sight. By continually focusing on the front sight, you can know where the sight is but not where the gun is pointed.

When you're going across a table of pins, the movement from target to target is so small that when you see the sight lift, you can just see the sight settle onto the next target without first having to actually refine a focus on the target. In that situation, your peripheral vision of each target may be all the target focus that's needed. It's hard to describe what your eye is actually doing there in that cone of movement. The gun's movement from target to target is so small that you could have the experience of seeing everything. But in my mind, by seeing the gun in focus, seeing the sight in focus, and seeing the way everything just comes so perfectly to the target, you had to have at least glanced toward the target. It's an orientation to the target rather than a fixed focus, and it's something that's happen-

You can shoot only as fast as you can see. High-speed seeing results in high-speed shooting.

ing very, very quickly.

For Type 5 from a freestyle position, the shot difficulty is at the highest possible level to where even watching the sight lift may not get the target. You also have to monitor the sight placement and alignment all the time that you're actually pulling the trigger. You can get a feel for Type 5 through shooting groups freestyle, and the most important thing is that you're not aware of a sight/trigger separation. Thinking of those two operations as being separate, plus the time pressure of hurrying up the shot, is what most often causes a miss on a difficult shot. So when I say that you monitor the relationship between the sights and the trigger pull, that's only possible through having a total desire to make the shot first and to do it quickly second. For the "textbook" Type 5 trigger focus, you must be in a stable, rested position—usually prone. In that situation, I'm still visually focused on the front sight, and will see it lift, but since my hold is stabilized by my position, I can focus on feeling every detail of trigger movement—just pulling it through until the gun fires.

Based on your practice and experiences on the practice range, you can, after time, look at any given stage and just by seeing the distance and the size of the targets you'll know what you'll need to see; you'll know what you can get away with to hit the targets.

Just your sights as they appear on the target is all the information your brain ever needs for it to know how difficult a shot is.

Your brain can fully judge the amount of quality of trigger release and followthrough that's necessary to hit a target. If your mind is just set in a state of observation, it can vary your shooting tempo for you without any thought at all just by being aware of how your sights appear on the target. There honestly is nothing more to shooting than what meets the eye.

You need to realize that you have to see something, you have to pick something, and if the targets are easy enough to allow the Type 2 target focus to hit them, then that may be all that you need.

Target Acquisition

The top-level shooters know that this is what really makes the difference. We're pretty close on most things—draw speed, strategies, shooting skills—so what really makes the difference in our times is target acquisition. It's always been like that but nobody really paid much attention to ways to improve it.

Rob Leatham was really the first IPSC shooter who just flatly admitted that he didn't necessarily need a sight focus to shoot, and that in a lot of given scenarios he looked at the target. And a lot of the traditional "front sight" shooters couldn't deal with that. The reason he's so much faster than most IPSC shooters on close stages is because of that focus—the vision he allows himself to use lets him acquire each target faster.

Being able to move the gun from the current to the next target smoothly and quickly reduces the amount of time you spend on any course. Even if your reaction time from target to trigger stays the same, the overall time will be reduced by being able to acquire the targets more quickly. This doesn't take a tremendous amount of athletic reflex; it only takes the determination to shoot the targets and an awareness of where they are in relation to you and your gun. A "shoot-move" mindset should be replaced with a "shoot-shoot" approach. My perception of the gun on the target adjusts my focus automatically. Practicing the *Awareness Exercises* in Section 6 will give you the confidence of being able to keep your gun centered and sights aligned as you move from target to target.

And that's where the speed comes from. If you want to learn to shoot multiple targets quickly, you've got to learn to acquire the targets as quickly as possible. And that's what this whole typing and classification business is about. Hopefully, it's letting you see that all these different focus and vision types are possible and that they're definitely intended to get you to not only hit the target, but to get you to the next target faster.

You can shoot only as fast as you can see. "Shooting fast" is a confusing term. To most people, *shooting fast* means *getting tense.* Shooting fast is just seeing the best way around the course and seeing what you need to see as quickly and clearly as possible.

Confidence

I experience these different focus types just based on what I see happening when I shoot. I actually experience a Type 2 focus, for instance, at times when a Type 3 might be called for, and vice versa. Sometimes a Type 4 focus may happen on something that's obviously a Type 2 possibility, but that's just the way it happens. I have to look back on what I saw, in retrospect, to know the actual focus I used. Again, being able to realize all these focus opportunities comes from a subconscious awareness of where the gun is and of what I need to see to get the target. It's also just the

Your eyes never stop looking, but you can let them stop seeing.

confidence that comes from experiencing the different focus types—trusting yourself to see what you need to see, and that seeing what you need to see will get the target.

Before my shooting had progressed to the level it is now, I can remember a point 4-5 years ago when I was going through a stage where I was learning in practice and at local matches to shoot close, easy to hit, high-speed targets by confirming alignment on the first shot and then shooting by just looking at the targets. At that time, most shooters always focused on the front sight prior to breaking the shot. When I was first learning to use Type 2, I remember that it was a major breakthrough for me going to the Steel Challenge where I had to do this for real, one time, and to trust myself to line up and focus on the target. I knew that if I could just see the target in clear focus on a lot of the shots—8 yards and under—I was going to hit the target. Pulling that off in the match was a big step for me. I really believed in myself and I knew this was for real; I knew that I didn't have to shoot every shot like the bullseye books told me I had to. It's a matter of turning over control to what you've already experienced—and to stop intellectualizing. You can just experience it and then trust that the experience is there. Again back to the problem of seeing something work well for you and then having that become the sole input that you'll allow to come in. If, for instance, you see that Type 2 works for you on a certain stage, you don't have to consciously try to see that or force that type of vision. You don't have to think if the experience is there.

The whole thing you have to get implanted into your brain is that *you do not have to see a front sight "focus" on a shot*. And you don't have to stay *totally focused* on the front sight all the time you're shooting. That's easily translated into that you don't have to see *anything*. And when you're in a match and you're tense and anxiety-stricken and your eyes are glazed over, you'll have the feeling of not seeing anything. And in that circumstance it's really easy to think, "I'm looking at the target," when you're not. You're just pointing the gun and firing hopers and listening for your hits. A relaxed focus on the target—being able to see the paint dimples or perforations on the target—is not an easy thing to do because your brain doesn't want to do that. When you're in a situation that would allow target focus to work, you're going to be shooting at your warp drive pace and that's the pace that causes tension and anxiety. When you tense up is when you stop seeing.

You can also just get lazy and let habit shoot for you. When you're shooting from habit, you just don't pay atten-

Pay attention! Nothing more really needs to be said. Most people aren't going to accept the truth of that because it is just too simple. They ask, *What do I pay attention to?* Just pay attention to what's happening. It's all right there before you. You must learn to see what you haven't been seeing. Find something that's out there and pay attention to it!

tion to your visual inputs. A good example is *Triple Threat:* you push the gun onto the first target and you see the sight drive onto that target and from that point on you may not see the sight again. I was burning out on that stage in practice one day seeing how fast I could shoot it, and I shot three or four runs in a row where I missed the second target every time. And that was from being lazy and just slinging a shot to that target. Shooting a stage like that becomes such a habitual routine that you don't really see anything; you just kind of point the gun in that direction and fire a shot. You've let yourself not see it. Rob Leatham, who was practicing with me that day, knew what I was doing and said, "Just see the target." It immediately clicked in my brain that I was in habit shooting mode and that I just needed to bring that target into focus and stop shooting without seeing anything.

Keeping in mind what I said in the *Introduction* will help you put all this into perspective—one thing you need to realize is that as long as you're going to be shooting a pistol you'll always need to do three things: locate the target, align your gun on the target, and hold it there while it fires. You'll always have to do those three things, and what you see in accomplishing them can vary in great detail depending on the difficulty level of the shot. But no matter how long you shoot, there's nothing that you can learn that will ever exclude any one of those three things. Everything you do is going to be based around your ability to see to get the gun to the target and to keep it aligned on the target until the gun fires.

You see with your mind. Your mind and body work together. When your body is tense, your mind is tense, "sticky" also. And when your mind is tense, so is your vision. Be alert for "tense" vision.

SEEING

In most shooting situations, the actual focus of your eye is the indication of the overall shooting focus. What you're actually seeing, in other words, is your focus. And it really doesn't matter what or where your focus is so long as you, first, are aware precisely of your focus, and second, that you are precisely focused.

At a match, the most eroded fundamental I see among shooters is *followthrough,* whether it's trigger or visual. Coinciding with that, your seeing tends to go in bursts. You may see the sight for a second, then you won't see it right before the gun goes off, then you may see it again, and then you won't see it again before the gun goes off. That fragmented seeing is something that you have to be aware of. Something that hopefully you've already made a practice through your group shooting and watching the sight lift is making sure you're always keeping your eyes open so you can followthrough on the sight (see page 94). The seeing or visual process needs to become totally automatic to where you're visually aware of everything that's happening from the time the gun leaves the holster to the time it goes back into it. Just be alert to that fragmented seeing, especially in a match, and you'll know where you need to place your attention.

Central and Peripheral Vision

Visual awareness filters down from peripheral to central vision in some types of shooting. *Peripheral vision* is a bigger space, a wider cone. It's also being aware of the *number* of things you see. It can be an awareness of seeing the target or an awareness of the gun in recoil on the target. On a close stage like *Smoke & Hope,* sometimes I have a remembrance of seeing my mount on the target, the slide operating, brass flying, the lead splattering on the plates. Sometimes you may see so many things that it's hard to recall or describe them. You're not looking for them; you just see them. All of those things you'll see are a result of being relaxed and letting yourself see them. *Central vision* is a narrower cone or plane. Central vision is the type of seeing you'll experience when you're narrowly focused and the only input you're actually aware of is the front sight or the textbook sight alignment on the target. If *Smoke & Hope* was set at 50 yards, all I'd see is my sight; I wouldn't be conscious of my mount, gun, or point.

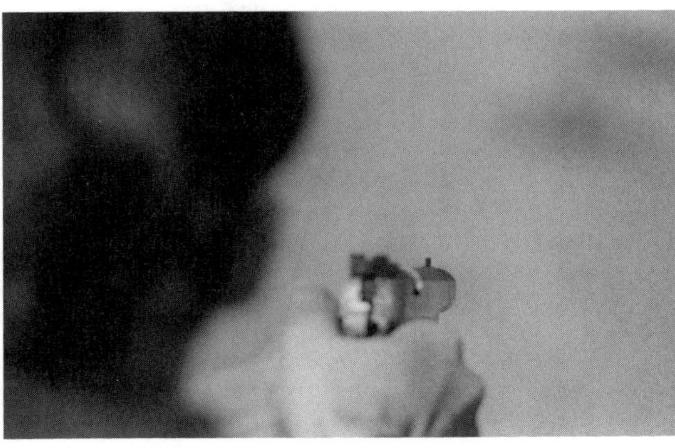

Relaxed, sharp visual attention—being able to call your shot at the last instant—opens up the possibility of high-speed shooting.

When you move off one target to another that's some distance away, your field of vision must open up peripherally to locate the next target; as the eye finds the target and the gun moves toward it, focus begins to filter inward to a point that's sharply in focus either on the sight or target, depending on the situation. When there's a big movement between targets, traditional "front sight" shooters often have problems acquiring the next target. With a totally fixed focus—staying with the front sight between targets—this shooter can't locate his next target accurately because he never sees it clearly, so the gun just sort of floats around out there looking for a target. This sort of disoriented limbo comes from the total Type 4 focus on the front sight when the situation calls for a Type 3. No matter how you look at it, staying with the front sight in that situation is slower and less accurate than shifting focus from target to sight. With a Type 3 focus, the gun and sights just snap directly and precisely to the next target. And your head does not move to see the next target. Your eyeball just simply swivels in its socket so it can see the next target. The eye then stays fixed on that point, and as your body moves the gun onto the target, the eyeball naturally swivels back to where it's looking straight ahead again when the gun is there.

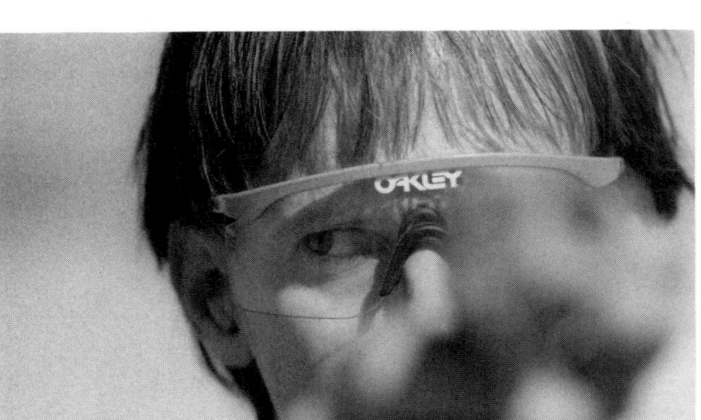

Your head doesn't move to acquire a target that's to your side. The eyeball just swivels in its socket to see the next target.

Your vision can change as you shoot. A good example is shooting a clay bird with a shotgun. My vision is very peripheral as I'm waiting to see the bird appear. Then as the bird goes out, my mind is chalking in the flight pattern, the gun goes on the bird, and I start tracking the bird. Then as I track it more, my vision gets more and more central to where I'm only aware of the relationship between the bird and the bead. That happens in pistol shooting too. My vision may be very peripheral on the first three plates on the *Speed Option,* and then I look to the next target and as my gun goes onto the bonus plate my vision changes and scopes right down to a more central vision. The feeling is like focusing a camera—something is slightly out of focus and then comes into perfect focus.

It's easier for me to go from a more directed focus to a more open focus. Let's say I set up targets at 40, 20, and 10 yards and shoot two shots on each. If I start on the 40-yard target, I'm going to have a pretty directed, Type 4 focus on it where I'll be watching the front sight come onto the target, hesitate, lift, and lift again for the two shots. If that's all I've seen there and my mind is quiet and relaxed, I'm usually going to be able to drive the gun real hard onto the next two targets without any conscious effort—it's just going to happen. Whereas if I start out on the close target, I'm going to come out tense and rushing. I have a more difficult time settling down by the time I get to the 40-yard target to see the things that I need to see there. My splits won't usually be as good on the close target in that situation either, also because of the tension. If I'm coming across the closer targets from the longer target, the splits will usually be faster because I'm more relaxed—I start relaxed and will stay relaxed. When I start on the close target, I start tense and stay tense. But that's just a personal thing; some people would much rather start on the close target and just crank on from there. For me, it's harder to pick up on the front sight for a Type 3, and especially to watch it lift on a Type 4 shot, when I start shooting with a Type 2 focus where I'm just blasting away at easy targets; it's hard for me to downshift those two gears and get back on the sight. One of the most difficult things for me is to shoot at warp drive and then shoot difficult shots on the same string—and to stay at warp drive when I should be at warp drive, not just at half-speed. I try to stay at the limit of function on all my shots, and being able to do that always comes back to how little tension comes into my shooting.

Visual Awareness

To shoot quickly you need to be able to see quickly—you need to heighten your *visual awareness.* For a simple exercise, hang a tennis ball by a string from the ceiling and swing it around and keep your eye focused on the ball clearly and sharply all the time it's swinging. But the best exercise is just shooting and being aware of what you *really are seeing* so that you'll start to learn from that. *You need to start to see things that you wouldn't normally see.*

If you move your eyes at a speed that approaches the speed a fan blade's movement, for instance, you can visually freeze the blades for a split second. Normal vision wouldn't allow you to see that. You're simply seeing something you don't normally see just by your eye's looking at it in a new way. A good batter can see the seams spin on the baseball and can tell which way a pitch is going to break. The power of your vision to intuit and process information like that comes from your being in the present tense state of meditation I described in *Awareness & Focus*. Again, these are things you can experience in everyday life that you can relate to shooting.

Don't ever feel content with what you see. You possibly could be seeing more.

At home or in your office, pick out a couple different spots at different distances and practice shifting your focus from one to the other. You can visualize one of the spots as the target and the other as your sight. You can define one object and then refine your focus on the next and see how quickly you can go back and forth. When you're shifting your focus from spot to spot, become aware of the time differences it takes to locate or define the object you're looking at and to actually refine a sharp focus on it. You'll see how quickly your eye can just look to and leave the object that you're just trying to locate and how it takes a little bit longer for your eye to actually refine the focus on the other spot. You can use one spot as a locator and one as a refiner, and then you can switch them—or you can refine them both or locate them both. You can change your types of seeing with this exercise to just get a feel for how your vision actually operates. Then try the same thing on the targets and sights. The more you do it, you'll see that you can do it faster and faster.

You just need to learn to see things that you don't normally see—things you haven't opened your mind up to let your eyes see. Your eyes are there looking all the time and seeing things all the time, and if you just open up your mind to allow yourself to see them, the visual inputs you will experience can be phenomenal.

Visual Patience

If there's any key at all to shooting focus, it's that you need to understand the meaning of the phrase *visual patience*. I first realized this at the Steel Challenge, but it applies to every type of shooting where you're under the pressure of your own time. *See what you need to see no matter how long it takes.* If you can just do that, eventually it will take less and less time because your seeing will become faster and faster and sharper and sharper. If you're having problems on a stage, or if things aren't going as they should, or if you're missing too many targets, you can almost always look back and realize that you just didn't have the visual patience to see what you needed to see. You're rushing. Your vision's not with the gun.

When you're in your broad spectrum, general preparation mode, "visual patience" is an easy catch phrase to run through your brain and relate to how you've done in the past on stages that resemble the one you're about to shoot. And knowing from your practice what you need to see, just keeping that visual patience in mind will tend to keep you in the real world. It helps keep the anxiety and tension down and keeps you from feeling rushed.

Are you forcing the shooting? When you let the shooting come to you, you will understand the meaning of visual patience.

Visual Acuity

Being able to see clearly is a central element of being able to shoot well. While that's a pretty obvious statement, a lot of shooters need to address it. The physiological facts of how your eyes see don't really have to be understood, but being aware of the practical effects of how different circumstances affect your ability to see clearly can really make a difference in your ability to perform and to experience these different focus types.

I use only my right eye when I shoot. The reason I do so is because I'm *cross-dominant:* I'm left-eyed and right-handed. This combination makes it difficult for me to shoot with both eyes open without experiencing double vision on either the gun or the target, depending on where I'm looking. In my opinion, a situation like mine is the only reason a person should *not* fire with both eyes open. If you're just beginning and you experience the same thing I do, you can learn to shoot with both eyes open by focusing with your strong eye. There are a few top shooters who do this, Chip McCormick and Tom Campbell for instance. I tried to focus with my dominant eye while leaving both eyes open for a year or so but found that, although my left eye could refine a focus to the same degree, the speed in which it refined that focus was much slower than what I experienced with my right eye because of the years of previous training my right eye had.

The solution for me was to block off my dominant eye's ability to focus. While this can be done by simply closing, either partially or fully, the dominant eye, that's detrimental for two reasons. First, when one eye is completely blocked off into darkness, that puts that much more strain on the open eye. Your eyes were meant to work as a team. If one eye is closed then the other's pupil dilates to gather enough light. When the pupil dilates, then it's not the correct size for optimum focus in that environment and both its duration of focus and ability to focus are impaired. The other disadvantage is that it's almost impossible to close one eye without subsequently slightly closing the other eye. Squinting with your open eye causes a straining of the eyelid muscle which causes the eyelid to exert more pressure on the eyeball which decreases its visual acuity. Closing one eye can decrease your visual acuity by up to 20% as opposed to simply blocking that eye's vision.

The best thing I've found to improve the performance of the weak-eyed shooter is to use transparent tape to block the dominant eye's focus. This blocks the eye's ability to focus, while it retains its light gathering ability so your pupils stay at their optimal sizes for the corresponding light conditions and let you focus as accurately as possible. Also, your eyes are more naturally open so there's no pressure on the eyeball from squinting. Tear off a strip of transparent tape about one-inch long and place it over the point where your eye looks straight ahead. Make sure you place the tape high enough so that you can look under it when you reload or have to perform a similar precise movement. The tape only has to block the point straight away from the eye to be effective. This trick allows you to focus with your weak eye without experiencing any of the problems associated with blocking the strong eye completely; both eyes function as if the tape wasn't there. Probably the most noticeable benefit you'll find when shooting with both eyes open comes when you're shooting groups. You'll notice how much longer you can hold your focus.

At first, you'll find it difficult to move around without stumbling, and the tape might make you feel uncomfortable. I suggest first using the tape while you're at home reloading or working on your gun to get used to it. In time it will go unnoticed.

This practice should be limited to the shooter who's only competition-minded. If you're a law enforcement officer, or if your motivation for shooting is self-defense-oriented, don't follow this practice. If you can't shoot without double vision, just close the offending eye.

For shooting glasses, the colors I've found to work best are gray and clear. If your eyes can stand it you're best off with clear. In the real accuracy world, most shooters don't use colors. For me, the "high-tech" lenses with the mirrored, reflective coatings cause distortion.

TRIGGER CONTROL

Trigger pull is a reaction to visual focus. Except for the rare, textbook Type 5 situation, I experience trigger control in all types of shooting as a visual process, although something that's such an impulsive technique as high-speed trigger control really can't be experienced as a process. But to break down and analyze visual trigger control, the technique can be looked at in terms of parts, but not in steps. I don't know the exact point where my visual awareness results in the physical action of pressing the trigger. Both these processes are really the same thing in that they deal with the relationship between trigger press and vision. But my attention is visual, and the actual order is eye-trigger.

Trigger control is born of a desire to hit the target. When you see what you need to see to hit the target, the gun fires. Look the shot off.

Looking The Shot Off

The different focal points are all a matter of seeing what's necessary to get the targets and get on with the shooting. When you're aware of a clear focus, the shot breaks. Knowing when to break the shot is a very important thing, but it can't be learned. Releasing the shot is totally a matter of awareness. It's a sense of clarity of focus, and then it's action. *I look the shot off.* Your attention and visual awareness of the clarity of your focus break the shot. It takes quite a bit of time to develop the sort of automatic trigger control that fires the gun in response to what you see. One way to work on that is to practice dry-firing the gun without aiming at any particular object, just focus completely on the top of the front sight. Keep your focus there until the hammer falls. Attempt to do that without any thought or direction whatever to actually pressing the trigger, and eventually you can make trigger release a response to your focus.

Vision controls the trigger. When you see what you need to see, the shot breaks. Trigger control is visual attention.

To just get a better feel of the trigger pull being separate, for mechanical improvement, you can practice dry-firing the gun without looking at it by just holding the gun in your lap, squeezing the trigger, and feeling every detail of the trigger movement. Your body can learn to pull the trigger accurately, smoothly, and quickly that way without actually having to shoot. You don't need to take a lot of time to pull the trigger. Then dry-fire while looking at the sights and experiment with seeing how quickly you can pull the trigger and not move the sight alignment. You'll see that you can pull the trigger really quickly and not upset the gun's alignment. If that doesn't carry through into your shooting, then you know that it's the gun actually going off that's causing you to flinch and pull shots—not trigger jerk.

To cure yourself of that, you can line the gun up on a target or even just on the berm. Get lined up and set up and close your eyes and squeeze the trigger, feeling its movement very carefully. Spend some time doing that and you can make your body understand that there's nothing there to be afraid of. You can also just fire into the berm with no directed visual attention toward anything—you're not trying to hit any particular object or focus on the front sight—you're just making the gun go off by working the trigger smoothly. Once you get a good feeling for that, then you can do that same thing by watching the front sight and looking the shot off. You're visually focusing on the front sight, and when it's in perfect clarity the gun should fire.

Trigger Speed

By pressing the trigger to the rear with a good amount of speed and followthrough, you're narrowing down the time frame in which you're allowing the gun to fire. In bullseye shooting, the competitor will align the sights and wait until sight wobble has settled down to an acceptable zone and then begin pressing the trigger. At any time thereafter, say from 1-3 seconds, the gun will fire. In practical shooting, we've just refined that process down to, say, 0.1-0.3 seconds. In other words, although you don't know *exactly* when the trigger is going to release, you know the range or the time zone in which the gun will fire. For higher speed shooting, that zone may narrow down to a variance of between 0.02-0.05. Likewise, the zone may move up to 0.3 and beyond for a really difficult shot.

This technique is difficult to explain. At the speed necessary to fire the shots, there cannot be the slow, deliberate squeezing of the trigger as is usually taught in other shooting sports. But, on the other hand, you cannot think in terms of *making* the gun fire at some instant; that would lead to trigger (and sight) jerking. Again, you know really *close* to when the shot's going to break, but you don't know *exactly* when it's going to break. Trigger control is a subconscious action that's directly linked to what I see; however, the physiological action is an increasing, constant pressure until the gun fires.

Where your finger rests on the trigger doesn't matter. It's best to just let your finger fall where it naturally does. I've noticed that the faster I shoot, the more my finger moves out towards its tip. For instance, I've noticed that my finger has moved out when I shoot a Bill Drill. And this is nothing intentional. When shooting a Bill Drill, you obviously have the desire to shoot the shots as fast as possible and your finger has more leverage and control towards its tip and can move the trigger faster. This is just one of the things that sorts itself out naturally if you'll let it. But regardless of where your finger rests on the trigger, make sure that's the only thing your finger rests on. Don't let your finger rub along the frame; the trigger itself is the only moving part on the gun that you want to cause to move.

Let the gun recoil freely. If you're neutral and relaxed, it will lift and return on its own. The gun can time itself.

TIMING

Timing is having a visual awareness of exactly where the gun is pointed at every millisecond it's in operation. Timing means everything to a shooter; yet it is, in fact, nothing. Timing cannot be learned, and there's no actual way to concretely describe it to the point where I could say, "...and that's how you time a shot..." You can never *know* exactly how and when to return the muzzle to the target, when to shift to the next target, or when to fire the gun. All these things can only be sensed and simply done.

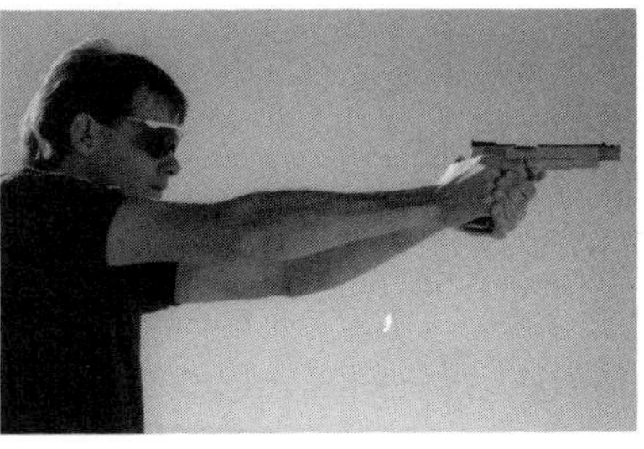

Timing comes from knowing where the gun is in relation to the target every millisecond. You time your shots by simply having the desire to get the gun on the target or to keep the gun on the target for each shot. Your wrists must remain flexible so you can visually control the gun's position. The gun must lift and return the exact same way and on the exact same path each shot. That way you just guide the gun with your eyes instead of your muscles.

Timing is the coordination of hands, eyes, sights, and mind. You're using timing when the gun is tracking onto the target. There you're timing the shot so it breaks the instant the gun hits the target's scoring surface. You're also timing a shot to where the visual awareness and focus of your eye sets the cadence for the next shot. This takes the form of seeing the sight lift up and down, coming back into alignment after the preceding shot. Each shot must break no sooner or no later than it's possibly able to. That's only possible if you're totally focused and aware of where your gun is aimed every millisecond.

If your gun tends to stay elevated after a shot, or if you find returning the gun to target is imprecise or inconsistent, tension is usually the cause. Some shooters who use a very tense grip can return the muzzle of the gun quickly, but not precisely. As I mentioned earlier in the book, when I'm able to shoot in my most relaxed state, my sight lifts and returns like it's spring-loaded. I don't have to make any alignment adjustments at all. The gun should recoil just as it does when you're shooting off sand bags. Neutrality in both the grip and stance makes this possible. A shooter who uses an excessive amount of pressure to grip the gun tends to experience inconsistent tracking which makes it necessary to realign his sights on each shot.

Your wrist's sensitivity and your visual sensitivity to the gun's movement control timing. The wrists must remain flexible for control of the muzzle. In this respect, what's necessary in shooting is very similar to what's required in many other sports—tennis, golf, baseball, basketball—in that the critical point of impact or release of the shot, swing, or throw must be done with a flexible wrist. In shooting, you're performing a similar fundamental with the muzzle of the gun. The grip remains constant, but the wrists must allow free gun movement away from the target in recoil, and, more importantly, movement back to the target as your vision dictates. In shooting, you time both impact (recoil) and release (return to target). If your wrist is tight or tensed in trying to stay rigid to "fight" recoil, you'll never realize complete, precise control. While on this idea, it may help you to think in terms of sight control instead of recoil control. The idea of "recoil control" leads us to think in terms of unidirectional control—stopping the muzzle's rise, while "sight control" is bidirectional—tracking the sight's rise and then its return to the target.

Although this may be a little difficult to comprehend until you experience it for yourself, allowing your gun to recoil freely allows you to get it back on target faster and more precisely. As I've said, the consistency of the recoil is more important than the amount of the recoil. From using a neutral grip and position, my gun lifts consistently, both in height and path, on each shot. That makes it easy for me to control my gun with vision instead of with muscle tension. Just let the gun recoil freely in your hands and guide the sight with your eye. I'll talk more about this in *The Shooting Tools* appendix, but this relaxed, neutral state is the key to shooting the .38 Super. That gun will almost shoot by itself if you'll let it work. Your gun can lift and return on its own much, much faster than you might believe is possible if you just let the gun work—let the gun time itself. The gun will lift and return by itself only if you're not exerting any excess pressure, especially side pressure, beyond what's necessary to just hold the pistol level, and if your stance and grip are neutral and very, very relaxed. You must give the gun the freedom to move on its own, unimpeded by any physical control you could exert over its natural path.

You can probably first experience this shooting groups off a rest. When you move to your freestyle platform, set up a target at medium range and just shoot at it. When you can relax and be neutral through your entire body, you'll find that the gun will lift and return on its own, settling right back on the center of the target. Keep turning up the speed so you can feel yourself relax *as* you are shooting, not just before you squeeze the trigger. If you tense up or increase the pressure in your grip, you'll notice that the gun no longer returns on its own; you have to physically steer it back into place.

The only true limit is in the body's nervous system. Anything less implies interference from lack of attention.

After time spent with this experience, regardless of the distance or speed you're shooting, you will intuit the actual amount of timing *you* supply. When doing a Bill Drill, for instance, I am aware of a huge amount of muzzle flip; I also know that I time the gun's return so the shots can come as fast as possible. But I *definitely* am not aware of forcefully returning the gun. In high-speed shooting, I'm driving the gun with my vision. For successive shots on the same target, in recoil I'm driving the sight onto the target with my eyes. And on separate targets I'm driving the sight or the gun onto a new target.

On occasion, I have shot with the intention of keeping the muzzle rise to a minimum. If I have the intention and if I'm working well and my timing is accurate, the muzzle seems to not even rise at all. Sometimes I might want that in certain scenarios—shooting doubles at close range on multiple targets or on small targets at longer range—and I am able to do that just by *willing* the muzzle to stay still with my vision. I'm just driving the gun where I want it to go with my eyes, and trusting my body to follow my vision. And when I've seen that, I've had the desire to see that.

My awareness of this possibility just came from a specific experience of trying to keep the muzzle low when I was shooting two shots on a 10-inch plate at 15 yards where my total emphasis was on keeping the sight on the plate. But beyond two shots on one target, I've found that it is extremely difficult to continue to drive the gun hard enough to hold the muzzle low without getting very tense on the gun. Beyond a couple of shots, just the speed of firing gives over total control to the gun itself where it just does the work for me, lifting and returning on its own.

But the whole point is to first experience the gun timing itself. When you experience that, then whatever timing that *you* supply is just as automatic. Consciously *trying* to time your shots will almost insure that you never will experience the gun tracking on its own. A relaxed, total focus on the gun's movement will allow your vision to control the gun so that it returns to the target as fast and accurately as possible. Your vision can control every aspect of your shooting technique so easily and so subtly that you'll never be consciously aware of any control coming from your muscles.

The whole timing process is made possible by your visual attention and acuity. Timing is *not* physical rhythm or cadence. Trying to time your shots with your hands and wrists, instead of your vision, amounts to nothing more than habit shooting. Timing is something that has to be learned by feel; it's not a fundamental component you can actually describe, because to execute timing you must be focused in the present tense—the shooting tense. You can't "think" about timing to learn it. Like shooting focus, you must think about what you saw in retrospect to know about your timing.

SPEED

The elusive absolute. A tremendous appeal of practical pistol shooting is that the perfect score is nearly impossible. I say "nearly" because in timed IPSC and Action Pistol events perfection can result from getting all As or all Xs within the specified time limit. But for most of the shooting we do, no matter the point score, you can *always* go faster.

Speed, by itself, is nothing; it's not even definable. Focusing on speed of muscle movement produces no outlet for applying that speed if the shooter will not maintain a focus that's related to firing the gun.

When I'm working as an RO at a local match, I see a lot of shooters of different ability levels come through a stage. It's really obvious to see how speed—shooting the stage quickly—not only comes from moving the gun quickly, but also comes from eliminating wasted movement. When the lower-level shooter draws, his gun doesn't move to the target—it makes all kinds of detours on the way. When he moves from target to target, the gun doesn't move smoothly, directly, precisely; sometimes the gun dips below his line of sight or he overswings targets, and so on.

As you remove the wasted movements through your attention, you'll notice that your speed will increase. You can't just go out as a D-class shooter and eliminate wasted movement and be fast. But by the time you get to the point where you've shot enough rounds and spent enough time to develop the body feel necessary to keep the gun between your eye and the target and have the sights aligned wherever you look, it will also have taken you that length of time to eliminate the wasted movement. All these things work together and filter down to the point where, as the gun handling and the reflexive skill develops, the speed of movement increases and the wasted movements stop.

Speed is a byproduct of your attention. That is: speed is a result of smooth movement which is a byproduct of relaxed visual acuity. If you're not focused, if you're tense and glazed over, you're not going to be moving quickly and smoothly. It's when you're relaxed and focused that high-speed movement becomes possible.

BREATHING

Respiratory control is a central point in most other forms of competitive shooting, but due to the intensity and speed of practical shooting, few of its players pay much attention to it.

Essentially, proper respiratory control achieves two things. First, it relaxes your body to give you the most stable shooting platform with the least amount of tension; second, breathing correctly means that you retain enough oxygen to keep your vision clear and allow your eye to focus precisely and quickly. Taking in a big gulp of air and holding it causes tension and pretty shaky shooting.

Ideally, you should shoot during the *natural respiratory pause* we all experience whenever we breathe. The natural respiratory pause is that transition between exhaling and inhaling. In normal breathing, as you're doing now, you don't breathe in and out continuously, and you don't hold your breath or exhale every last bit between breaths. You should breathe the same way when you shoot. The only difference is that you'll hold that natural pause while you shoot. The natural pause is usually at about the level you'd have if you were just talking to somebody, but just hold whatever amount of air that's comfortable. You'll be able to comfortably hold this natural pause for at least 15 seconds. Especially when shooting groups, you'll notice a big difference in your ability to hold the gun stable and to maintain a focus on the sight. If I'm trying to do a really high-speed draw and don't have to hit a lot of targets, as I'm moving toward the gun I may exhale slightly more air from what I normally hold. For some reason that seems to lower my tension.

You might want to watch how the RO runs his commands so you can practice your breathing rhythm to where you can time your respiration so that your breath will be exhaled to your natural holding level just before the start signal. I try to time my breathing to where I'm holding a comfortable breath when the buzzer goes off. I'll usually inhale more than that and then exhale to that point shortly after the *"standby..."* signal. And at that point—as my air is settling in my body—I can feel how much tension there is in my body, especially my face, stomach, and arms. I can feel a *set*.

In practice, exhaling that little bit of air and feeling my set gives me a point of reference. Then when I draw the gun and fire, or when I finish a string, if I hold my position I can compare the breath, the way my stomach feels, and the set or feeling I have now as opposed to what I realized before I started. If I exhale or inhale when the buzzer goes off, it's harder to have a reference point to make this comparison because you don't really get any feel for your body set if you're exhaling or inhaling sharply. Through my breathing I try to set everything at an equilibrium, and in practice I use that reference to see if I can keep everything at that equilibrium while I'm actually firing.

On mid-range targets it takes 1-2 tenths longer to set up before shooting (to let the gun settle in the aiming area as opposed to just getting it into the aiming area). Use that time to relax; it's time well-spent.

RELAXATION

A normally tense shooter who's working to reduce his tension level often feels that he's going slower in the draw and on fast, close stages. The reason explosive, tense movements might feel faster to this shooter is simply because he'll feel more muscle strain. His muscles are already wound up, so when they're stretched or contracted more, the extra effort will be perceived as speed. After you're able to feel relaxed, watch the clock for a few runs and find the answer. (However, as I'll make a better point of later on, the timer itself can cause as much tension as anything else.)

In any sport, "touch" is a valuable quality. You can't throw a punch, a ball, swing a bat, or perform most any other precise, quick motion if you start with tension in your muscles. Likewise, you cannot perform one of sport's ultimate speed moves—the draw—with tension coursing through your forearms and shoulders. Along with the easier, and therefore quicker, movement of relaxed muscles, the extra precision of movement further adds to speed. Through a relaxed draw, the pistol will find its final position more quickly and more directly; there won't be as much pre-shot fidgeting as is made necessary by a draw that jabs the pistol out in the vicinity of the target, but not on it. A relaxed draw leads into a relaxed mount so the shot can break almost immediately when the gun is leveled. And that pace continues on, especially by helping your vision relax so your eyes can bring inputs in clearly and quickly. That's speed. If you *look* fast, you're probably not.

If you're diligently practicing with a focus on relaxation and you don't see your times drop and accuracy improve as you expected, rest assured that they will. Often a shooter who is extremely tense when drawing and shooting needs some more time to allow himself to re-direct his mechanics. In extremely tense shooters, the actual motions, and of course rhythm, timing, and even balance, will naturally change when his overall shooting becomes more relaxed. For a time, he might experience difficulty in getting his hand on the gun properly, difficulty in getting the gun to settle down on target, or trouble with the natural direction the gun points when he mounts it. All these things can be affected by pressures and tensions; therefore, when the pressures and tensions change, so can these mechanics.

Our sport is a tension sport. And a lot of shooters may not feel their own tension because of that. People who come into IPSC from no other competitive shooting backgrounds have usually not been made aware of the importance of relaxation. And they *won't* learn relaxation in IPSC;

they'll have no clue that it even matters. It's crucial that you do learn to relax and that you learn the feelings of relaxation. Get the feeling of just floating the gun out there with only enough tension to keep it from dropping down. Get the feeling of gripping the gun with the same tension you'd use to drive a nail with a hammer. And everything can happen from there.

When I'm shooting at my fastest possible, tension is the hardest thing to fight. See how relaxed you can be.

If you are tense, and have always been that way, then you won't be aware of being tense. In practice, you need to just see how relaxed you are. Notice things about tension. Notice tension especially in your biceps, stomach, and face. Check for tension in your jaw and see if your tongue is pressed up against the roof of your mouth. Just see how relaxed you are.

Mostly, if you can keep your stomach relaxed your whole body will be relaxed. It's difficult to draw the gun quickly without tensing your stomach. You think you should be able to turn the draw into just an arm movement, but it's really difficult to do. I'll accept that tension as I go down, but as the gun goes out, I want to feel my stomach relax with a normal breath of air in it.

Learning about tension in my stomach was a major discovery for me. I was practicing several years ago for the Steel Challenge and my partner had to leave for a while. Since this was in the days of the stopwatches and we had to run each other through the course, he told me to take a break. So I decided that I would just shoot the stage we had set up without a timer at all. That was the first time I ever did that—just draw the gun and shoot on my own command and I won't know what the time is. The first time I did that I noticed how much more relaxed I was. So I did it a couple more times and noticed how relaxed my stomach was. And that was a major turning point for me. I started experimenting with that feeling and experiencing my new awareness.

A recognition that you are too tense and that you move so much more smoothly and accurately when you're not so tense could be a major discovery for you, and not only in shooting, but in any physical action.

CALLING YOUR SHOTS

In this sport, you have the easiest means at your disposal for feedback: *call your shots.* It's so easy to do—your sights were printed there when the gun went off. An ability to call shots accurately is something that's usually lacking in the shooter who's hovering around the upper-A/lower-Master level. And that deficiency comes from having had too little disciplined accuracy work where that fundamental is instilled. Don't just take it for granted that, "Well I saw the sights there, so that's where the bullet must be..." But if you miss the shot, you didn't *really* see the sights there the instant the gun lifted. If you really think about it, it's not possible to miss a shot if you saw the sights on target when the gun went off, unless you *really didn't* see the sights there at the instant the gun fired.

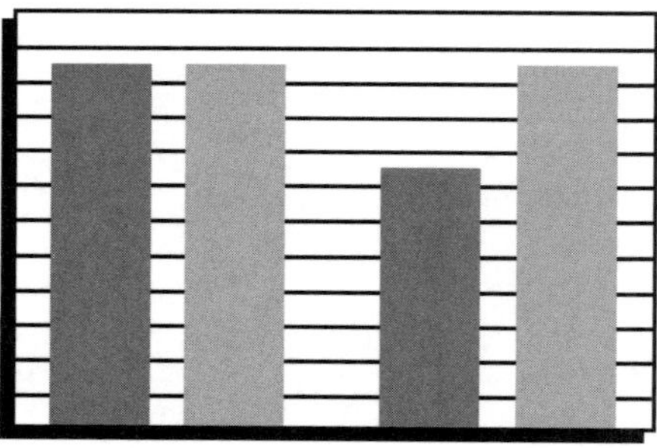

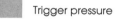

When you're in a match (right), your visual attention tends to go in bursts. To be able to call your shots accurately, the trigger pressure bar and visual attention bar must both peak together, as they usually will in practice (left). If your vision shuts off before the trigger pressure peaks—even for .01 seconds—you won't *really* know where the shot went.

You feel anxiety in a match and you don't followthrough like you do in practice; you lose your visual patience. That's why shooters say that the shot "looked great," but the shot's not there. I've done it myself where I've shot, and in my mind's eye it looked perfect, but the paper doesn't lie and the hit just was not there. And the reason that happens is because the followthrough is bad. If you were to put your attention level on a graph like the one shown on this page where one bar represents your visual attention to sight focus and the other shows your finger pressure on the trigger, if you're giving the shot your full attention, both bars are at peak levels when the shot breaks. As your sight focus becomes more and more refined and your trigger pressure is going higher and higher, before the trigger pressure bar can get to the point where the shot breaks, your vision stopped somewhere. The visual followthrough on the sight stopped, the inputs stopped. The shot went off and you may have seen the gun recoil, but if you really look back and recall it in honest detail, you really didn't see the sights in a lined up position at that instant. So you get the idea of *that looked good, looked perfect,* because you never quite made it all the way. You may have only had to see it for .01 second, but your vision may have lost it as you tripped the trigger.

Missing one hundredth of a second of visual input is enough to make you have no idea where that shot went. If that shot wasn't where you thought it was, then you weren't paying attention. When you don't see that point in a match situation, it's normally because your eyes are glazed over—fuzzy—and you're not seeing accurately. You don't see the followthrough; your vision just doesn't stay with the shooting—it becomes fragmented and goes in bursts. And that's because your eyes are not relaxed. Remember, you must see continuously—stay in a state of constant observation—to shoot well, and your eyes must be relaxed to do that.

It's really valuable to be able to tell you're jerking the trigger, for example, not by any feeling of convulsing on the trigger, but by watching the trigger jerk move the sight out of the notch before it lifts. When you can see that happen, you know that you're following through on the sight. And usually just the pure attention of holding the front sight aligned in the notch stops the trigger jerk. If you can't tell you've jerked the trigger by watching the sight, then you didn't see what you needed to see.

FLINCHING

If you ever see a good shooter "fire" a shot that doesn't really happen and the gun dips down, such as when the gun has a malfunction or runs out of ammunition during a stage, that may not be a flinch. The shooter might be just anticipating recoil in the amount that he knows it will lift the gun. In that case, it's the shooter's timing that causes the gun to dip. But uncontrolled flinching comes from different causes and must be eliminated to shoot well at all. Some shooters flinch at the pure impact of firing a handgun. Especially with a Super, there is a tremendous amount of blast that, admittedly, is a little hard to deal with at times. Realize that is something that happens after the trigger is released. If the gun is going to blast you, at least avenge it with a hit. Hit or miss, the blast is still there in full force.

Other times flinch can come from just pure anxiety. Anxiety over firing can cause a shooter to quickly hit the trigger in fear that he must do so to get the shot over with. This sort of trigger jerking can't be solved directly through work on the mechanics of trigger control. The shooter is usually not comfortable with the relationship between his sights, the target, and the ticking clock so he rushes up firing because he thinks he has to. The truth is that refinement of a sight picture can happen in hundredths of a second. Tension and anxiety can cause the shooter to overlook that fact. This shooter needs to relinquish control of his shooting to his vision. A relaxed focus on seeing what he needs to see—having visual patience—will allow him to fire at the right moment without ever being consciously aware of it.

If you can't call your shots, then you don't know where the gun is pointed when it fires.

An extremely valuable shooting lesson for a lot of people is that if you didn't see that point in the graph, it may not be something as complex as shutting off your vision. With new shooters, a much more simple possibility is that you're just closing your eyes when you fire. I've caught myself doing it on certain days, or with a certain gun—or for some reason—I blinked as the gun went off. And that, along with the group shooting and calling your shots, is a major point that you need to work on before you can really start on any of the fundamentals of practical shooting. You have to be able to keep your eyes relaxed and open to where you are able see the sight lift. Even if seeing the sight lift is not central to the shooting focus, you must retain the ability to see it. If you're unable to see the sight lift when you watch for it, you are quite possibly blinking.

Spend a lot of time with this and get a real feel for whether you're always able to keep your eye relaxed and observing. If you're shooting at an indoor range, you can watch for muzzle flash. If you're seeing orange, or if you're seeing the front sight come up in the rear notch silhouetted against orange, then you're not blinking. You can't see that if you blink at all. You can sometimes even see the sight silhouetted against the flash in the daytime. From talking to bullseye shooters, they say that a real important day for them was the first time they saw the muzzle flash in daylight; they knew then that they were really following through. It's amazing how fast you can blink your eye and open it. You'll never even know without the muzzle flash check. Look for it.

If you are blinking, the best things you can do are looking for the flash and looking for the sight to lift. My solution is to always look for the sight to lift. If I can see the sight lift out of the notch and the shot is right where I called it, then I know I'm not blinking. If the shot's where I called it, but I didn't see the sight lift out of the notch, I may have blinked. I may have gotten the shot where I wanted it to go, but that's not enough. Just because the bullet hits where you want it to go occasionally doesn't mean that you're out of trouble. You want to get to the point where your eye can be dead calm and relaxed and watching all the movements that are going on. And that's harder and harder to do the more you tense up. The more tense you get and the harder and faster you try to go, the easier it is to blink your eye.

If you can't keep your eyes open when you shoot, there's honestly not much more you can accomplish until that ability is acquired.

FLOATING THE GUN

When I shoot my best, I don't hold my gun—it's *suspended,* floating in front of me. *Floating the gun* is something that you can only begin to experience after you've developed a neutral, relaxed stance to shoot from. You also must be to the point where you're so relaxed that your eyes are totally attentive and focused on the gun's movement. Then your mind and body as a whole are so completely focused on the gun that it seems to float between your eyes and the target with no conscious energy exerted toward controlling it. I move, the gun moves; my visual focus shifts, the gun shifts.

All the things in this section, and the one that preceded it, could actually come down to experiencing this level of shooting. I call this a level of shooting because, to me, it's attainable only after time spent in experience of bringing all the objective and subjective components of shooting together. Since this is a sensation, I can't tell you exactly how to "do" it, but you'll know for yourself when you do.

Floating the gun is a state. The sensation allows me to shoot my absolute best. When the gun is just suspended between my eye and the target with no conscious effort at all, my eye can just drive the gun wherever I want it to go, and my body follows.

When the gun is suspended, you reach a state where you are not separate from the gun; you're no longer just this person back there trying to control it. The gun, the target, and your vision of all those things, become one unitary process. Your awareness of that process allows the feeling to take place.

Achieving this level of shooting is a good example of what I meant by meditating as I shoot. Reaching this level means that no matter the speed, precision, or conditions, the shooting takes place with its optimal result. Even from an unbalanced position where I'm not able to stand solidly, such as leaning around a barricade or kneeling under a boundary, or even hanging from a parachute, then that position doesn't affect my shooting. The gun is always out there—suspended, aimed where it should be, ready to fire, and totally controlled with my eyes. Watch for it, but don't *try* to make it happen. Just knowing about it will allow it to happen. After you experience the sensation of floating the gun, you will discover your own way of finding it each time you shoot.

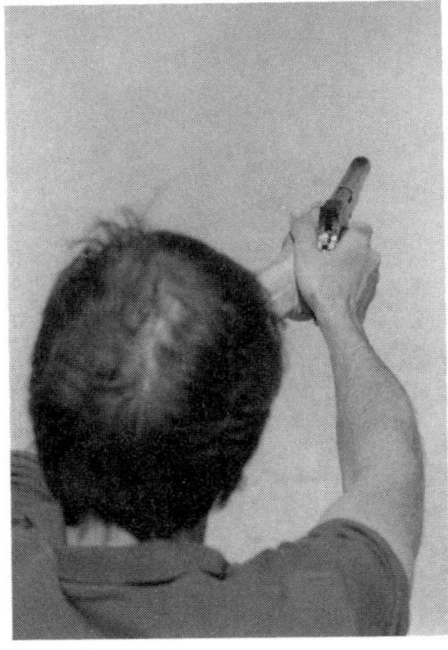

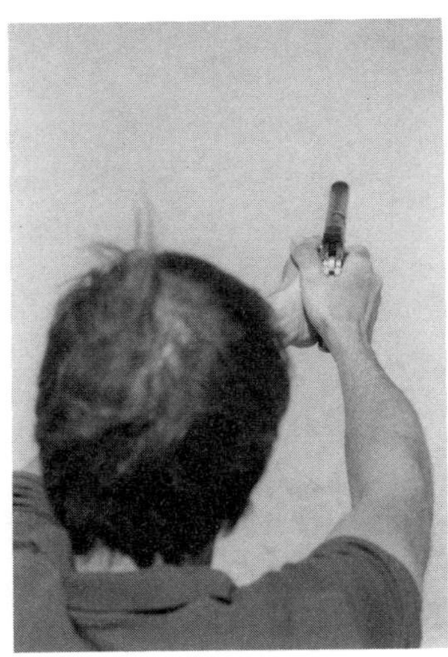

Since I don't have any limiting ideas on how to hit the targets the fastest, I've actually seen my wrists break to hit a stop plate before I was indexed on the plate. And it's only something I've seen... Driving the gun is simply getting on and off the targets as quickly as possible. It's a state, not a mechanic.

DRIVING THE GUN

In this book, I make a lot of references to *driving the gun*. This is a main fundamental in my shooting, but it *definitely* is not a mechanic, and it's *not* anything I ever practiced. Driving the gun is a good example of undirected focus that I've seen in practice and in matches. Because my only goal is to shoot the targets as quickly as possible, and because I don't have any limiting thoughts about how to do that, while my gun is moving toward a stop plate, I've actually seen my wrists break to point my gun toward the plate before my upper body was lined up with the target. That type of action would never happen if you were in a state of concentration—say if you were concentrating only on your front sight. But if you're visually aware enough to let it happen, your body can find a way to hit the targets. Trust it.

But driving the gun is not limited to something as unorthodox as my wrists breaking at an angle to get to a stop plate before my body is indexed on the target. I also have the sensation of driving the gun into the first target. I have a zone focus on the A-box, and when the gun gets up and into my focus, it just follows a track toward the box; I steer it in there with my eyes and the gun centers itself. Then from that first target, I often feel like I'm just driving the gun onto the others too.

Driving the gun comes along in the exact same frame of mind as floating the gun. It's just a mental state where you're *visually* directing the gun anywhere you want it to go—much the same as when you're driving your car down a crowded city street. You're aware of *all* your visual inputs. You're simply responding to your seeing; it's direct action. When you're driving the gun well, you're not thinking at all; you're simply steering or driving the gun with your eyes. You're driving the gun in recoil where you're driving the sight back down on the target; then you're driving the gun to the next target. It's just a total frame of mind.

When you combine driving the gun and floating the gun, to me that's the highest form of pistol shooting. I really can't overemphasize this. When you've practiced all your techniques and you understand all the things that you see and what you do here and what you do there and how this affects that—when it gets right down to it and you're out in the match, if you're going to perform your best, *you're just going to drive the gun onto the targets as quickly as possible.*

Section 4: SPECIFIC CHALLENGES

Learn the mechanics of technique. That will leave you free to focus on the mechanics of the match.

In this section I'll give you some ideas that will help you face the specific challenges routinely encountered in practical pistol shooting and help allow you to realize the ultimate goal of always being able to adapt to the shooting, without thought, without hesitation, and without limitation. While the techniques used to conquer different specific challenges are, to the last one, really just different ways to apply the same comprehensive ideas we've discussed so far to different situations, I put these in a separate section because many of the different components of technique are unique in themselves and have their own set of mechanics and own points of focus.

You cannot "think" your way through using these different techniques; you can only do them when they're needed. Therefore, your practice should include both the physical exercise of installing each technique into your inner repertoire, as well as the free application of experiencing the different focal points, mental sets, and body feels each specific challenge requires. And make sure that you practice them. You have got to practice what you can't do if you want to be a successful practical shooter. Never take these techniques for granted, because the more a stage requires a mastery of a specific challenge, the more distance there's going to be between different levels of shooters.

Prior to shooting a stage which will make necessary the use of any of these techniques, visualize as fully as possible how you will use them as you move through the stage. Spend as much time as you can using this form of observation. Avoid hitting a stumble because you hadn't prepared yourself to act.

It's important that you understand that some of these things *you just do*. You know what you need to do, and you just relax and get it done. Something like a turning draw, for instance, can be done so much easier and faster than I can think through it, much less write it all down in

detail. Such a movement is totally a feel process, and the inputs you get that create your feels are bound to be different from anyone else's. But, even though a lot of the things in this section fall into this category, the real purpose of my technical, step-by-step descriptions of them is that you may understand where any negative inputs that could inhibit developing your feels might originate.

MULTIPLE TARGETS

When I have to shoot more than one target I use what might be called a "turret" rotation to position the gun on each target. But, and this is important, 99% of the time, once alignment is confirmed with the first shot, *nothing moves from the waist up*. Unless I'm shooting at my fastest possible on easy to hit targets where I might be driving the gun toward the targets, everything from the waist up stays neutral. No matter how little or how much I'm turning, the rotation is all done with my legs. I want to keep exactly the same upper body relationships and feels as when I'm just shooting one target. When you keep your legs still and twist from your upper body, your arms change in their tension and relationship to center. And that's what you cannot have. You want to get started from your relaxed, neutral position and keep your knees bent enough so that you'll have plenty of latitude to move so that by the time you've swung as far as you can go, you can still keep your position. You don't want to have to change your stance at all—you lose your index that way. It's harder to acquire targets by just looking at them if your gun isn't mounted the same way for every target. Flexing your knees allows you to pivot and keep your index. The faster I need to shoot and the farther I need to pivot to get the targets, the more knee flex I use.

Making the big swing to target 3 on the *Speed Option*, I maintain a neutral upper body index by moving from my legs. The knees must be flexed to do this.

"Index" denotes the shooter's point. Once you're lined up and have confirmed sight and body alignment on a tar-

get, then that's your index. And then, hopefully, wherever you look is where that index always follows—you can move up, down, left, or right and still see your alignment. That's why there can't be any movement from the belt up; all movement must be done with your hips and your legs to keep your index correct.

If you're a beginning shooter it will really help you to work on the *Awareness Exercises* in the *Development* section that deal with learning to move the gun and keep the sights lined up—learning to keep your index. Through your experience with those exercises, you'll discover on your own how important it is to move the gun from your legs instead of your waist or upper body.

Moving Your Head

In a scenario where you're faced with two targets that are close enough to you and are spaced far enough apart from each other to where a simple movement of your eye within its socket can't acquire the next target, don't be afraid to move your head.

To reach that second target, you can keep your head fixed in its relationship to your upper body triangle and move that "unit" across the open space until your peripheral vision has finally acquired the target—quick intentions, but slow body and gun movement. *Or* you can snap to it by swiveling your head so that your eye can immediately focus on the target. By the time your eye has got the focus on the target, the gun will be there. If you'll study the pictures, you'll notice that my upper body "unlocks" slightly so I can move the gun this great a distance as fast as possible.

When the targets are too far apart for my eye to acquire them, I move my head. I slightly dismount the gun to make the movement as fast as possible.

This is an advanced technique that requires extreme body feel and awareness to preform consistently. If these haven't been developed to an extremely high degree, this technique won't be consistent, and it would probably be faster for the beginning and intermediate shooter to just pivot until he sees the next target, rather than unlocking any part of his upper body. I included this technique to dispel the notion that your upper body has to remain rigidly locked in position continuously from the time you've indexed on the first target. The goal is to shoot the targets as quickly as possible. If something works for you, and you can do it consistently, use it.

THE DOUBLE TAP DELUSION

Hopefully by now you've worked and experimented with your grip, position, and tension enough to know what your front sight looks like when it's tracking consistently. Your body and eyes are aware of where the gun is each millisecond it's rising and falling and it's the observation of that process that sets up the timing of shooting two shots on one target.

There is no such thing as a "double tap." There's just two shots on one target. Whether the break is .11 or .30, your eye is looking and has the ability to see more than you could possibly imagine. So if you can just watch without putting any limitations on yourself, through having a visual awareness of the gun itself, you can see where it's pointed, the front sight, the relationship between the sight and the target, the gun tracking in recoil, the sight lifting—you can see the gun in every single detail of its movement. You may as well see it—you've got to see something. The idea of pointing a gun at a target, confirming sight alignment, and then hitting the trigger twice is ridiculous. It's so limiting that you're never going to progress past your self-imposed pace. You could work yourself down to where you could hit a 12-inch circle at some certain distance, maybe 10 or 15 yards, reliably at a certain speed, but you're never going to get out of that cage. It's a trap; it's just a self-imposed trap that you place on your vision. Just shoot. Two shots.

There's no such thing as a double-tap. Although the shot split will be under .15, I see what I need to see for "each" shot.

I'm always aware of what I see prior to releasing either shot. I retain the ability to separate the pair of shots to whatever interval is necessary to see what I need to see to keep them on the scoring surface. I'm asked that question a lot: do I actually see the sights—or see anything—when I shoot a double? I do. And if it's central to the type of shooting focus I'm seeing, the sights will be razor-sharp. I've just refined the sight-tracking process down to where I'm aware of the gun's position in .01 second increments. This sort of high-speed seeing is only possible when you're relaxed and focused entirely in the present tense.

The term "sight picture" will be a stumbling block for some people in understanding what's in this chapter. Many shooters are only aware of "sight picture" when they think of "sights," and ask, "Do you see two sight pictures?" No, I don't see two sight pictures—if we define sight picture as being the relationship between the front sight, rear sight, and target in a paused, or stopped, state. What I'm actually observing is the sight's *relationship* to the target, so when I say that I see my sights when I shoot doubles, that's what I mean.

It's helpful to monitor your split times when you're shooting two shots on one target. The time between shots is usually a good indication of the levels of attention and relaxation you're experiencing. I haven't yet been able to get below a .11 split. An average Master-class shooter will be in the .14-.16 split zone with .18 being acceptable for most types of shooting.

For normal single-hand shooting, I quarter away from the targets at approximately a 45-degree angle. There's a little more pressure on the gun and my arm is extended more straight. I don't quarter away from the targets strong-hand if I have to reload or make a transfer to the weak hand.

SINGLE-HAND SHOOTING

Whether in IPSC or Action Pistol, a good deal of the courses require you to fire the gun with either hand. The fundamentals of firing stay the same; however, there are a few differences between single-hand and freestyle shooting techniques.

Most changes are in the shooter's setup. For best results, it's advisable to stand so that your firing side is closer to the target. I stand at approximately a 45-degree angle to the target. Quartering like this helps keep the gun from destabilizing your stance. Since you don't have the other arm on there, you don't want recoil to tip your shoulder back, which it would if you stood in a freestyle stance and fired one-handed. Experiment to find the position that allows you the most comfort, best natural aim, and most consistent sight tracking.

But whether or not I quarter away from the targets depends on two things: how easy it is to hit the targets and whether or not I have to reload or transfer during the stage. If the targets are close and open, I'll usually just stand about how I would to engage them freestyle. And if I'm shooting strong-hand and need to reload or make a transfer to the weak hand, those processes are a lot easier and faster when done from my normal freestyle stance. When the shots are more difficult, and when you have to shoot more of them, though, you'll have better control by quartering away from the targets.

You should find a position that allows you to maintain a secure base for suspending the gun without requiring you to overly tense your arm and shoulder. I extend my arm out more straight by locking my elbow, but I don't allow my shoulder to move farther forward. A major fault is stretching the shooting arm too far forward, unplugging it from the shoulder joint. From that position, the shoulder and upper back muscles can't contribute to supporting the gun. The shooter begins to really strain and the gun becomes unstable, especially when it must be moved from target to target.

I cant the gun slightly shooting weak-handed. This feels very natural to me, plus it keeps my head relatively upright. It's better to tilt the gun than to tilt your head.

When you shoot one-handed, use the same shooting grip you use freestyle. For me, the most important thing in controlling consistency of recoil is to not force the pistol out there in an extremely tense position. I get a firm grip, relax, and just extend the gun. When the gun is extended naturally, the bicep of my shooting arm is relaxed. Again, be alert to feeling any excess tension there; it's very detrimental. The head should be positioned so that your eye is looking directly through the sights, and the head should be erect as possible. I cant the gun over slightly when shooting weak-hand. I have to tip my head quite a bit to the left to see the sights with my right eye if I don't cant the gun. Tilting the gun to the right lets me feel that I'm in a little more of a compromise position because I'm not having to tip my head radically just to keep the gun straight up. Most of the shooting we do weak-hand is close enough to where any impact change that canting could cause is not even worth mentioning. To me, slightly canting the gun feels very relaxed and natural.

If you're just standing and shooting, position your non-shooting-hand somewhere on your body. This is done so that the free hand and arm can't act as a pendulum and destabilize the stance. It doesn't really matter where you place your hand so long as it isn't being forced against the body with any excess pressure. But if I'm moving and shooting from my strong hand, I won't secure my free hand; I use my free arm like a rudder to help me feel more balanced as I'm moving.

A problem many shooters have when firing one-handed, especially with the weak hand, is holding the pistol with a death grip. Since you only have half the support, the sight will move more on the target than when using both hands. But controlling that movement is what counts—making it consistent. A super tight hold on the gun makes it very difficult to hold the pistol steady and to execute good trigger control—two critical components in a good single-hand technique. Relax and pay attention to trigger control, or more specifically, the relationship between your trigger press and the sight's position on the target. Press the trigger straight to the rear when the amount of sight movement is acceptable. I use a slightly more firm grip, but the extra pressure is added only by my perception of my hold. In other words, it increases naturally and uniformly through my awareness of the larger amount of gun movement.

Trigger control is critical when shooting with one hand. Since you don't have the extra support, the gun is more free to move, or be moved, in response to a poor trigger technique. A common mistake in a weak-hand technique is sticking the finger so far through the trigger guard that the finger makes contact with the gun. If you do that, your whole hand starts "milking" the gun as opposed to just the pad of your finger moving the trigger. If you get poor results in weak-hand group shooting, this is a good thing to check.

If you have to make difficult shots one-handed, you can focus on feeling yourself pressing that little bit of takeup out of the trigger. That's something you're normally never conscious of in freestyle shooting. A lot of times if you're aware of having that sensation from the time you touch the trigger to taking up its free travel, just that feeling alone will quiet your trigger pull down from a jerk.

Practice firing groups with each hand to help you discover weaknesses in your overall technique. Shoot groups from long distance as well as at higher speed from close range. Focus particularly on the consistency of the sight movement before, during, and after the gun fires.

Weak-Hand Transfer

The weak-hand transfer is definitely something that needs to be practiced over and over. For safety's sake, as well as for improved performance, this motion isn't something to be fumbled through. The actual technique of the transfer, though, is really a simple process; precision of movement is far more important to speed than is sheer speed of movement.

To make a transfer from the draw, on the start signal, I move both my hands into the same positions as I would for a freestyle draw. As the shooting hand withdraws the gun from the holster and begins moving it upward, the weak hand moves towards the gun as normal.

The transfer occurs when the gun is pushed slightly away from the strong hand, exposing a gap underneath the grip safety. The thumb of the weak hand moves through this gap, and the "V" formed by the weak-hand thumb and forefinger slides firmly up against the grip safety. The positive contact of the weak hand up against the grip safety is important to insure that you reach a good final hand position. The hand should be placed as high on the pistol as is comfortable to improve control.

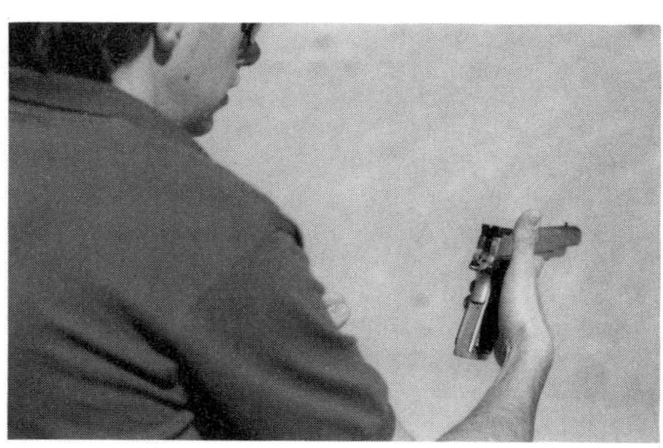

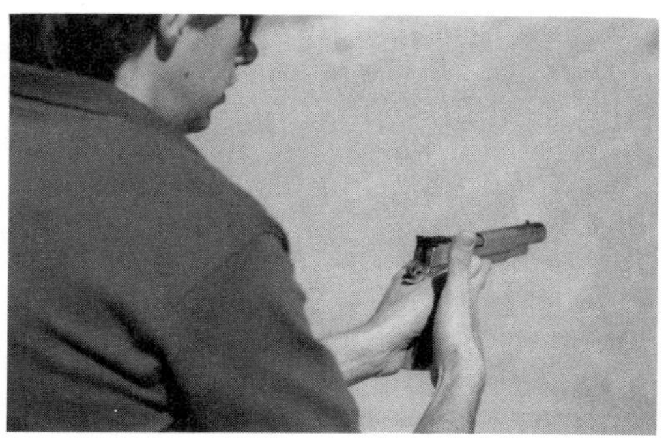

The transfer occurs when the shooting hand exposes enough room for the weak hand to grasp the gun. Relaxation and precision are the keys.

For a gun with a single-sided safety, the lever should be released at a point just before the hands meet for the transfer. With an ambidextrous safety, you can either do it then or release it with the weak hand when the gun is transferred. If you do that, you can go ahead and leave the thumb on top of the safety if you prefer.

When the weak hand is moving onto the gun and the strong hand is loosening its grip, there isn't really a secure hold on the pistol; this is when relaxation and precision of movement are most important. Just as with the reload, the transfer must be done in a very relaxed state. The final transfer is a "wiping" motion of my weak hand continuing forward and my strong hand beginning to move rearward.

On a stage that requires you to make the exchange at some point in the shooting—after a reload or shifting sides on a barricade—both hands are brought back to about the same position where the exchange took place as I described above for the draw and transfer technique.

The actual motion is very simple and certainly takes far less time to do than to detail. It is a "feel" movement, and is, therefore, very difficult to actually describe in a fool-proof way. The main thing is that you're relaxed. That's what allows you to make this fairly complicated move safely.

These are the two basic methods for going prone. Neither one offers any real advantage in itself, but you need to learn to do them both since they can be used to your best advantage in different situations.

PRONE SHOOTING

Whether it's required as part of the stage or required by the conditions of the shooting, the prone position is a major specific challenge you'll definitely face.

I've never been that much on going prone. I will go prone by choice only if I have enough time so that going prone doesn't make me feel rushed. I usually feel more comfortable just standing and working from a relaxed position within a time limit that I know I have plenty of time on than I will pressing myself to go prone and then maybe having to rip off the shots to make the time limit.

There has got to be a bottom-line comparison of accuracy and speed in making a decision to go prone. If multiple shots are called for at long range, and there's not a lot of gun movement from target to target, sometimes the extra stability of the prone position allows you to shoot faster and more accurately beyond the extra time it takes to go prone. Only experience, experimentation, and your own confidence can determine whether or not you should go prone in a scenario where the position isn't stipulated. Unless you're at a level where you are extremely confident in your performance from that position, and you can go prone very quickly, you're probably better off using the extra time to shoot more carefully from your freestyle platform.

When I go prone, as soon as the buzzer goes off the immediate input in my mind is that I just go straight to the ground and somehow snatch the pistol out of the holster while my body is still fairly erect. The main thing is to get the gun out of the holster *immediately* and get your weak hand going toward the ground. I'll be more tolerant of an initially poor grip on the draw when I'm going prone because from when I get the gun out of the holster to when my weak hand gets up onto the gun in a shooting position I've got a lot of time to change my grip to what I want.

There are two basic methods for going prone. You should experiment with both for two reasons: first, you'll be able to see which method you're more comfortable with; second, you need to be able to perform both methods because they both need to be used in different situations. This gets back to being a well-rounded shooter. You don't want to give anything away to a stage, or to the other shooters, by not having the confidence to simply perform in the best method possible.

In the first method, the weak hand goes down and the strong-side leg goes back at the same time. The leg goes back as far as it can go and the shooting arm stretches forward and completely extends all the way out before you lay your body down so you don't have to push the pistol along the ground. Then you kick your support arm out, and at the same time, the weak hand grabs the gun.

In the other method, the basic difference is that you don't move either foot initially. The first part is the same: you get the gun out as quickly as possible and your weak hand goes straight to the ground. Then just as the weak hand is touching the ground, you kick both feet out behind you at the same time. At the same time you kick your feet, the shooting arm comes down with the gun to a point fairly close to where your weak hand has hit the ground and you have moved your body all the way back. Once your body is on the ground and your legs are back, your weak hand is right next to where your gun is so that you can get your shooting grip a little bit faster.

It's possible to engage targets at extreme close range by wedging the gun up in the air by sliding the support hand down on the grip. To get your head lower, you'll need to move more around toward your weak side.

Those two methods offer the same overall amount of speed. You may want to use one over the other under different circumstances. Using the first one, I go prone a little smoother. If I'm not trying to go prone in any certain area, for example, if I don't have to go prone starting in the confines of a shooting box, I'll usually use the first method because I "float" down to the ground more as opposed to the second one where I hit the ground quite a bit harder.

When shooting prone, it's critical that the gun and both your forearms rest on the ground. You never want the gun dangling up in the air or to have your elbows on the ground and your arms off the ground. The whole point to the position is stabilizing the gun, and there is no stability in holding the gun up off the ground.

For medium- to long-range shooting, I drop essentially straight down so that my body is almost in line with the target. My neck relaxes and my head just rests against the inside of my upper arm. In a situation where you have to go prone and shoot close targets or targets that are at a high angle to your position, your body can move around to your weak side, allowing you to move your head farther over onto your shooting arm or even onto the ground on the other side of it. This lets you lower the support hand on the grip to wedge up the muzzle of the gun to a point where you can effectively engage targets at extreme close range. Both arms and your support hand are still on the ground, but the gun will be off the ground.

Notice how you need to stand to be able to just drop down and be lined up. When you're learning (which is continuously, don't forget), you can rehearse your prone position in reverse from down to up to discover how to get where you want to end up. Practice not only getting to your prone position, but practice the position itself. Shoot groups from your prone position and see how fast you can fire accurately. Give yourself a time limit and compare your results to what you get from your freestyle position.

Kneeling with one knee down isn't as stable, but it's much faster to get in and out of and to draw from. And always put the strong-side knee down.

Kneeling with both knees down and sitting back on my heels gives me a very stable position, but I'll only use it if I don't have to get in and out of the position quickly.

Again, in the prone position it's very important that once your body is in position that you stay relaxed and keep your arms relaxed—just as relaxed as you would be in a freestyle position—so that the gun can recoil and return on a natural path. You should feel totally relaxed when prone. When you're lying on the ground, just pay attention to yourself and see what kind of tension you're lying there with. You want your body nice and relaxed with its full weight on the ground. You don't want to be tense and have your legs pulling up or your stomach curling in. You just want to flop down on the ground and let your arm lay out there nice and straight and be relaxed. A common problem I see is shooters who are really tense and fighting their prone position—having to tense their muscles to hold the position. Just because you're down and stable on the ground, it doesn't mean that muscling the gun can't still have the same effects as it could if you were standing. Fighting and muscling the gun totally defeats the position.

KNEELING

The kneeling position, for me, offers no more stability than my freestyle technique; therefore, I'll only use it when the stage makes it mandatory.

If I'll finish a stage in a kneeling position, or any time I can economically get into a position with both knees on the ground where it won't cost me any time in having to get back up, I'll use both knees down because it's much more stable; I can get behind the gun a lot better that way. With

1. Neither the gun nor the shooter should touch the barricade. Try to ignore it as much as possible. 2. Stand to the back of the barricade and bend your knees so you'll have flexibility to reach the targets. 3. And don't rule out the possibility of engaging targets that are at an awkward angle by shooting one-handed and gripping the barricade with the other for stability.

this method, I hunch back and sit my rear-end on my feet so that my body is just slightly curved forward.

The only time I put just one knee on the ground is if I need to get in and out of the position quickly and if the shooting is not that difficult. If I have to draw from a kneeling position, sometimes I feel more comfortable with only one knee on the ground. And if you're only going to touch one knee down, use the strong-side knee; it's a more comfortable position to shoot from.

BARRICADE SHOOTING

For those interested in Action shooting techniques, there is a more specific breakdown of using the barricade in those events in the *Revolver Shooting* appendix. But for this section, I'll discuss using the barricades as we find them in IPSC.

Unlike in Action Pistol shooting, the first rule in IPSC is to not allow your hands or the gun to touch the barricade. Although it may feel more stable to rest the gun on the barricade, the recoil will be directed differently.

Stand as far back in the barricade as you can and try to just ignore the barricade as much as possible. Keep your feet set a little bit wider and bend your knees a little bit more so your center of gravity is lower and you'll be more stable if you have to reach or lean around the barricade to get to awkward targets. And if the targets require you to make really awkward leans from your freestyle position, don't ever rule out the possibility of engaging the targets strong-handed or even possibly weak-handed. Getting into a strong-hand barricade position by using your weak hand to grip the barricade for stability can be done pretty quickly and is a real possibility as long as the shots aren't difficult.

Top: When I have to pick up the gun from a table, I use my thumb and index finger.

Bottom: You'll always be able to shoot faster and more aggressively if you stand rather than stay seated.

TABLES & TRICKS

If a stage requires you to begin from a seated position, with the gun on a table or in a drawer, or requires you to perform some action prior to the draw or in the course of moving through the stage, remember that those things are designed to "upset your concentration." And now if you're no longer concentrating as you shoot, there is nothing to be upset.

When you might have to move through doors, shoot from a perch, or negotiate your way under, over, or around other obstacles, take a look at solutions instead of problems. And in the case of moving through swinging doors, for instance, don't overlook the importance of actually getting through the doors. That would become a main point of your observation and visualization preparatory to your shooting. Mentally work through whatever it is you have to work through by visualizing in detail how you will overcome it and get to the shooting. Think it through until it's no longer a concern. Don't dwell on it though; just give it enough attention so that you know you can do it—and then just do it. *Just getting to the shooting should always be your simple goal.* If you can get to the shooting as easily as possible, and then just shoot the targets, you'll be way ahead at a match.

A really popular thing in IPSC matches is shooting from any number of "table" scenarios. Sometimes you begin seated with the gun in the holster; other times the gun is placed on the table or in a drawer. If the gun is situated like that, use your thumb and index finger to pick up the gun, grasping the pistol by the grip safety and the front of the trigger guard. As the gun comes off the table, it just pops right into your hand.

When you must begin from a seated position with the

gun holstered, just stand up, draw, and shoot. Don't make this simple act any more complex by worrying about kicking away chairs and other similar things. Again, you have got to just work through whatever stipulations the course has designed for you and get to the shooting.

Years ago, Rob Leatham and I did a lot of experimenting with table scenarios and determined that if you're allowed to do anything you want, you'll always shoot faster if you stand and shoot rather than remaining seated, especially if you have to move after you're done shooting from the table. You'll shoot the targets more aggressively from your freestyle platform.

It always helps, especially before you travel to a big match, to go through a few scenarios like beginning from a seated position. Don't, however, spend a lot of time trying to develop a "feel" for deploying a technique in the specific instance you're practicing. That becomes wasted time when you discover that at the match the table height is different, and so on. Show yourself that you can handle any curves that are thrown at you and that you can get onto the shooting. Make that your goal in practice when rehearsing an oddball stage: see how quickly and consistently you can get to the shooting.

No matter how you actually move, the most important thing in the turning draw is that there is no lateral gun movement. My holster just pivots on a straight line to the target.

TURNING DRAW

One of the most famous IPSC courses, the *El Presidente,* requires you to begin with your back to the targets. This isn't a common starting position, but you definitely will encounter it. Even if only practicing the *El Presidente,* which is a good idea since that course really gives your gun handling a workout, being able to get to the shooting means that you need to learn this maneuver.

When I start, I have the majority of my weight on my left foot, and at the sound of the buzzer, the first thing that happens is that my right knee bends down and my right foot pivots on the ground to get my right leg turned around. My left foot pushes off at the same time and pivots me around to the right. My left leg swings around, and when my left foot lands in position, my right foot just turns out again to complete its pivot.

From the instant I begin my turn, the gun is never facing uprange even when it's in the holster. I start the draw movement immediately on the sound of the buzzer, and by the time my hand gets on the gun and the gun starts to come out of the holster, my right hip is pointing downrange. The gun just lifts out of the holster and goes directly to the target; there is no lateral movement of the gun at all.

Some people use a technique in which they step their strong leg around behind their weak leg and then pivot both feet. That doesn't work as well for me, but it's very popular and you should experiment with it. But no matter how you do it, the most important thing is that there is *no lateral gun movement.* You want your body pivoting into your holster and you want to have the gun lifting straight up out of the holster and then going on a straight line to the target. Your hip is just essentially pivoting around that straight line. The gun is *always* moving in a straight line to the target.

This maneuver takes some practice in order to get to the targets with the minimum amount of stance adjustment. But again, on a course like the *El Presidente,* there isn't any need to refine your stance. Relaxation will allow you the speed and precision of movement necessary to perform the turn as efficiently as possible, and efficiency means that you're shooting as soon as you're facing the targets.

RUNNING & GUNNING

Where the movement is forward, such as in the basic IPSC assault course, *just run*. I dismount the gun and bring it back closer to my body in about the same position it's in halfway through a draw. I've practiced my reload to the point where it's fast enough that the reload is in before I can take my first couple of steps. In the end, it's faster and more consistent to perform the reload before you really get started running. That way you can get the reload out of the way and put your attention on running. If anytime you're moving and fumbling around with the load or you're not loaded when you get there, it costs you major time. That's why it's so important to really perfect your reloading so that it becomes a reflex; you should be able to have the reload in before you take the first step out of the box, never later than the second step. When you do start running, take long, smooth steps—but *run*. Make the running and movement part of your visualization prior to shooting the stage. The running is part of the course. Don't overlook it or be unprepared to go.

No matter what they throw at you, just get the gun into your hand and onto the targets—just get to the shooting.

Anytime you're moving from point to point, the main thing is that you have to be ready to shoot and have the gun in front of your face and between your eye and the target immediately when you step into the box; just as

you're taking your last step in, you want the gun in position. Don't wait until you're all safely tucked inside the box before you mount the gun on target. But don't extend the gun before you're one step away; that slows you down and unbalances your running. About one step before I reach the next box, I extend the gun into shooting position and focus on the target. If the targets are easy, I'm able to shoot the instant my feet are inside the box; if the targets are more difficult, I've got a head start on acquiring whatever shooting focus is needed. You should be able to intuit the position of the box and your feet position relative to it by at least one step away. You don't have to slow down and tip-toe into the box. *Get to the shooting...*

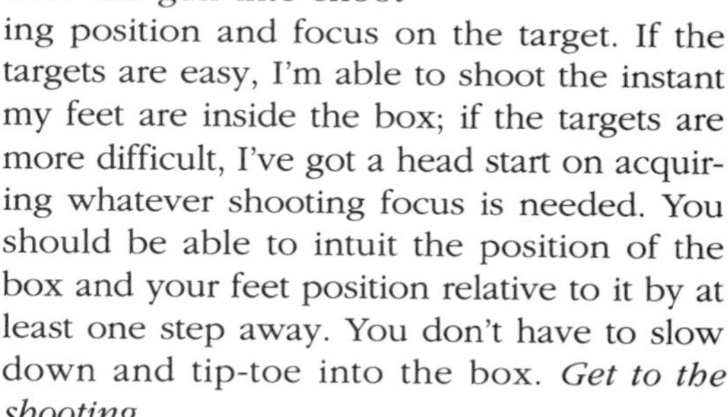

When you're moving from box to box, the gun should be extended by at least one full step away. That way you're ready to shoot as soon as you're in the box. Up to this point, though, the gun is dismounted so I can move faster and smoother.

Probably the best way to shave down your movement time from box to box, provided you can move smoothly and that you've got the gun in position when you get there, is to be able to leave the box as soon as possible, and that usually means getting your body moving before you've made the last shot or two shots. That possibility is something that's extremely variable and just depends on the target scenario. If you're just going to draw, shoot two shots, and move, and if the shots are easy, Type 2 shots, you can pretty much start moving as soon as you draw the gun. You can make those shots while you're leaning and your body's already in motion. If the shots are a little more difficult, you have to experiment to see what kind of movement you can get away with. It also depends on whether the targets are steel or paper. If the targets are steel, and if it's a more difficult shot, you need to weigh the factor of possibly missing and having to come back into the box. It may be worth it to keep your body stable while you're still firing the shot. Leaving the box while you're still shooting is an advanced technique and you have to experiment on your own to see what you can get away with.

When it's actually possible to shoot the gun *as* you are moving, your footwork may become a central focus. Rehearse your steps as much as possible; you may need to develop a cadence where you're having to vary the length of your steps so you can time your shooting with your target acquisition. This is an advanced technique that you just have to work with. The best advice I can give is to just keep the gun between your eye and the targets and move as smoothly as possible so your steps don't cause you to jog up and down. You're attempting to move while keeping your upper body as stable as possible, and the only way to do that is to bend your knees so you can just float your upper body across the ground. If you want to practice shooting on the move, you can hold a glass of water with your hands in a shooting position and see how fast you can move without spilling any water. That will help teach you to move your feet without disturbing your upper body.

When you're in a position where you can't support the gun using your normal freestyle technique, achieving the sensation of floating the gun as I described in *Creative Shooting* becomes central to your performance. If you can reach the level where you're able to float the gun before you in that alive, undirected state, then it's possible to shoot well from any stance.

At the West Coast Invitational, they've had this stage where they strap you into a parachute rig and then slide you down a chute so you're dangling by the parachute straps after it hits its stop at the end of your fall. They've got targets everywhere, no-shoot targets, and a stop plate with a no-shoot by it, and in the meantime, you're swinging back and forth trying to shoot it all. And because of the way the straps hold your arms out away from you, the gun just flies all over the place; you have no control of the muzzle.

I've always done really well on that stage by just staying relaxed and watching the gun's movement. I just let the gun dictate the pace. Each time after I shot, people were saying "Wow, you went three seconds faster than anybody else...," but it didn't feel like anything to me. All I was doing was just letting the gun tell me its story. I had no idea of what the gun was going to do; I had no way of predicting what I was going to see. I just had to do it as it came.

Anytime you're faced with a specific challenge, the first awareness of how you're going to handle it should ideally come from experience. If you're a new shooter, the only way to get that experience is to set up scenarios in practice and work through them. You don't have to set up actual match situations; just devise your own tests of your ability to meet the challenges. But every year, I run into something somewhere at a match that I haven't seen before or tried on my own. When that happens, I look for my best opportunities to make myself as comfortable as possible on the stage—and find a way to get to the shooting. When faced with a totally unfamiliar situation, relax and rely on your awareness to intuit the best way through the challenge. Really open yourself up to all the inputs coming from your environment rather closing your mind down to concentrating on the difficulty and unfamiliarity of the stage. In a totally off-the-wall stage, focus on making the most of your *shooting*. Don't let the anxiety of indecision get in the way of accuracy. You'll find that shooting through an oddball stage clean usually puts you very near the top. I'll talk more about this in the next section, but don't ever let a difficult situation affect your awareness of your shooting focus on each target. *Find the targets and shoot them...*

CHALLENGE YOURSELF

Once you feel that you're to the point where you can handle the specific challenges that are normally encountered in practical shooting, start coming up with your own. Create things you haven't encountered yet at matches. You can't help but learn when you try something different. Although what you try may not have any direct application in that you'll be developing some specific skill you can put to use, you are looking at things in new ways and the more you can experience that the farther and farther you'll be from the cage of doing everything in the same, certain, specific way. It's called *creativity...*

If you ever hear yourself say, "I know all there is to know about this or that technique," that should be your first clue that you really don't know anything. Don't get stuck in the rut of working on only those things that you know that you need to know. Once you've gotten beyond all the mechanical details, what you really need to know about is *you*. You can only find out about yourself by continually learning and trying different things and monitoring your perception. There's no other way to see your limitations. And there's certainly no other way to pass them by.

There's always something that can be done differently, and maybe better, and rest assured, they'll keep coming up with different things to test us with. This sport can be wide-open. There is still a lot of new ground to be covered in practical shooting, and I plan to cover as much of it as possible. I'm working on a lot of unconventional things—

prone positions where I'm lying on my side like in a normal stance, target acquisitions while I'm running, switching gun hands while I'm moving by targets. For instance, if I'm zooming by a section where they've got the target hidden behind a no-shoot, I'd like to learn to run by that target and shoot it at a full run. I'd like to add all that to my repertoire. There is always something to learn if you never stop experiencing, and never stop appreciating your experiences.

Section 5: COMPETITION

To the competitive shooter, performance in a match is the culmination of shooting. It's the whole thing. It's the reason we're here...and it's the reason you're reading this book. Perhaps this is the section you looked the most forward to reading, and I hope you won't be disappointed. But if you skipped straight here, I recommend you return to the beginning and start there so you will understand my ideas and what my descriptions and terms mean to me.

In competition, you must let your bodily awareness and your visual acuity work in relation to the training they have undergone.

All the questions and understandings, mechanics and methods, and functions and forms we work through—and all that practice—lead to standing in the shooter's box, whether at a club match or at the Steel Challenge. And the point I'll make in this section is that whether in practice, at a local match, or at the Steel Challenge, *the shooting is all that matters.* Nothing else. If you can focus yourself in the present tense, nothing else *will* matter.

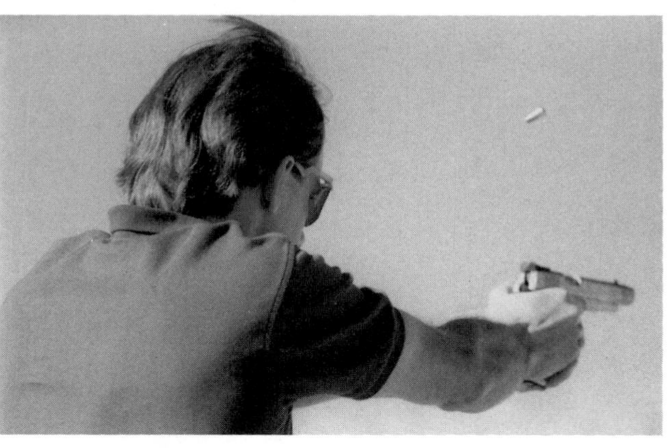

Detach yourself from conscious thought. Conscious thought is always going to be your greatest limitation to match performance.

I don't make any distinction between *match* shooting and *shooting.* I don't "use" a different attitude at a match than I do in practice; I am only one person and I only have one attitude. Ideally, you should shoot in a match or in practice as if nothing in particular were taking place at the moment.

Conscious thought has no place in shooting—not as the shooting is taking place. Focusing in the present tense removes you from conscious thought and allows your mind and body to operate intuitively and creatively as was your original nature. Your mind is unlimited. It is the thoughts that you put into it that are limiting. Take a look at your thoughts. Take a look at your limitations. Try to understand where they are and why they are. Facing and overcoming your own self-imposed limitations is always going to be the biggest barrier to realizing your potential.

MONITOR THE SHOOTING

One of the problems—*the problem*—with classical concentration is that it separates the action from the actor. In classical concentration, your brain is usually focused on a thought of one type or another as to what you're going to see or what you're going to do.

IPSC or Steel Challenge shooting, or any type of high-speed shooting where you fire more than one shot, is such an ever-changing game that there's no way you can ever have any positive prediction as to what you're going to see or what you're going to do. So instead of trying to concentrate on one of those things, you need to open your mind up to become just an observer or a monitor for what's actually going on in all your senses. Your eyes are especially tuned in to monitoring what the gun is doing and the gun's relationship to the target at all times. And in that choiceless, complete awareness, you've no longer separated the action from the actor. The action and the actor become unitary. This is what some people refer to when they use the word "feel." It's hard to describe, and that alone should tell you that feel is not an intellectual process.

If there is a key in practical shooting, it is to just become attuned to all your senses as they are monitoring what's going on as opposed to focusing on any one specific thing. Because it doesn't matter how well you're focused, as soon as that first shot goes off, *nothing* that happens from that point on is predictable—even if you're only going to fire two shots. You need to turn yourself into a continually observing, monitoring, awareness machine that perceives and processes information by sensation and sight and doesn't make any attempt to steer or guide your body's reactions by any type of thought.

The only type of beneficial thoughts that can ever come into your mind at a match, and even these can be turned into visual focal points, are those that deal with the procedures of negotiating a particularly complex stage. For instance, where you need your foot to be at this certain position to see these targets, or where you need to be to have the advantage on these targets, and so on. But as far as the actual shooting goes, anytime you make an attempt to *try* to do or see any particular thing, you're going to lose. When those things *come* to you, it's a totally different experience. Anytime you have a particularly amazing run and can recall all the things you saw in great clarity and great detail, without exception, all those things you saw just came to you on their own through paying them your undivided attention. And never will they come to you as a result of any sort of planned program that you force yourself through. The bottom line is that you just need to open up all of your mind and all of your senses to receive all of the inputs and information possible.

Get comfortable with being aware of what your mind is thinking as you're preparing to shoot. Be on guard for any kind of attempt your mind makes to try to *do* something. When your mind tries to do something it becomes rigid and doesn't flow. Open up your mind so that you can discern and intuit everything that happens. Be aware of your mind's wanting to expect something, but never expect anything. It will come when you least expect it.

Mental Observation

We hear a lot about mental control and mental preparation or conditioning, and there's a lot to be said for it prior to a match as long as it helps you relax or puts you in a more tension-free state. However, I don't follow the idea that there should be some separate mental programming that is followed for a match that isn't followed for my everyday shooting. I would never try to transform or manipulate my mental state at a match to the point that it's separate and distinct from what I sense in practice. The essential attitude will prevail. I associate the terms "mental control" or "mental preparation" with conscious planning, concentration, and other similar things I feel are too limiting. I prefer to think in terms of *mental observation.*

To me, mental observation means that before I shoot I need to be aware of all the things that come into my head—observe what my mind is going through. From experience, I know that these are going to be thoughts that usually try to get me to do this or that, try this or try that, bear down extra hard on this or ignore that. I look at every one of these thoughts very carefully to see if it's actually valuable or not. Most of the time these are things that your brain comes up with that it may think you need to try to do, and if you screen them pretty carefully, you'll realize that they'll be more a hindrance than a help. It takes experience, and often bad experience, to learn that.

Ideally, you should be able to shoot in a match or in practice as if nothing in particular were taking place except the shooting.

When I'm at the match or when I'm around the area of the match—at the hotel, for instance—my whole "mental plan" is to just be alert to my mind's own workings. When thoughts about the match come into my head, I go ahead and load them up, run them on through, and try to understand where they came from. In the past, a lot of times I noticed myself getting all worked up or pressuring myself about a match when I was back at the hotel, and, in retrospect, I wasn't really paying any attention to all the things that were going through my mind that were putting pressure on me—my brain was just sort of chattering away—and that just made me more tense and more tense and caused more stress and more stress. But I have found now that anytime something comes into my mind about the match, no matter where I am, if I will just let it run its course and just be aware of what it is that I'm actually thinking, then its true value will reveal itself. But when you're not aware of it and you're not aware of how many times during a day you might have thought about one particular thing in a match you're going to shoot tomorrow, it goes on as a chattering reflex, and then that's when you heap a lot of unnecessary anxiety on yourself.

You need to learn to be able to really observe what your mind is going through so you can read through it and, in a non-biased way, pick out the things that can help you—techniques and tricks and things like that—and you need to get past the things that aren't going to help you by carefully understanding them and realizing that they have absolutely no beneficial value to you.

It's just getting to the bottom of a problem... If you are alert and aware of your mind's workings in dealing with a problem—if you're conscious of it, so to speak—if you work through the problem, stick with the problem, and get to the bottom of the problem, the problem will drop away on its own. However, if you're not aware of how your mind works in handling a problem and you have a problem that's running around in your head and that problem just keeps coming back, and coming back, and coming back, it's no different than anything else in life that you have a problem with, whether it be a relationship or a job; if you just keep ignoring the problem—even though the problem is chattering away in your head—over time the problem may *seem* to disappear, but if you never understand the problem and never get to the bottom of the problem, it will *always* return.

Any time you plan for action based on an idea, what happens? When you actually meet the idea—down to the finest detail—it is never the same as you had pictured it, and so your response will be lacking in creativity.

Comparison

Comparison is another killer. If you want to watch other people shoot, be aware of how what they do can affect your own performance by the way your thoughts can relate to that. You need to teach yourself to be able to very detachably observe another shooter. I can watch other *Super Squad* shooters and learn things about the stage or pick up on key ideas that I may have missed in my rehearsal of it, and I can use what I see to constructively help me. But if you just look at their performance on a stage, it's real easy to be intimidated. You may know that someone who's shooting the stage doesn't have your skill level, but they may do something that, for some reason, you judge as exceptional, and the process of self-doubt begins. You start wondering if you can do that, when, in fact, you know you're at least as good as that other person. Watch yourself as your mind sizes up and compares. If you want to make a comparison, at least make it in a positive way. If you see a shooter who you know doesn't have your skill level do something you judge as exceptional, that should give you *more* confidence.

One of the main problems in making a judgement like that is that you don't have all the information necessary to actually make a judgement—you're going on a hunch. When you're watching a stage being shot, you're not seeing it through the shooter's eyes, and when you actually get up to the line, it's amazing how often the course of fire looks so much easier than when you were back there watching. Sometimes you can watch a person move and he may look fast, but what does that really mean? Did you actually see his time on the timer or know what his actual time was from target to target? Sometimes a guy may look like he's got an amazingly fast draw and first shot and you may look at that and say, "I can't hit that first target that fast," but in actuality you don't know anything. You don't know anything about what his actual time was or what his actual skill level was, and even if you did know, it doesn't have anything to do with your own performance.

Confidence is an emotion created by conscious thought. By its very nature it can work for you or against you. When you step up to shoot, let the emotion of confidence yield to pure action.

Judging Your Shooting

At the Bianchi Cup in 1988, I shot a numerical score of 1912-150X. As far as I'm concerned, that's all that happened. And every year I will shoot an undetermined numerical score. Period. Winning or losing is up to someone else's judgement. But at Bianchi, or any other match, the most important score is that shot that I'm firing now. And now it's over. And my next shot, and next shot, and next shot are all over. The point is to make each shot the most important one—the one in which your awareness is at its peak and your focus is most clear.

The only pressure at a match is that which you bring

with you. You should design all efforts to bring as little pressure as possible. Shooting in practice and at matches with a high level of awareness and razor-sharp focus will insure that you experience as little pressure as possible. Awareness places you in the present tense, where pressure cannot exist. *Pressure can exist only in your mind,* and only then when you devote conscious thought to the matter. In the present tense—the shooting tense—there is no conscious thought.

There couldn't be a good performance without a bad; likewise, a good shot without a bad. Both are illusions, dependent on someone's judgement for their definition. *Simply shoot, without judgement.* Many times a bad performance will follow an exceptional one. The mistake there is in judging the exceptional one as exceptional. Let's understand what happens in that thought process, and the fact that it is a thought process is the first clue...

When you do something that can be judged as exceptional, the first thing you do is try to recreate that the next time you shoot by concentrating on whatever you were aware of at the time of the exceptional performance. You feel like that's going to make another exceptional performance, whereas that will destroy your next performance because you won't be focusing in the present tense. You'll instead be concentrating on what you were focusing on last time, which may have no bearing on what you're doing this time—even if it's on the exact same course of fire. So in the performance that was exceptional, the main difference there was that the things you were aware of and the things you remember about that performance *just came to you.* When you try to recreate something, you're not letting anything come to you; all the inputs are out there, but they're not coming to you because your concentration is screening them through your previous inputs. Never try to force a pattern or a plan. Shooting well requires clear thinking and focusing on what is actually happening. Any interpreting or judging blocks clear understanding of the truth of that. The shooting, as it is happening, is all that matters. Don't *you* tell the shooting the story. *Let the shooting tell you its story!*

Wanting to win is a contradiction. The desire imposes a limit on your actions. There is only the shooting.

Something that's also related is judging a poor performance as poor. And we all do that because we all have performances that aren't what we wanted. But your feelings about that shouldn't affect your next performance. They won't if you really do have the right attitude about shooting, which is having the right attitude *as* you're shooting. I've gone away from practices before just disgusted and complaining about it to a friend, and my friend will say that's a bad attitude. I don't believe in that. When I'm out there on the line and I'm ready to shoot and the gun comes up, *that's* when my attitude is going to matter. Whatever I say doesn't mean anything. If I had a bad experience, I had a bad experience. I don't care if I trash the match or if I don't. If I don't, I don't—if I do, I do. But what I say away from the line doesn't affect that at all.

A Nationals Disaster

I had a pretty dismal performance at the 1987 IPSC Nationals. I don't usually like to talk about dismal performances, but there's a pretty valuable lesson to be learned from what happened there. This was just a major caution that I experienced once before in a match a good while ago that had to be relearned again at this match. The caution is that *you can be too prepared*. And at this match I felt too prepared. Basically, I just never allowed myself any creativity in my shooting there because I didn't feel that I needed any. And that's interesting because I had been in an extreme state of learning prior to that match and was experiencing a lot of new, different feelings that I hadn't felt in years, or ever, and I had been shooting better in practice than I had ever shot. That all gave me such an extreme feeling of confidence going into the match that when I went in, my main focus was in *trying* to reproduce these feelings that I had experienced in practice.

Always be on guard against *trying*. When you sense that happening, just back off, watch, and see what happens.

Trying. The very word trying implies contradiction. If you've already decided that you're going to try to make something happen, as opposed to just seeing it as it's actually going to happen, in that trying, all you've done is put pressure on yourself. There's a major difference between trying to do something and actually doing it. The difference is in the thought process that goes into it. Before you actually try to do something, your conscious mind comes up with all sorts of programs and plans and reasons and judgements as to a way to try to do something or for a reason to do it. Whereas if you just have the desire to see what actually happens, you'll operate without the pressure of having to accomplish anything. You'll just be a passive witness to what actually happens.

Trying to do something not only refers to trying to do something mechanically or physically—maintaining a certain position or a certain rhythm—it also can be something as subtle as trying to *see* a certain thing. For instance, you might know how the sights move in your peripheral vision when you're engaging certain close and easy targets. Well, *trying* to see that can be disastrous. Trying to see something puts just the same limitation on your mind as does trying to do something physically. Anytime you catch yourself trying to do anything, stop it. Back off and turn down to about 85% or so and just watch what happens. See if the smoothness doesn't take over and tune in your vision. Just kick back and watch and see what's really happening instead of trying to *make* something happen. This is something that you always have to be on guard for, and when you're practicing, or especially in a match, it's really easy to forget to not *try* to do anything.

If something occurs that's extraordinary in your shooting, it's always something that's just occurred. And it always seems, in retrospect, that it was just something that you noticed; you didn't try to make it happen. When you're aware of certain visual things that you see when you're operating at the extreme envelope of your performance, it's not because you *wanted* to be aware of them—it's just because your brain was quiet enough so that you *could* be aware of them. And it's that state you need to enter into in the competition. You need to have the confidence to just *see what you see* without putting any particular emphasis on *this is what I should see here,* because you may find that you might see things that are totally different from what you planned on seeing and that actually are more suitable to the scenario. Always be aware of your brain. Every time your brain tells you that you need to do this to do that, that's a good sign that you need to take notice of that process starting to happen so you can deal with it prior to shooting.

In a match, shoot at a pace that you could shoot successfully every time. Let the adrenaline of the match and your heightened sense of awareness enter your score.

The Truth of Fact

You get trapped by questions and explanations when you lose sight of what really happened.

A good example of that is when you hear the stories about a 90-pound, 70-year-old woman who lifts a car off her grandson. The first thing everybody wants to know is *how* she did that. *"Explain to me how she did that..."* When you really get down to it, it really doesn't matter *how* she did it. Maybe God came down and gave her the power, or adrenaline, or some chemical in her body just poured loose and turned her into Superman, or maybe it was just a total process of visualization where the car never was really as heavy as you've been taught to believe it was, or maybe you're 1000 times stronger than you've been taught to believe you are. It could have been any of those things, but the point is that *it doesn't matter* which of those things it was. If you think like that you're missing the point that *she did it.* If there's anything to be learned there it's that you can do it—if you just let yourself do it. Your brain has got to get away from the little sphere it's trapped itself in of, "How do I do this, why do I do this?"

If you start asking yourself, "How did I do that..?," you've just about sealed the fate that you won't do it again. That's what you've got to train your mind to see. Open up your mind to see the limitations of your own hows, and whys, and thoughts. If you don't see the limitations that you put on yourself in things you normally do, then you'll not see them in shooting; you're going to be trapped in your own questions. The whole purpose of your attitude is to learn to see the limitations that your thoughts have trapped for you. When you face those limitations, you'll see that the only way to break free of them is to focus yourself in the present tense, where they don't exist. Conscious thought, which constructs the limitations (which *is* the limitation...), doesn't exist in the present tense.

VISUALIZATION

Visualization works well for me. If I can look at a map I never get lost because I've got the image of the map in my mind. As it applies to shooting, visualization, essentially, is mental rehearsal. Its benefit comes from the hope that if you can mentally rehearse something well enough, then you can physically do it just as well. Visualization doesn't really show you *how* to do something—it only shows you that you *can*. But with open-minded experience in your visualization, you'll soon find that what you can imagine is what you will actually see.

I think we all can use visualization to one extent or another. It just takes practice. You need to become more aware of how you do it and when you do it. You need to become aware of how exact in detail your visualizations are. Can you focus exactly and make a perfect mental image of the alphabet, for instance—all the letters at one time, then capitals, small letters, then each in color? Can you visualize things in color or only black and white? How quickly can you pull up an image that's exact and full of details? Can you visualize only things you suggest to yourself, or, with a blank mind, can you let visualization turn up its own images? Can you actually feel that you're *experiencing* what you're visualizing? Just see what goes through your mind, what images it forms.

There are all kinds of things you can do to practice visualization. But the important thing is being able to use your visualization to your real advantage when you're preparing to shoot a stage. And sometimes that means being able to turn it off. If it's a simple stage like something at the Steel Challenge that you've fired thousands of times—something that doesn't involve anything but drawing and firing the gun on some single targets—then your visualization or mental rehearsal is quite a bit simpler. You don't need to overburden yourself and run it through your mind again, and again, and again. An exception would come from an insecurity that you're not going to get it right. But it doesn't take that long, especially if it's a course of fire you're familiar with, to get it right. I've proven that to myself in match conditions.

The best two examples I can think of both happened at the Steel Challenge. One year I shot *Outer Limits* and *5 To Go* both in the same day and set records on both of them. That was probably the single best shooting day I'd had to that point.

The first day I didn't do too well on any of the stages. I had over-rehearsed them and dwelt on them too much. Even though I'd fired them thousands of times in practice over the years, I still rehearsed them to death mentally, and I didn't need to do that. I knew the courses of fire, I knew what I needed to see, I'd trained for them, and I was very disappointed.

When you're shooting in a match, don't tell yourself to slow down, hurry up, watch the front sight— don't *tell* yourself anything. *Show* yourself what you want to do.

On the second day, I didn't do all the mental rehearsal. *5 To Go* is my favorite stage. Every time my mind started to go into some insecurity rehearsal, I was aware of it and I stopped it. I understood why I was doing that and I'd just go on to something else. When it came time to shoot, I walked to the line and then just started from there. "Shooter make ready," and I just sight-blacked the gun and got my natural point of aim. I knew exactly what to do, and the only thing I wanted to be aware of was that I just wanted to see the gun stop on each target and see a sight focus on each target. I was also really aware of the target focus on that stage, and that's the thing I remember the most clearly about it. The targets just looked huge; I never really had the feeling that I could miss. I was very connected. There was no directed effort at all towards doing any one thing.

My third run was a disaster. I had several misses, missed on the stop plate and recovery, but that run had no effect on me at all. Even though I knew I had to keep the next two runs, I didn't change my shooting or my general plan—I just stayed with seeing what I wanted to see. I burned the next two runs. And after that people commented that they were impressed that even though I trashed the third run, that I just kept with it and didn't let up. Well it had nothing to do with that. It had nothing to do with letting up or forcing myself to bear down. My mind was so attuned with what I was doing that there was never a change of plan.

I went on to shoot *Outer Limits.* And by then there were a lot of things going through my mind: *I had just set a record on 5 To Go, amazing time, it's pulled me back into the match...*

Going to *Outer Limits*, I knew that I had shot that stage a lot of times, but I'd always been intimidated by it and had always trashed it at the match. But I did the same thing as for *5 To Go*. I didn't rehearse it; I didn't pay any attention to it at all until I stepped into the box to shoot. I just knew exactly what I wanted to see. At that time I used a Type 4 focus for *Outer Limits* and could see the sight lifting and tracking from target to target really well, and that's all I wanted to see.

The first run was a total disaster: I missed shots, stepped out of the box and then had to step back into the box... But again, it had no effect on me at all. I didn't slow down, throw the brakes on, or anything. I just saw what I wanted to see and I never missed a single shot after that; they were perfect runs and I remember them in great detail.

These two descriptions are perfect examples of when to curb your visualization and stop rehearsing something you already know that you know how to do. And they're examples of using mental observation prior to shooting so that you are aware of things coming into your mind and you stop and consider them for what they are. After the first day at that match I thought to myself that I had spent time mentally rehearsing stages to death that I'd shot thousands of times and they were total hatchet jobs, so obviously rehearsing myself to death doesn't play a role in my performance. There's something else that's going to play a part in it and make the connection between knowing *how to do it* and being *able to do it*. Trust yourself to have that connection.

There is no place for using effort when you're shooting. If you're not aimed at the target, aim at the target.

FEEL

Because I've been opening myself up to it, I've been noticing more and more that being aware of the sensation or feel in certain types of shooting works better for me than a visual image. On certain high-speed IPSC-type stages where I'm more aware of driving the gun, or on the barricade at Bianchi, it's more a feeling than a visualization. I want to be aware of the feel of the gun in my hands and have a total awareness of exactly where my gun is pointed. This sensation is equivalent to being able to hit a 10-inch plate at 15 yards with my eyes closed. It's a feel of position—a total body feel right down into the muscles of my legs. Your body has to be very neutral to develop that type of feeling. To have some understanding of that awareness, a person with vision needs to try to read braille sometime to realize how poor our sense of touch really is. When you look at braille markings they're like night and day, but when you touch the markings you can hardly distinguish them. It's almost unbelievable that a person could ever read braille; it's amazing how much power the mind has to channel its energy.

I often integrate an awareness of feel with my images so that when I'm getting ready to shoot I'm not always so aware of a 100% visualization. I may have it split 50/50 on a visualization and a feeling or sensation, or I may have it all on a sensation. It just depends on the scenario. A shooter should try to be aware for himself which of those two modes he's more familiar with and more comfortable with—not so he can force and plan things with it, but to help him as an aid to finding his "set."

When I get ready to shoot, I am in a *set*. It may be a visual set or it may be a sensation set. My set is hard to describe because it's my perception of being attuned or connected to what I'm about to do. But there's definitely a feeling there, and everyone needs to learn what type of mode he prefers so he can find his own set. Imagine yourself drawing your gun. Can you visualize every detail of the draw or is it just more of a feeling? To me, the draw is more of a feeling than a visualization. But certain aspects of my shooting are more of a visualization, so my set may switch from a feeling to visual, and then may switch back again on different targets.

What you are seeing matters more to your shooting than any other input you get.

If you're aware of how your body likes to intuit those things, it can then use them to its maximum advantage. And the whole point to finding the set is so you don't have to think about shooting. The set puts you in operational mode to where your focus can meet the shooting. You're

not trying to "use" it to recreate anything; it just puts you in the vicinity of the answer.

Most things can be done with equal success through either a visualization or sensation. Again, it's the unforced details you conjure up from each type of awareness that should guide you to which mode may work best for you. A good example is learning to reload: the angle your shooting arm has when it reaches the spot it needs to be in, and the exact amount the gun needs to be rotated so you can see that line in the mag well I described earlier, can all be talked about step-by-step. But after you learn the exact position you need to bring the gun to, the whole thing can happen as a feeling; likewise, you can visualize that spot and visualize seeing that line in the mag well. Both have the same effect: you feel it or visualize it, and the magazine is in. Again, you've replaced thoughts and words with visualizations and images so that you can act instead of question.

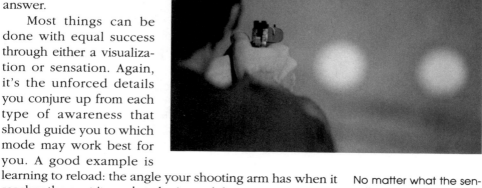

No matter what the sensations are prior to shooting, during the actual shooting, the seeing is it. I process information by sight alone. An awareness of feel can enhance the vision.

Although I often have an awareness of feels or sensations to the point of making them a central focus to help me find my set for different scenarios, my vision controls my shooting as I am actually shooting—*I process information by sight alone.* The awareness of feel is my perception, and my perception intuits my feels, but the feels don't actually control the shooting. What I see controls the shooting. You really can't say that you're going to feel something instead of see something as you're actually shooting. The different sets help get me in the best frame to see what I need to see, but the seeing is it.

A really direct insight into the relative importance of the set or the vision is kind of a tricky thing to reach. I think that the vision is what's occupying my focus, but there's still the feeling there of being a neutral observer or of almost a non-trying third party. I don't know if the feel or the set of being calm and relaxed enhances the vision or if the vision enhances the relaxation. I've experienced it both ways. My main focus has been on being relaxed and then I've seen extraordinarily sharp vision. And I've seen extraordinarily sharp vision with no directed effort and then noticed the effect of the calm-observer feeling.

REHEARSAL

While rehearsal and visualization of a familiar stage can sometimes hurt you, when you're faced with an unfamiliar situation, both processes can be necessary to get you ready to shoot. Rehearsal and visualization work together to help you decide the best way to shoot a stage and then to get comfortable with that decision. Rehearsal is objective; visualization is subjective. Once rehearsal has shown you the best way through, then visualization takes over to help you be aware of things you might experience and the set you might want to open yourself up to that will help you experience them.

If there are a lot of alternatives in how you can shoot a particular stage, you might want to rehearse it over and over until you feel that confidence. Then your visualization process will become very acute. But up until the time you decide which way you're going to shoot the stage, you need to sit back and be objective. You don't want to actually visualize all your options too intensely during the decision-making process or you might end up running the stage in a way you don't really want to.

Once you've come across the best solution, then really try to get comfortable with that through your visualization. When I've made up my mind as to which way I want to shoot the stage, then, as time permits, I'll continue to visualize it until I feel comfortable. When I feel relaxed and can see that my movements and the gun movements are all good and my timing movements are perfect, then I find the feeling of anxiety over shooting it the way I've chosen disappear. Then I know I've rehearsed it enough. Visualizing the stage to that point keeps indecision from creeping in at the last moment.

A good example of this process happened at a stage at the World match where they had moving targets and targets swinging in and out of places and it was totally up to you as to how you wanted to shoot. There were 16 shots in the stage and just a multitude of possibilities of which order to shoot, when to reload—more possibilities than I'd probably ever seen. There were places where you had to take some chancy shots to where you'd barely be able to get to one target as it was disappearing, for example, but was still the best way to go if you wanted to shoot the stage the theoretically fastest way. Every shooter in the *Super Squad* seemed to shoot this stage differently. Usually we'll each go one of two ways, but nobody could agree on this one.

And as I'm standing there on the line and the RO is telling me to load and get ready, I'm still rehearsing it in my mind—I still don't know the best way to do it. And I finally just had to stop and say *this is the way I'm going to do it.* I had to pick a way because I'm sight blacking my gun now... It was the only time I'd ever been on the line and did not know what I was going to do. I focused on it a couple more times and visualized my way through the string of fire as fast as I could because I was starting to hold up the show. I just totally let my mind open to be aware of what I was doing. All I wanted to be aware of was just the gun coming onto the first target and just staying with it after that. I shot the stage exactly as my last visualization showed me, and it went as well as it could have possibly gone. If you've developed a visualization process, you can make it work for you even if you don't have a lot of time. If you just have to make a decision that you're going *this order,* then visualization is something to help you; it's something to fall back on. Again, it just gets you ready to experience what you might feel or see.

Sometimes you may look at a scenario you've never shot before and be able to relate it to something you may have shot in the past. For instance, you'll look at the shootoff at Bianchi and might say it looks like *5 To Go* or *Roundabout.* And you'll remember the kind of vision, awareness, feeling, or body set that came to you when you shot those stages, and you can apply it to that. I shot a stage once in an IPSC match that had five targets lined up in a row with no-shoots positioned between them; the only thing visible on the targets were the A-boxes. The stage was set at 12 yards. That scared a lot of shooters and made them back off or really bear down and watch their sights because they had all those no-shoots everywhere. But I looked at the stage and thought that it really looked like *5 To Go* on paper. And I decided that what it's going to require is a nice, precise stopping of the gun on each target—just like *5 To Go*—nothing more, nothing less. You didn't have to dress anything up more than you would on *5 To Go;* the shot difficulty level was just about the same. Little visualization relationships like that can really help.

I don't want you think that there's a contradiction here between my always telling you to just let the inputs come to you and then telling you that you might shoot this stage like *5 To Go.* I mainly use these relationships if I'm a little uncomfortable with something or if I don't really have time to look through the stage or if I'm not really getting any feeling on what I need to see or how I need to feel as I'm shooting it. So I'll use the familiar stage to give me some type of feeling that I can relate to, while at the same time,

I'm still open for any feelings that I do have. I'm still open to every visual input, but I may see more or less than necessary. In the above example, I may actually see more like Type 2 or even Type 4. So on one hand, I'm totally open to whatever I see, but on the other hand, I may use the comparison feeling. But the thing is that I'm really not on either hand. I use *everything* that I can feel or see.

A final bit of advice that's related to rehearsal is to watch the ROs. At a match where the ROs aren't well-trained, a lot of them have a particular rhythm or cadence they go through. That's something you should watch for. There are some guys we actually try to avoid at matches because they start you as fast as they can say *Shooterstand-byreadybeep!,* or they try to hold you for four seconds, or always have some trick up their sleeve.

If I'm in a big match and the start really means something, I'll usually spend some time watching the starter. I won't do that near the time when I shoot, but when there are several shooters ahead of me. I try to get a feeling for his rhythm or to see if he has a particular cadence so my body can adjust to it. If a guy's a quick buzzer, it will really help you if you're ready for that. You don't have to really think about it that much, but if you've already stored it away, it can help you to not get caught. If he catches you, a guy can get you for a half-second sometimes in scrambling your brain, and there's no telling what the damage from a silly start signal can do in the actual shooting.

BEYOND VISUALIZATION

Earlier I said that you could visualize a feeling as well as an actual "picture" image to help you reach your shooting set. Breathing can sometimes help you visualize feelings and images in combination. When I was practicing for the Masters *Precision Event* in '89, I found that anytime I had to raise the pistol and shoot a shot quickly and accurately, my breathing could coincide with my arm lifting to where—although I'm backwards according to the Olympic shooters—I took in a little bit of extra air before the buzzer and then exhaled that extra air to my natural holding level as the gun came up. That just controlled the whole movement of the gun for me. When you incorporate things like breathing and body feels into your visualization, it becomes much more than a mental picture; instead of your mind just being full of a picture, it's also full of a feeling that you get with just that breath. Breathing adds to that picture and makes it more "feelable" for me. My mind's eye is just totally full of picture of the sight coming up and stop-

ping at the bottom of the plate, but breathing is adding to that picture by also helping my body reach its set.

Shooting the *Duel* string at the Masters, I don't remember a single conscious thought for the minute or so I was there shooting. I had really worked more on this visualization and feeling in practice than I did on my score. I worked on getting myself just totally absorbed in that image to where in the match I was able to not think about anything. One minute is a long time to shut your brain off and make no corrections and have no second-guessing, especially in a match.

No matter what it is you want to pay attention to, find a way to replace words with pictures. Anytime any words are in your mind, you are at a conscious level of function and are limiting your performance.

I was invited once to shoot a local "dot" match where they have this sheet of 15 tiny circles at 7 yards. It's a *very* difficult game. I sighted in my .45 and practiced a little bit so I wouldn't make a fool of myself. But in practice I couldn't hit anything.

I got up to shoot at the match, and as I raised the gun I had this feeling of it coming up in stages each time I would breathe out a little bit—and all of a sudden I had this image of a hot air balloon. To make a balloon rise, the pilot turns the gas on a little bit, and I could hear that noise. Each time I would breathe out a little bit I'd hear the burner turn on and raise my gun. My gun became the hot air balloon, and it was just hanging there steady like a balloon. I could control how well it could hang there by just hearing that noise in my brain. I shot 11 of 15. I had never even hit close to that many before in practice. And that visualization was something I never had thought about; it just came to me at that moment.

You can use different combinations like that to do more than just visualize what you want to see. You can also visualize how you want everything to *feel*. When you shoot an air gun, if you're relaxed and neutral and not muscling the gun—it's just sitting in your hand and the only thing moving is the trigger finger and there's no attempt to force the shot into any area; it's just simply a break that happens—you'll feel the gun recoil. You'll feel it lift and settle in your hand, you'll see the sight lift about halfway out of the notch and it's very repeatable. It's really difficult to perceive that. To feel it you almost have to just aim at the wall. If you muscle the gun at all the recoil goes unnoticed because there isn't any. *But there is...* There's a lot to perceive there that's not just in your vision.

Chip McCormick's visualization trick for the draw was seeing a thread running from his eye to the target and having the gun come up and get on the thread and then just drive the sight down the thread. On my own, again from shooting the .22, I've noticed a similar plane. It's not very wide, and I can see it run from my eye right down the top of my rear sight and down the top of my front sight and onto the target. When the gun is sitting very steady, the flatness of the sights just seems to sit in that plane. And I can actually *see* it. It's a real visualization, and it's never something that I make myself see.

I've had many other visualizations come to me in the past. And some of the most memorable have come when I was playing pool because I'm very open to my inputs then. One day I could see the line that the object ball was going on to the hole. The line was actually a groove that looked like it was made into the table. The ball was just riding in that groove and I could see that very accurately. And it was *there...* Even beyond that, sometimes I would see the ball rolling into the pocket even before I shot it; I could see the stripe on the ball rotating in really amazing detail, and I never missed a shot like that. Anytime I'd have that clear of a picture, I just let the shot go and let the ball absolutely follow my mind's pattern. One time I stepped up to shoot a really difficult, critical bank shot, and as soon as I looked at it my mind saw something that looked like a board going from the bank to the pocket at whatever angle I needed to shoot the object ball. I looked at that and second-guessed it for a minute, then looked away and looked back and it was still there. So I said that if it's still there, then I'm going to shoot it like that. And it went straight in. I couldn't even shake that image.

But the most important thing about all this is that the images all just *come to you*. And the real power of visualization is always found through images that just come to you. When I'm shooting I don't ever pre-plan my images. I'm just alert to any that do come in. If I've had some visualization in the past that might help me shoot a stage, I'll watch for it to come in, but I won't try to force it in if it doesn't just naturally turn up. For instance, there was an old TV commercial that had a bouncing ball going over words like a sing-along. I've had that image of front sight movement reoccur many times in the past before shooting *Outer Lim-*

its or shooting bowling pins. I've had the image before of making an extremely mechanical-type movement as if the gun was being retained by a robotic person who had just a trunk and straight arms with joints that were just circles. For draws from the surrender position I've had the image of my wrists being held up with strings by a puppeteer who cut the strings when the buzzer sounded.

If you replace your thoughts with pictures, then when you see what you want to see, your body follows—without thought.

But since images must just come to you to be really effective, and since they'll come to you only when you're in a very relaxed state, images like those I've had for the *Duel* and the dot shooting don't really come to me that well in speed shooting. I can get pretty good visualizations on Bill Drills sometimes, but relaxation is the hardest thing to find in super-speed shooting and that's why it's more difficult for images to just turn up.

Visualization takes you beyond conscious thought. It gives you a way to quiet your mind and remove all the chatter by removing all the words. And it's the words that go through our minds that block our awareness and present tense functioning. If you want to think, think in pictures; think with visualization instead of thinking with words. Any time *any* words are in your brain, *you're absolutely, 100%, positively in a conscious state of mind.* When the words are there you're at some conscious level of functioning which is going to limit you and not open you up to your best potential, so just be aware when you're shooting if you're able to think in pictures. Whatever you're doing, you can find some way to look at it with a picture in your mind rather than with a thought in your head. And, if possible, that's where you always want your brain to be—geared to some sort of picture or some sort of feeling, which is an even harder thing to describe because there's really nothing there. (Or is everything there?)

On stages that have a lot of shooter movement, it's often important to be positioned in a box a certain way to see certain targets better or to move through a door with your feet in a certain way. Your body positioning can be very important on certain stages and you need to rehearse that mentally through visualization before you shoot.

As you're rehearsing it, visualize yourself moving and stopping and having your feet where you want them to be. Imagine it all visually with no thoughts at all, and then as you move through the stage, you just simply direct your body's movements with your vision. As you're moving into a box, you don't ever think *stay to the front of the box*—it's all done with your vision. You look and you go there without thinking about it at all. This is an important point in the value of visualization. Since your emphasis in shooting is always on what you see, "programming" your plan for a stage can be done with no conscious thought (words) through using visual images. Again, your body's movements are then simply directed by your vision.

Probably the best image I have in my mind's eye when I'm waiting to shoot is seeing the sights on the target. And I see the real thing there at real size—not just a picture of the sights, but what they will *really* look like on the target. The other images I've mentioned are always spur of the moment things that pop in when I'm waiting to shoot, but I can't usually remember them. But in really high-speed shooting, I've mostly got a set of how I like to feel and I stick pretty conventionally to what I'd like to see.

WHERE'S YOUR BRAIN?

Shooter ready...standby... Where's your brain *right now?* That's a difficult thing to describe. Again, probably the best thing to say is where your brain is not. Hopefully you're not thinking about anything; hopefully there's not a single thought in your head. Hopefully your mind is totally open to whatever you're about to see before you.

If you are tense, you are probably concerned over results. Only when there is no concern over results can you perform to your maximum potential. Results aren't found in the present tense.

You've already rehearsed your plan of what you're about to do to the best of the scenario's limitations. Ideally, your mind will be in the state it was when you tossed the keys in the air—you're watching the keys and waiting to catch them with no anticipation, no focus on one key versus another, no focus on how high you were going to toss them, just a total open focus on whatever you threw. That's as close as I can describe as to where my mind is immediately prior to shooting. It's just totally alert and open to the situation at hand.

I usually narrow myself down to that state. When I'm behind the line, my attention is general and I may be focused on different things about the stage—things I'd like to do, or things that bothered me in the past, or what I'd like to see. And the closer and closer I get to shooting, the more narrow my focus gets to where eventually when I'm in the box, I'm hopefully not trying to make any major decisions.

Where's your brain right now? Hopefully, there's not a thought in your head. You're just prepared to see what's going to happen. Just watching...

I have my plan sorted out and am only aware of what I'm actually doing, whether I'm sight blacking my gun or getting my natural point of aim or indexing on the first target.

Then as the gun gets into the holster and my hands are up and I'm ready to go, my attention is narrowed down again. At this point there's no need for any thoughts. The only thing that I need to perform to my maximum potential is just turning up my total awareness. I need to have weeded through all my thoughts and have everything sorted out and then just let everything drop away. Until finally at the time when the buzzer goes off, everything has dropped away and I'm in a total state of observation. *I'm just watching,* with a very attentive focus. I may be focused on the target and waiting for the buzzer, but that's something that takes no conscious thought or anticipation. The audible start takes absolutely no attention at all.

Something else you might be feeling when you're immediately preparing to shoot is *nervous*. You can still shoot to your maximum potential if you're nervous, but you can't if you're *tense*. I've shot some of the best scores of my life when my knees and hands were shaking. It doesn't matter how nervous you are as long as you don't get tense—don't let the nervousness turn into tension. I've proven to myself over and over that it doesn't matter how nervous you are if you are focused in the present tense and are determined to see what you need to see. Tension and anxiety don't exist in the present tense. The nervousness will work for you. It can actually heighten your awareness.

When you shoot a stage particularly well or feel that you shot a stage to the limit of your current ability, you'll want to remember where your brain was then. Don't worry if you can't remember. When I think back to try to see what I was thinking about or to see what I was doing when all that happened, most often I have no remembrance of anything beyond just what I remember about the stage itself and the inputs I got from shooting the stage, but not the actual mental process that was happening as I was shooting. When you first start experiencing that, it can seem frustrating because your conscious mind naturally wants to think back and remember what it did to perform so well. And it can't remember anything. And the reason it can't remember anything is because *there's nothing there to remember.* When your mind is in a total state of awareness—when there are no thoughts going on—there's simply nothing to remember.

ROUTINES

I have never consciously developed a routine that I follow before I shoot. I think that's something that should be left up to each person because it's not a fundamental in that it's not something that everyone should try to do in essentially the same way. Some people will really benefit from following a set plan of counting down a predetermined pattern of actions so they'll have all those things mechanically out of the way and forgotten about. But I've never functioned that way. I've experimented at times with trying to come up with a routine of stepping in and out of the box, and sight black and holster, and so many dry-fires, and so on. And all the experimenting I've done just didn't make any difference at all for me. I've often shot the very best scores I could shoot just rushing up to the line late and scrambling and making sure I had all my stuff together. If I know what I need to do and then can just stop and shut my mind off, I can shoot just as well that way as I can by following the most methodic routine.

But there are other championship-level shooters who believe that their routines are very important. They've got everything down to how they load their gun, where their extra bullet comes from, where they sight black—the whole shooting process is a routine. If you feel comfortable like that then you should, by all means, develop a routine to suit your own personal taste.

For people who need to follow a set plan of action, the routine can definitely be a calming influence. A lot of shooters who develop and follow strict routines say that their biggest benefit is that finishing the routine gives them a "go" signal; everything is set and they're ready to shoot as soon as the routine has run. You should know what kind of personality you have to make the decision as to whether following a routine will help you. If you're a planner and make lists of everything you're going to do, then you'll find some comfort in following a specific routine. For the opposite-type person who doesn't know what plane he's getting on until he gets to the airport, and who has all his things seemingly disorganized but always knows where they are, following a routine probably won't do that much. For that person, operating from a routine could even be detrimental because it becomes just another thing to think about that won't influence his shooting.

To me, the actual worth of a routine is to make sure that you don't overlook something. Having a routine helps make sure that you don't experience brain-fade and just overlook something important, like loading your gun or exchanging magazines between runs. But beyond that it's purely personal.

TRICK OF THE DAY

A lot of shooters believe that some day they're going to find The mechanical trick. And I must have found 200 of those. I've tried every mechanical trick that I or anyone else could think of. And it's really remarkable how they always work so well that first time you try them, but then the next day it's hard to duplicate the result. That has to do with focus. When you're trying something new, your focus becomes very clear and directed. Rob Leatham and I always came up with the *Trick Of The Day* because we knew what effect that had on focus.

One time at the Steel Challenge I decided to change my grip halfway through the match. I was shooting terrible and went back to the hotel room that night just disgusted with myself. And I wanted to try a new trick. I wanted to find the Trick Of The Day for getting me through. So I changed my grip completely. I shifted from a low grip to the high grip I use now and then went out to shoot the rest of the match. I dry-fired for *hours* that night trying to get the change worked in. To go out the next day at the Steel Challenge and run with that change required an amazing amount of attention on just the feeling of the new grip.

It was amazing. I shot great that day. I shot great for the rest of the match. That first day, though, I shot especially well. At least I had *something* to focus on. My mind was so confused that it had nowhere to go and was so cluttered with junk from the first day of the match that I couldn't shoot at all. And that was the Trick Of The Day...that day.

But remember that no matter how long you shoot, no matter how many tricks you come up with, no matter how many mechanical techniques you'll come across, you're always going to be locating the target, aiming at the target, and holding the gun on the target until the gun fires. *There's nothing you'll ever do that will stop you from being aware of that process as it's happening.* That's something that you have to realize. The value of the Trick Of The Day is that it's a temporary distraction that quiets your mind down. But as a last resort, *look at the front sight and squeeze the trigger*. It's funny, but it's true. Sometimes.

STEEL

The Steel Challenge is a shooting skill test. The requirements are always single shots on steel, there's very little movement, no reloads, but the match itself is probably the finest test of a shooter's skill and his ability to shoot creatively that we have today. It's just pure shooting. The stages vary and there's always different priorities. Each stage can allow you to see different focus types. The *Speed Option* takes a different type of shooting than a real speed stage like *Roundabout. Smoke & Hope* takes a different focus than *5 To Go*. They all require different emphases or points of attention, but the shooting is very similar. If you shot every stage in the match and just let yourself shoot a Type 3 focus, you'd do fine. The competitive level in the match is such that the winner never shoots a faster pace than you could using Type 3. You don't have to do anything tricky: focus towards each target and see the sights stop on the middle of each plate. If you do that you're going to be right in there for your own level.

The main thing for the Steel Challenge, or for any other similar event, is to *shoot the match with your eyes instead of your ears*. Shoot the targets as if they were made of paper. Tell yourself that you're going to call your shots and then you're going to walk down to score your hits when you're through shooting. That's an easy thing to understand, but it's difficult to do. It's so easy to let yourself go into hearing mode to tell if you hit the targets or not. And that's what makes that match so difficult.

What you need to have your mind open to is seeing what kind of vision you can get away with on different targets. You learn that in practice. Do you have to see the gun stop completely, or can the gun almost have the appearance of not stopping on the target? There's hardly any time on any target where it's easy enough to hit that you don't need to move the gun directly to the target and at least have the *feeling* of stopping the gun there. But if you're practicing the *Speed Option,* for instance, where there's a lot of swinging going on, you'll notice that your shots are always on the left on target-2. There may never be a shot right of center on that target because the gun goes to the target and pauses, and by the time you break the shot, the gun is already leaving the target.

In *Creative Shooting* I talked about how being able to move your eye in sync with a moving fan blade allows you

These photos were digitized from video tape, so their quality isn't perfect, but they show the effect of shooting steel with your eyes instead of your ears. 1. On the first plate on the *Speed Option,* my gun stops and fires. 2. I saw what I needed to see there so the gun goes to the second plate. 3. I'm over halfway to the next plate when the bullet hits. Since I'm shooting steel loads, the total elapsed time for the three photos is approximately .045 seconds.

to visually freeze the blade's motion. I believe that same thing happens with the sights on some of the targets at the Challenge. I say that I believe that's what happens because it's probably impossible to actually measure. I remember seeing the gun pause, but on a video tape it's obvious that the gun never comes to a complete stop. When the gun is moving onto the target and reaches the target, there's a point where my vision freezes the scene and "backs it up" for me, holding the target and the gun together for a split second—it's like a strobe flashing when the gun touches the target—and that's plenty of time to shoot. I can see what I need to see while the gun may still be moving, so stopping the gun can be visual rather than actual in some cases. One year after Jerry Barnhart made a fairly amazing run on *Roundabout,* someone came up and asked him the inevitable question of, "Do you see your sights on every target?" Jerry's answer was perfect: "I saw what I needed to see." End of story.

When I'm practicing for the Challenge and am getting to the point where I'm about ready to shoot the match—I've got everything worked out mechanically and I know exactly what I'm doing on all the courses and know exactly what I need to see on every target—I quit using the timer my last few sessions. I just shut it off. I don't use the timer anymore to push myself or to refine anything or to make any more decisions. I'll shoot the match and never look at a single time. And I don't care about the time. My total emphasis then is on what I'm seeing—I gear *everything* to what I'm seeing. And I've got the confidence and the experience to know that if see what I need to see, I'm going to be fast enough. When you get right down to it, it's what you see that really matters; that's what controls the shooting. When you're in the match, you don't care about your times and they don't tell you your times. The only thing you're going by then is what you're seeing while you're shooting, so I get myself into that frame before the match.

If you want to shoot at warp drive on steel, first break the sound barrier. Shoot with your eyes, not with your ears.

Pace and Rhythm

These are the performance killers on steel. You really need to be on guard against firing shots without paying attention and turning into a pace shooter or a rhythm shooter. It's so easy to do on some of the stages. On the second shots on *Speed Option* or *Roundabout* or on one of the big targets on *Smoke & Hope,* for examples, you get into the habit of just pulling the gun out and maybe firing an accurate first shot, but then just sort of slinging shots at a predetermined rhythm and you realize that you're not actually aiming at the targets, you're just firing. And that just comes from the fact of shooting the course of fire too many times to the point where it becomes a habit. And since it becomes a habit, sometimes you don't realize that you're doing it.

In the next section I'll talk about the game that Rob Leatham and I play before the Challenge. It's called *Break Out,* and it will help you to pay attention to the targets and to what you see. Through playing the game, you'll find that it doesn't take any longer to see the target, see the gun stop on the target, pick up the sight on the target, and fire the shot actually aiming at the target than it does to just rhythm-fire a shot in the direction of the target.

IPSC STRATEGY

IPSC is a strategy game, but only to a point. It's easy to get so wrapped up in your strategies that you can start seeing too many options, which leads to indecision at best. At worst, that can lead to total confusion and having to think your way around a course. The important thing is to make a decision as early as possible and get that intellectual process out of the way so you can spend the rest of your time getting comfortable with what you've chosen through your visualization.

If you're having trouble finding your own way, it will help to watch some other shooters go through the stage. If you notice most all of them shoot it in one particular way, then that's a clue that might be the best way, but it might not. If you see a way that you think is better, then go with what you want to do. And always go the way that's most comfortable for you. If you see everybody shooting something one way, but you're not particularly developed to do it that way—maybe you're not comfortable shooting on the move and you'd rather stop and shoot these targets rather than move by them—the best thing to do is to just shoot it your own way. I've seen countless examples of that with myself and with other shooters where we broke outside the traditional way of thinking on a stage and just did it the way we wanted to do it because we knew we could do it better that way, and we accept that. You may not do the stage as fast as Rob Leatham is going to if the stage happens to suit his strong points, but you are just going to take what you can do and you're going to do *that*. You're not going to try to be somebody else for that time; you're just going to do exactly what you know *you* can do. And I've seen a lot of stages won by that exact attitude.

Set up different scenarios in practice that will help you

When the middle target is down low, I'd hit it first, then left, then right. If the middle target was more level with the others, I'd shoot left to right. The reason I'd go for the low target first is because that would allow me to acquire the other targets faster. If I started out on the left target, my mount would obscure my vision of the low, middle target. When it's possible, I always move the gun up through a stage.

see where your shooting preferences are. You shouldn't necessarily reproduce actual match stages, but you should practice situations you'll encounter. For instance, find out which target order you prefer: long shot, then short, or left to right, or whatever. Check your split times; they give you the most important information. Then when you're faced with a scenario that allows you the flexibility, see if your preference will be competitive. If you'll follow the photos, you'll see what my mind goes through when I'm given an option in target sequence in a simple scenario.

But the final point to make on strategy is that you have to be able to handle any situation and every situation in the best possible way if you want to be a top-level competitor. That takes confidence and experience in showing yourself that you can handle whatever they throw at you. You have to learn to do what you don't do well until you get to the point where you handle a stage not just the way you want to, but the absolute best possible way. To a top-level IPSC shooter, objective decisions are immediately met with a subjective reference.

Shooting a match can be likened to a professional motorcycle roadrace. The overall winner does not concern himself with beating every rider in every corner. Quite possibly some riders may be faster in certain sections of the track than the winner. However, by the end of the race the winner will have built up a certain lead by a consistent performance on every inch of the track. In the same way, the match winner should not expect to win every stage (lap) or be the fastest on a particular string (corner). Interestingly enough, the attitude necessary to put into practice the above is the same attitude that will allow you to win most of the stages (laps).

Acquisition Splits

Drawing and shooting the closest target first is not always the fastest way. For instance, put two targets at 7 and 12 yards and shoot two shots on each. Depending on your skill level, it may be faster to shoot the 12-yard target first, especially if that target has a no-shoot over part of it, because your split time is going to be so much faster if you're moving to a full target at 7 yards. You're going to acquire that target in a heartbeat, whereas if you're moving from the 7-yard target onto the 12-yard target, you're going to have to ease the gun onto it a little bit to avoid the no-shoot and make sure that you get an A-hit. You'll see a major difference in the split times in that scenario.

Let's say that you put up targets at 10, 25, and 50 yards. You're going to be slower shooting your first shot at 50 yards, obviously. But you possibly can make up the time in target acquisition coming back to the others. This is something you have to experiment with because there aren't any hard and fast rules; everybody is different and you just have to get a feel for what you're comfortable with. You'll have to make these decisions a lot of times in IPSC matches when you have the choice of which order to shoot the targets. You make your decisions by paying attention to your target acquisitions when you practice so you can get as much of that information stored away as possible.

Only experience and what you actually see once the gun is out and going can tell you which focal points will work best on a stage. And the main thing to remember with focal points is that they are only your own suggestions to yourself as to what likely will be required from your vision.

Alignment & Index

As I described earlier, the relationship between natural point of aim and index is that npa is your original, basic lineup, while index is wherever you're actually pointing your gun and body from that.

Where I line up is just a total comfort factor. I will favor the first target that I have to shoot a lot more often than some people will, and especially so if that target is to the right of the centerline of the stage. (Although this chapter is about IPSC, I'll use a couple of examples from the Steel Challenge since it's probably easier to relate this information to a fixed scenario.) For instance, on the *Speed Option* you shoot the target that's to the extreme right first. So I'll line up almost off the first plate on that stage and index or pivot to all the other targets. The other targets aren't that far out of my reach, and the farthest target to my left is a 10-

The advantage to lining up on the most difficult target on a stage is mostly just theory. I much prefer to get started shooting comfortably. On the *Speed Option,* for instance, I'll line up nearly on my first target, the one to the far right.

yard, 12-inch disk, so if I can see that target I can hit it. On *5 To Go* where the targets are spread out over the same amount of range, but now I'm starting on the left side, I'll line up on the center target and index to the left to start. Drawing to my left is very comfortable for me; drawing to my right makes me feel cramped. I feel more comfortable indexing to the left and that has to do all with the draw. My body just doesn't want to stay in position if I feel like I'm indexed very far to the right of my npa. It's the same for reloading. If I have to make a mandatory reload on a stage and it gives me some latitude as to where I'd like to reload, I'd rather have finished the shot before the reload to the right because I'd rather reload going to the left. I prefer to have the feeling of pulling the gun in as I'm going to the left, whereas if I go to the right I feel like I'm cramping myself; it just doesn't feel as smooth. If there isn't going to be any penalty target acquisition-wise or time-wise, I'll always reload going to the left.

If I can ever feel comfortable with having my npa on the most difficult shots on a stage, I'll do that. If I could have my npa on the bonus plate for the *Speed Option,* I would. I'd let my body just naturally uncoil to that target, but I don't on that stage because it's not as important to me as getting out and shooting comfortably on the first targets. But if a stage has some 50-yard shots or an extremely difficult stop plate, I may sacrifice a little bit to line up for the hard shot. Lining up on the hardest target comes from a theoretical idea that if you do that then *maybe* it will let you settle onto that target the quickest. You would had to have been very relaxed and neutral and really paying attention to even know if you were actually able to relax onto the difficult target. But it's always more important to me to get started shooting comfortably because that allows me to stay relaxed for *all* the targets. I don't like to feel forced or cramped or tense from indexing to some awkward starting position. Once I've mounted the gun I can move anywhere and keep my index. I can swing up, down, left, right, and it doesn't matter how far I have to swing because I'm using my legs to hold me in position as I pivot.

Virginia Count & Comstock

When I'm allowed to shoot more than the specified number of shots on a stage if I want to, I really don't let that influence my shooting or how I'm going to approach a stage. I'm always shooting for at least 90-95% of the points possible anyhow, and it doesn't matter if I'm shooting comstock or Virginia Count, I'm going to be calling the shots and the sights and watching where the gun goes. I'm not going to hurry any more and take a risk of dropping a shot for comstock than I would on Virginia Count. Neither one matters to me; I'm just shooting at the speed I can engage those targets at. If you do choose to make up a shot, it should be done immediately off of a visual input that the shot was questionable—just like the example I gave in *Awareness & Focus* of making up a shot on a missed steel plate. If you're stopping after you've engaged all the targets to look back over them and decide if you need to improve a couple of hits, you didn't see what you needed to see when you were shooting.

I'd like to give you a little insight into the comstock scoring system that might help you put some stages into perspective. Basically, you need to look at a stage and determine how much the points are worth to you. To do that you first make an estimation of the time it will take you to shoot the stage. You can do that by watching other shooters, or if it's a simple stage, you can probably do that just from experience. But come up with a time that's within one or two seconds of what you think it will take you to shoot the stage with good hits—mostly As—and then take that time and come up with a *factor*—score divided by time. Take the number of points possible on the stage and divide it by the time that you think you can do it in to get the factor. Then put a 1 over that number to make it a reciprocal. Now you've got the time in seconds that you'll have to shoot an A instead of a C. If that factor comes up to 4, for example, you've got .25 seconds to fire an A instead of a C. The balance in the stage between time and points is going to be at that tradeoff. So you have to look at that now and decide if you can do that or not. And almost always you'll be able to shoot the A instead of the C, no matter what the time limit is. Even if it turns out to be a 10-factor stage, for a Master, .1 seconds is a lot of time to have relaxed and shot an A instead of forcing or muscling a C in an attempt to hurry up because it's a fast-paced stage.

For a Master, the break-even speed where it's pretty important to shoot the majority of the shots As is around a 5-factor. You don't see 5-factors very often unless there's a lot of movement in the stage. If there's a lot of movement in the stage, that's just something that you'll have to use your own judgement on because if you're moving and all the targets are at 3 yards, but you have to run 25 yards to get to the boxes, then the factor is not accurate. The stage may work to a 4-factor, but the actual shooting times may vary down to a 10-factor, so you have to use some common sense there.

You can figure factors all you want, but what it really always comes down to is that, no matter what the speed factor is, if you shoot the targets with 90-95% of the points possible, you're never going to do anything too wrong. But sometimes determining a factor can give you a clue if you have no idea how to interpret a stage. For instance, if the stage comes out to be a 2-factor, that's .5 seconds to shoot an A instead of a C—you'd better not be firing *anything* but As. I've seen stages where you only draw and fire one shot into the target and you do that, say, five times. And if you're only going to draw and fire one shot at a target, even if it's only at 5 yards, the factor is going to be really high—it's going to be a 5-factor if you can shoot the shot in one second flat. So on that stage, if you fire any shot but an A, you're really going to lose. Even on a 10-factor stage where each point is worth .1 seconds, if you beat me by .5 seconds but are 5 points down, we're going to tie. Basically, you need to rack up as many points as are possible without milking the stage too much.

People are always talking about how IPSC has gotten to the point where you can just sling shots all over the place, and that's just not true at all. We were shooting a side match once, a *Vice Presidente* (an *El Presidente* without the turn), and our times were all the mid-4s. But because we got to do it over and over again, what that stage came down to was points. We could all function the gun across the targets in the same time, so you had to have all As. As I remember, Rob Leatham won the stage with 4.3 seconds and two points down; I was one-tenth faster but with three points down. And that shooting was at the absolute envelope of our performance; we couldn't do any better. So even at the fastest speed I've ever seen, it came down to points on the target being the deciding factor.

If you're not forcing or trying, I've proven it to myself over and over that it does not take any longer to shoot an A than it does to sling a hit.

Area Aiming

You may have heard about the concept of "area aiming." This, in essence, means that there is a certain acceptable area on each target in which a shot will score maximum value. The idea is that when the sight rests anywhere in that area it is okay to shoot. In fact, this concept is valid; however, in application, it can be only another limitation. When you're sizing up a stage, making a note of available scoring areas on each target can serve you; however, when you're actually firing, your awareness, observation, and perception must be what tells you when you're effectively using area aiming; your visual awareness and *visual acceptability* constantly define the target area. Visual acceptability is what you allow yourself to "get away with"—it's your interpretation of what your visual inputs show you about the gun's relationship to the target. React to the target area that's available by being aware of where it is. And define the target's scoring surface by what it presents you, not by what surrounds it as a boundary. Look for targets, not obstacles.

While on the subject of targets, here's a tip that might help some shooters: take a close look at an IPSC target. The whole design intent of the IPSC target is to obscure the scoring areas so there's no clearly defined spot to direct your eyes to. You've probably heard people suggest shooting "center mass" of an IPSC target, and that's good advice. But be aware of what actually is the center of the target. Many shooters see the center of the target as being in the middle of the large rectangle that makes up the "body" portion. But the actual center of the A-box is measured from the top of the "head" rectangle to the bottom of the "body" portion. That means that the true center of the IPSC target is actually 6 inches higher (the height of the "head") than the center of the "body." You can get a feel for this by marking the center of the A-box with something you can easily see, such as a piece of white tape, and practicing that way for a while.

SHOOTOFF

I don't think that there are many good shooters who can honestly say that they don't make a strategy change when they're in a shootoff. And the change will be geared to the person they're shooting with. An example is the Bianchi shootoff. The top-20 shoot qualifying runs to make the top-6; out of those 20 people there may be only three or four who are up to current speed. So the last thing I'm going to do is to do something stupid, like have a fault, shoot an extra target or leave a target up and not even qualify. In that scenario, there's no sense leaving any shots to chance, because by hitting every plate right in the center, you know that you're going to qualify. If I'm in that situation, then I just make a visual change; I don't make a speed change or a pace change. I'm just going to stay relaxed and shoot the center of each target and have the visual patience to do that. I may want to be aware of a Type 4 focus and see the sight lift even though the targets are so easy that I don't even need to see my sights on the targets, let alone see the sight lift. You actually can allow yourself this flexibility very seldom in an IPSC shootoff, but sometimes you can make decisions like that there too.

But when it starts getting to where your opponent can match you in speed, that's when no changes are necessary. That's when you just shoot. If anything, you just need to be finely focused; you don't want your brain to be in indecision mode. The last thing you ever want to do is miss a target and find that your gun starts to move to the next target and then have to come back to hit the target you missed. That's such a time-waster. You're shooting by hearing when you do that. You want to have your vision turned up to its maximum acuity to where the gun never comes back to a target.

In a shootoff on falling steel targets, I feel that I need to be totally focused on shooting the targets as if they were paper and my vision needs to be extremely high. Every decision as to where my gun goes needs to be made from vision, nothing else. It doesn't need to be because I didn't hear a hit. My vision is totally controlling the gun's movement. I try to have my vision very high because there's a lot of noise going on. The other guy's shooting and you're shooting and you're hearing his hits and your hits, his shots and your shots. With all that blasting going on, you really need to have your vision turned up as high as it can go so you can shoot every shot just like it's on paper.

If you called a shot a miss, go ahead and shoot the target again without waiting to see if it's falling. I shoot as fast as I can call the shots. I call them up until the stop plate (I call the stop plate too), and if I saw what I wanted to see up to the stop plate, I'll go ahead and shoot it. I won't check to see if the targets have fallen. That's something in a shootoff that confuses a lot of people. At Bianchi, you're both shooting five pepper-poppers and are working toward the center where the stop plate is the center popper. The poppers fall very slowly. You will have hit the stop plate before the first popper hits the ground. On the last two or three targets, if you're looking to see if they fell, you may never be able to tell; it just takes way too much time. Your vision then just totally scrambles your brain. You need to shoot each target as if it were made of paper, call your shots, and just trust yourself. If you call a shot and the target didn't go over, then you didn't call the shot correctly.

Visual Acceptability

I would say, and I'm sure the other top-level shooters would agree, that we vary the speed we're shooting with depending on who we're shooting with. And that's true even if we're shooting against someone who's relatively at the same level. For me personally, turning up my shooting speed means turning up my vision. If I'm shooting against a guy who's 10% slower than me, I'm never going to accept anything I see unless I *know* it's going to fall. Against a shooter who I know I can beat, I'll never turn my vision up to its maximum *acceptability*. But when I'm shooting against a guy who's at my pace, someone who I know won't be holding back, what happens then is that I just get less picky about my acceptable visual inputs. I won't try to refine the shots to where I'm *absolutely* sure the targets are going to fall. I'll take a chancier shot so my speed will go up.

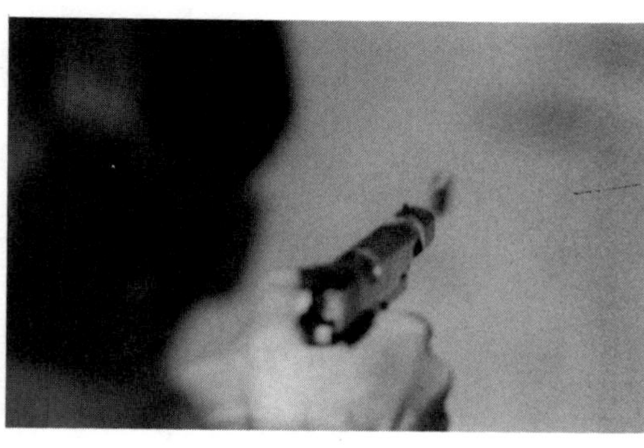

In a shootoff, I turn my vision up to its *maximum acceptibility*. Turning up my vision lets me see more so I can accept less. Against a top shooter, the visual inputs I will accept as a shot possibility are much less clearly defined than normal.

You can only shoot as fast as you can see. If my vision is turned up very high, then I can discern the gun being on any part of the target that will drop it. With a fast shooter, I will accept the gun being on *any* part of the target; with a slower shooter, I only accept the shot when my vision sees the gun aligned on target *center*. My visual acceptability—what I'm willing to accept as a shot—is higher against a slower shooter than it is for a fast shooter. It's really not correct to say that I turn up my speed against a top shooter, but that's the effect of turning up my vision.

It's hard to explain why I shoot a faster pace against Rob Leatham, for instance, than I do with a guy who's 10% slower than me. But what's happening there is that I'm trying to go across the targets so quickly against Rob that I may not have acquired each target in clear focus. And if I didn't acquire a clear target focus then the gun probably didn't completely stop on the target (which are the necessary ingredients of a Type 2 focus—the target *focus* allows the gun the time to hesitate on the target). I may have only seen the target as a blur peripherally, and then from seeing that blur on my gun blur, I may accept that as an acceptable shot. It's because I'm trying to see as fast as I can possibly see that I may not get all my inputs. I become very visually *impatient*.

I'm always shooting as fast as I can see, but against a slower shooter I'm just more particular about what I see. Against a slower shooter, my visual acceptability is actually turned *down,* in effect. As you go from Type 2 to 3 to 4, in a way you could say you're turning *down* your visual awareness "rheostat" so you can see more and more and more distinctly. When I'm shooting at my maximum warp drive, I've turned my seeing up to where what I'm actually able to discern from my visual inputs is at the absolute borderline of what I need to see.

If it ever seems like you're making things too complicated or too hard on yourself, just get behind the gun and drive it onto the targets.

It's easy to see the speed turn up at Bianchi because there are a lot of different skill levels involved. In '89, Rob Leatham and I were the only two speed shooters who made it; the rest were Bianchi specialists. Shooting against guys who didn't have our backgrounds, we were just going through the course and our vision was nice and precise. Then when we got to ourselves, all of a sudden we went from a 2.6 run to a 2.2 run. Someone asked me about that after the '89 Bianchi shootoff. He didn't understand how we could just turn up our pace just like we were turning a dial. And the thing to understand is that you're not turning up your pace; you're turning up your vision to accept less. You're just making a visual input change. And the ability to do that comes only through a lot of experience with visual awareness as to literally *seeing* what you can get away with.

This difference in visual acceptability in the shootoff can also be applied to other scenarios. You may want to make differences in things you see to control your pace. For example, if you've got a time limit to shoot a string of standard exercises and you've got more time than you know you'll need, instead of *telling* yourself to slow down, just shift to some point of focus that *will* slow you down. Just keep your vision very relaxed and watching the sight and watching for it to lift so you can call your shot at the last instant. Whereas on a comstock string you may not see that, but if you've got time to see it, go ahead and look for it. That may give you a little insurance for shooting better shots without trying to make some sort of a pace change like consciously telling yourself to speed up or slow down, which really has no meaning. If, for some reason, you feel that you need to try to really burn a stage or feel like you can't make the time limit, you could lower your visual acceptability to where you're seeing only just the minimum of what you might need to see. I really don't recommend that, though, because when you feel that higher speed is needed on a stage, it shouldn't be gotten at the expense of accuracy. Against Rob Leatham in a shootoff, it's do or die, so turning up my vision past the edge of certainty is a risk I'll take there, but not for a stage in the match that preceded the shootoff.

Section 6: DEVELOPMENT

Keep yourself open to your experiences. Never accept or reject anything —just pay attention to what you are seeing and what you are feeling —the learning will then be continuous.

Actually learning to shoot is, for me, an impossibility because I learn on every shot I fire. But learning *about* shooting is possible, and it's not difficult to do. Hopefully what you've read so far has opened you up to some ideas, given you some tangible concepts, and, otherwise, has shown you some directions you might go to help you learn more about shooting.

This section deals with learning about yourself as a shooter. Developing yourself as a shooter really comes down to experience, and experience as I define it is something that's happening currently; it's not just a history of so many years behind the sights. Experience the shooting by opening up and allowing the experience to come in unfiltered—no screens, no preconceptions, no limitations. Through awareness, you can reach any level in practical shooting you're willing to believe you can reach.

You'll be concerned with whether or not what you're practicing or what you're trying to do is "right." See for yourself... If you keep yourself open to your experiences, there's no right or wrong—there's only what you're doing. Right, wrong, good, bad, fast, and slow all exist in comparison, which exists away from the experience. Your perception of your shooting—what you are feeling and what you are seeing—right when it's happening, is all you need to know to answer that question.

There is a place for conscious thought in shooting and that place is away from the range. In an environment where you're removed from the actuality of shooting, thought on the subject can be sufficiently broad, or specific, in nature to where details and understandings can make themselves very clear. I learn the most about my shooting on my way home from the range after a practice. All the things I was working on all seem to come together then, and during that time I usually have a lot of insight into a particular problem I might be having. I'll just tune in and let my mind go wherever it goes. My notebook is always handy when I get home so that I can write down things that were important to me. I really recommend your keeping a notebook. Not only is it important to record your thoughts on shooting for future reference, but you'll also find that taking the time to organize them so that you can write them down will help you to make sense of them and understand them that much better. In the course of entering in your thoughts, you'll also find that other thoughts and different ideas will come out too. (Sometimes seeing these thoughts shows that your limitations may even be in what you're writing down.)

TO BE A SUCCESSFUL IPSC SHOOTER...

IPSC can tax you in so many different ways. To be a successful IPSC shooter, you must be a well-rounded shooter. You can't have any weak points that are going to get you, because a weak point will always catch up to you somewhere at a match. If you want to be really competitive, you have got to get to the point where you're not afraid of anything.

If you're not able to shoot quickly on close targets, not able to shoot accurately on long targets or on no-shoot targets, not able to shoot reasonably well while moving, not able to shoot weak-handed or draw quickly, or not able to analyze stages and lay out a careful plan, work on it. A lot of times, you'll go to a stage and just take it haphazardly and you'll miss some kind of technical thing you should have done there that a novice shooter saw and did. You weren't paying attention. You not only need to have the mechanical qualities of being able to technically do anything that could ever be thrown at you, but you also have got to keep your mind open to stay sharp.

To be a successful practical shooter, you work on what you can't do until there's nothing that you can't do.

One of the hardest ways to have to look at yourself and one of the hardest things to do is to practice what you don't like to do. If you don't like to shoot weak-hand, you'd better practice it. If you don't like to shoot at 50 yards, if you're not good at it and there's no confidence there, then you'd better practice it. The things that you're having problems with are the things you need to practice. It's all too easy to fall into the trap of only practicing what you like to practice. And that's typical: you keep developing and refining things that you can do well while ignoring the things you can't do well. The best quality a practical pistol shooter can have is being consistently able to do anything that any stage requires of him. So to be competitive, you need to develop and refine every single aspect of your shooting, not just the ones that you like to do or are the most comfortable with.

EXPENDITURE

For those of you who have heard all the stories, I'd like to put to rest one prevailing myth. To become a top shooter, you don't have to fire 100,000 rounds a year, stand in the shooter's box from sunup to sundown, shoot until you're knee-deep in brass, or pay any other unrealistic dues. Over the course of the time it might take to develop your skills as a shooter, there will be enough spent brass to fill up a dumpster, but just firing until you're shell-shocked will not make you an accomplished shooter. I shoot relatively few rounds now, and even in the so-called learning stage, I fired far fewer rounds than many top shooters.

For a couple of years I kept up with how many rounds I fired. In 1988 I shot almost 25,000 rounds. That was 17,000 rounds in practice and about 7500 in matches. This counts .22, .38 Special, rifle, shotgun, 7BR—everything I shot. Approximately 12,000 of those went through my .38 Super. I fired an average of 275 rounds per practice. In '87 it was about the same thing: 6000 in matches and about 19,000 in practice. I don't really practice for any matches at all with the Super except for the Steel Challenge. I'll shoot it a little bit before the IPSC Nationals. If I've been shooting a lot of matches locally and have my equipment ready, I may shoot two days, 300-400 rounds each day, to maybe work on a few specific challenges that I might expect to encounter there—seated draws, barricades—or I may work up a couple of comstock standards to just work on a few specifics like weak-hand shooting. If I haven't been shooting that much and am feeling a little bit rusty, I might shoot a week's worth of 300 rounds per day. But I don't go out and shoot working on the basic drills anymore like I used to where I probably shot closer to 25,000 practice rounds in a year.

If you'll just work with the right ideas and fundamentals, keep yourself open to your experiences, and can use awareness as your learning tool in your practice as opposed to the number of rounds you fire, you don't have to shoot a tremendous amount of ammunition. Everyone has heard the expression that it's the quality and not the quantity of the rounds fired in practice. And it's so simple and so true that it's hard for some people to believe.

A PLAN FOR DEVELOPMENT

I don't really think anymore about goals. I'm never really trying to accomplish anything in a tangible sense as far as actual match-scenario performances go or meeting any "standard" skill levels. For example, instead of wanting to shoot an *El Presidente* in 5 seconds, I have the goal of wanting to see or feel something in that time. I do still set tangible goals, but they don't have anything to do with any feeling that I *have* to learn something or reach some measured skill level. For me, tangible goals are fun. Doing a 10-shot Bill Drill is *fun*. Doing an 18-shot Bill Drill is *fun*. Just to fire that number of rounds in that time into the *dirt* is hard enough, let alone do it in the A-box of a target. It's something that's just on the absolute edge of my skill and ability, and it's like a very rewarding fun. But they don't have any great meaning; they're just fun to do and to talk about and to try.

But when I was learning to shoot, I did have more tangible goals to help me reach the level of competency in different skills that I felt I needed to be competitive on a technical level. And I'm sure a question that's on the beginning shooter's mind is whether or not there is a system, a plan to follow that will take him to the level he wants to reach as a practical shooter. It's a pretty common thing to talk about setting goals and reaching goals. But to me, goals, no matter how high they are, can often just become limitations. But at the same time, the new shooter needs to have some direction or otherwise he'll never get through the basics so he can move on. Just make sure that you understand when setting and reaching goals can be beneficial, and, more importantly, understand how placing too much emphasis on achieving a particular goal can be limiting.

There is a time and place for everything. Dry-firing at home is the time and place for thinking; shooting at the range is the time and place for experiencing.

As I said in the *Tools Of Shooting,* learning to shoot accurately is the first step. Believe it. Before you start developing specific practical shooting skills, you should be to the point where you can consistently call your shots.

Next comes following the ideas in that section to develop a freestyle platform you're comfortable with and one that is fairly reflexive. If you're at the beginning level, it's really important to use imagery, dry-drawing, and all the different drills and visualizations and awareness exercises that can allow you to mount the gun with your eyes closed and have the gun in line with your eye whenever you need to. You have to develop that skill level; without that you're never going to progress past anything besides "see the sight on the target." You'll never learn how to let your body feel do any shooting for you.

For the shooter who has already developed his freestyle platform and can pick up the gun and find the sights are always in alignment, then his goal may shift to just becoming more well-rounded. You need to work on specific challenges like weak-hand, strong-hand, prone—you don't ever want to be in a position where you can't do something as well as anybody else. You have to develop every aspect of your technique down to where they're *all* down.

And once you're at that level, you might have a goal of being able to feel comfortable with yourself when shooting from unorthodox positions—crouched down, leaning around, falling over, unbalanced, on the move. You may want to spend some time practicing things like that since you may normally only get a chance to do them in matches.

Your focus may then eventually switch toward more internally-oriented goals such as shooting at your current level and not letting yourself lose your center in a match—being happy with your own performance in a match.

These goals aren't limiting; they're not milestones. Things like doing a one-shot draw in so much of a second are limiting once they're reached because someday you may be able to go twice that fast. Based on your own perception of your performance and of your general ability to do all the things I've talked about, you'll also discover and define any specific things you need to work on. Never stop questioning and facing your limitations. And make sure that any goals you set are geared to take you beyond them, not just to them.

Shoot every run as if you were on your last magazine before quitting. Shoot every shot as if your life depended on the attention you were giving it. Never get caught in the trap of practicing haphazardly.

PRACTICE STRATEGY

I've said that my attitude doesn't change from practice to match. That's only possible if you can devote full attention to your shooting in practice just as you should when shooting in a match. The only real difference is that in practice you can focus on whatever you want to, whereas in a match, you're going to be focused on what you need to do or see to shoot the course. But the quality of the focus is the same.

When you go to the range, you should have something in mind that you're trying to accomplish. But don't limit yourself only to one, specific thing that you're trying to force into your shooting. You might have an idea that you're trying out and, in the course of your experience, discover that idea has led to a focus on something else. Depending on how related the new focus is to what you originally started with, you might want to stop and take a look at it and see where it's coming from or where it's leading you. But don't ignore it. Keep yourself open to your experiences, no matter what they are.

I recommend practicing on paper targets because paper is so unmerciful in that it shows you every shot exactly where it went. I always practice on whatever IPSC target is in vogue at the time. The only time I ever practice on steel is right before the Challenge. Steel doesn't show you where your hits are as accurately as paper; after you get a few hits on a plate, it's more difficult to call your shots. Shooting paper forces you to go down and tape the targets and gives constant feedback in the shot-calling process. That's the major thing. Some people practice on steel in the belief that the smaller plate will make the larger IPSC target easier to hit, but I don't go with that: the A-box is smaller than most plates. Practicing exclusively on steel can tend to shift a shooter's feedback from sight to sound. As difficult as that is to fight in a match, you don't want to further habituate it by adding it to your practice. Shooting paper keeps you open to your visual inputs.

A POSSIBLE APPROACH

When I go out to the range I usually have a specific problem in my mind that I want to work on. Speed on the first shot, speed in acquiring the targets, accuracy at 50 yards, going prone, weak-hand, doubles at close targets, or whatever. I'll always set up some type of scenario to test some particular skill level I'd like to see or refine points I'd like to work on. And then I'll shoot that until I think I've learned what I set out to learn. Sometimes I've gone out to shoot Bill Drills and set up at 7 yards with the intentions of shooting them at 15, 25, and 50 yards. But if I'm not really happy with the way I'm handling the gun, I may shoot all my rounds at 7 yards. Once I feel like I've received the inputs I was looking for, then I'll switch and set something else up. I use practice as just pretty much as an experimentation ground, nowadays at least.

When I first started out, I shot much more general drills—general IPSC-type practice—draw and fire two shots at 25 yards in 3 seconds, or one shot in 2 seconds, or two shots in 1.5 seconds at 10 yards, reloading drills, and just specific skill-test, time-limit type drills—whatever was current at the time. Once I'd gotten past all those fundamental, skill-test drills—shooting any target at any distance in any realistic time limit—I began to structure my practices so that now instead of trying to acquire a certain level of measured competency, I'm usually just trying to acquire a certain feeling or observe a certain focus. Now I make up my own tests so I can see my own limitations, not those of the people who invented the drills. Therefore, I don't really have a specific system or set of drills, standards, or exercises that I'd absolutely say to follow, because I hate to recommend anything like that for you and assign time limits to them. If you're a Master, the drill won't mean anything if I have C-class time limits on it. If you're a C-class shooter and I've got Master-class time limits, you're going to be getting D hits trying to make the time limits. For the beginner, though, I would like to offer some suggestions for practice to develop the fundamental skills and skill levels you'll need to acquire. Looking back on my own development, here's what I'd suggest following if I were starting the game all over again.

Structure your practices so you're working on developing real general shooting skills that involve targets from 5 to 50 yards. *Always* shoot with an accuracy goal. You always want to score at least 90-95% of the points possible. For instance, if you draw and shoot an A and a B, that's 90%. Two Cs, 80%, won't cut it. You want to keep at least 75% of your shots in the A-box. And that's the speed you want to shoot. You don't want to be concerned with plugging little groups in the A-box or seeing how fast you can squirt hits all over the target. *You never want a D hit on an IPSC target.* A D is *never* an acceptable shot. If you're shooting Ds on a target, you're shooting past what you're capable of on that particular string. So you might want to start out shooting single shots at 5 yards, seeing how fast you can work down to keeping with your 75% As goal. Then do doubles on the same target.

You always need to set your own time limits because everyone is going to be at a different skill level. When you first start out, you may need 1.5-2 seconds to put a shot in the A-box. Eventually you'd want to work down to where you're doing that under one second at more of a Master level. Then you can move to 7 and 10 yards and do the same basic drills. Draw and one shot; draw and two shots. Then move to drawing and firing on two separate targets that are about 3 yards apart just to bring in a little gun movement and target acquisition into it. One shot on each, two shots on each. Same thing at 15 and then 25 yards. Then skip out to 40 or 50 yards. You need to work on shooting the same type drills at 40 and 50 yards. At 25 and 50 yards, you'll also need to start getting into a little more special position work by going prone because that will be required of you.

Out to 15 yards, you need to practice drawing and shooting strong-hand and the transfer to the weak hand. For instance, shooting at three targets at 10 yards—one on each weak- and strong-hand. And, again, the whole key there is keeping your shots in the A-box. Don't sacrifice accuracy for speed. Just keep pushing yourself until you're just able to hold that 90-95% point score.

There are so many different drills you can do within these parameters that it's too much for one practice session.

When we first started shooting, our philosophy was that if we just practiced long-range, then anything up close would be easy. We figured that if we could hit the A-zone consistently at 25 yards, then we could hit anything any closer than that, and that's where the matches are anyway. That worked 6 or 7 years ago, but then we started breaking out of that phase and seeing the speed that was really possible on the close targets. And it's gotten to the point now where we're almost doing a reversal. The hardest thing for me has now become the highest speed possible type shooting where I'm just pitted against myself. And the reason it's become the most difficult is because it's the hardest to fight the tension in. That's a performance killer on close range.

I spend probably 75% of my IPSC practice time now shooting close-range, multiple shots, with most of the drills emphasizing relaxation. I still shoot some long-range 25- and 50-yard practice, but not nearly what I used to. Because now if you can only shoot at 25 and 50 yards, it just doesn't matter—you're just going to be too slow. The top shooters are just too fast in target acquisitions and speed on the close targets. You have to keep up with what's happening and develop the full spectrum.

Work on what you can't do. Don't try to be a specialist. Vary your shooting. Work on your weak points. If you can hit the A-box quickly on close targets, don't shoot close targets. If you can't keep your shots in at 25 yards, work on that. Then when you can keep the shots in at 25 yards, you can go back to the close targets and work on hitting them faster. And you need to try everything. Expose yourself to every condition you can dream up. Make up your own time limits, create your own drills, make up your own scenarios that test your skill on specific challenges. *And learn from them*. Set up a scenario that just tests your gun movement from target to target—maybe two targets 5 yards apart at 15 yards—and in shooting that test, maybe you shouldn't even care about your draw time. Just look at your split time between shots and be aware of any inputs you get that could increase or decrease your split time. Just work on that specific skill test and stay focused.

You have to be creative and come up with your own tests. Have some fun and find out what's possible. There is no set of standard drills you can do that will teach you everything you need to know to be competitive in this sport. If you're not afraid to try anything your mind can come up with just to see if you can do it, your development will be that much faster and your skills that much better.

TIME LIMITS

When you're practicing specific drills or skill tests, my advice is to *always* put a time limit on them and to always figure *your own* time limits. On a lot of things at the more advanced level, I'll work purely against time; I'll see how fast I can do a certain thing with all As, for instance. But if I'm trying to learn a specific skill, I'll always establish a time limit and work within that time limit. And I'll make the time limit comfortable enough to where I can see and feel the things I need to. That way I'm not crowding myself so I can get some grasp of what I'm trying to learn. There's no sense in trying to shoot 6 shots on 3 different targets at 40 yards in 4 seconds if you're just barely able to hang the hits on the paper. You might want to try it in 8 seconds or try it going prone. You need to blend it with your own skill level, but set your limits at a point where you don't have enough time to just casually shoot As in the center of the box. You'd like to think that your time limit is allowing you just barely enough time to shoot As, and then you'll realistically see some shots that aren't As. And if that's kind of the parameter that you've established for setting your time limit, then you'll be pretty close; you just need to be honest with yourself. Time limits aren't goals—they're just ways to help you practice. When you can comfortably make all your A hits in the time limit you've established for yourself, whittle the time down so you always feel pressured.

Time limit exercises are back in vogue in IPSC because they've learned how to make the time limits tight enough to separate the scores. If the time limits are too lenient, the scores are going to be separated in the B and C classes, but the Masters will shoot the same score and it becomes a non-stage. But with really tight time limits that push a Master to the edge, the standards are a measurable stage and are a factor in the match. When you're practicing time limit exercises, make your emphasis on what you're seeing. What you see should tell you where you stand in relation to the limit.

For practicing comstock standards, it used to be that the big emphasis was on speed. For a while, the current thing on those was to practice and practice them at warp drive. You'd hear of guys who had been practicing them to death and how fast they were running, and then all you'd become concerned about was the time you could shoot each string in and whatever hits you get...that's just the way it goes. I think that a much better way to practice any comstock string of fire is to establish some kind of base time limit to work from. Shoot the string of fire and arrive at some pace where you can function at about a 90-95% score and come up with par times for each string. Then shoot that stage as a time limit exercise and shoot for points only, functioning within those limits and making your emphasis on what you're seeing instead of how fast you're going. The more you see, the faster you'll go. Focusing on your visual inputs will help remove the barriers to your performance on these stages.

USING THE TIMER

I always use a timer when I practice. I won't usually program a stop beep to tell me when my time limit is up, but I'll always look at it to either see my raw time or to see if I'm within my limit, depending on what I'm practicing for.

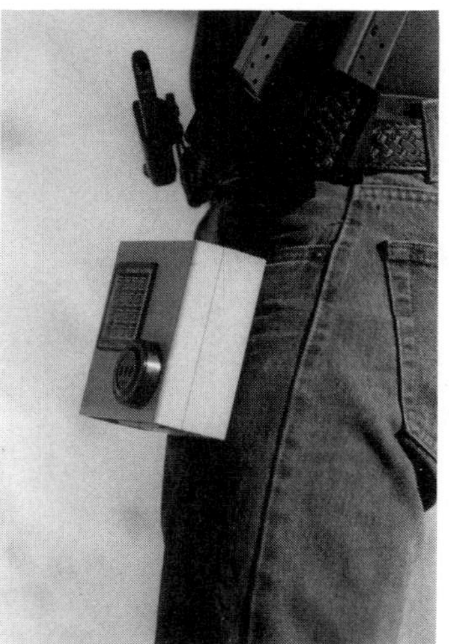

I use a timer when I practice, and I won't use one that's not user friendly. It must show the split times easily and quickly.

Some timers are user-friendly and some aren't. You should have a timer that's easy to use so operating it won't ever get in the way of your practice. And the timer *must* be able to show you the time in between each of your shots—the shot breaks or splits—not just the overall time you've done. That's *the* most important feature. Your timer display should let you review the time of each shot in a string as the split between it and the last shot and as the overall time up to that shot. And it's much more valuable to get that sort of information out of a timer than just your overall time.

It's a good feedback process to watch your splits to see how fast you can your fire shots on one target and on multiple targets at certain ranges. The timer can show you how well you're moving on a course, such as from box to box. The splits can tell you which targets you're having trouble acquiring. The splits can tell you so much more about your shooting than just how quickly you're doubling up on a target. If you're shooting a couple of shots and doing a reload, you need to be able to call up that reload time instantly; you don't want to have to play with the timer and wonder if you went past it. And you also want to be able to review your first shot time easily; that's always a good thing to monitor on any string.

In the old days, we used stopwatches and whistles and things weren't quite as precise as they are now. The modern timer may have pressed us into the warp zone as far as speed goes because it is so relentless in reading out the time to the hundredths of a second; it never gives you a break. There's never any doubt about what your true time is as there was with the stopwatch. And if you're not careful, the timer can drive you nuts. The timer can turn the time into an end in itself. I've caught myself practicing where all I cared about was the time and just kept working a drill down and down until I could get The Time. In that mindset I'm not really concerned about my technique, or what I'm feeling, or what I'm seeing—all I want to do is shoot and push the button on my timer and see what my time is. If you get obsessed with the timer like that, the best thing to do is to just take a break from it. If I get in that mode, I'll just use the timer as a start signal, and then I won't look at it after that. It's a great tool, but because of all of our thoughts that we can come up with, we can just get carried away with it.

BAD HABITS

Some aspects of your shooting will become habits. Trigger pull can become a habit, but that habit can sometimes hurt you. For instance, if your finger automatically pulls the trigger every time your sights are aligned, sometimes you may want to wait on that for a no-shoot to get out of the way or for a target to appear. Your finger needs to feed its information off the total environment, not just off of sight alignment. Every course of fire is going to be different. Whether it's on your range or the next guy's range, it's going to be different—even if it's supposed to be the same stage—and it's going to take awareness and observation to successfully negotiate it.

Do not become caught up or attached to the idea of knowing how to do something. The knowing is not it. There is only the doing.

For instance, if you shoot a Steel Challenge course at your range and your range inclines upward at a 5-degree angle, then all your targets will be high, and at 40 yards there may be quite a difference. But on your own range it feels normal to you because you're sensing the height of the targets from the ground level. So if you go shoot the same course at a range that slants upward as your range did, but now they've adjusted the targets so they're level with the shooter, now that 40-yard target may be sitting almost on the ground, but it's level with you, and there's a major difference for your body to deal with.

This is always something to be aware of when you're trying to duplicate courses of fire. If a match has a published course of fire, the last thing you ever want to do is get too attached to its specifications. Because when you get to the real range it's never like it is on the drawing. And if you set something up incorrectly and you practice it to death, it can really hurt you. Practicing like that can program a motor response and program a rhythm into you for that one stage, and when you get there and it's nothing at all like what you've trained on, it's really hard to break free of the program and just shoot the stage as it now appears.

A really top-flight IPSC shooter can go through a fairly complex stage and on his first or second time through it can usually run it about as well as he can run it, period. You've got to have the attitude of keeping your senses and your mind completely open to intuit the situation and the needs as they arise. That sense has to be very finely honed. A person who's too programmed just cannot do that.

OVER-PRACTICING

If I'm practicing for the Steel Challenge, I'll shoot through the whole thing like a match just to pressure myself to see how realistically I need to shoot it. After they're knee-deep in brass and have fired 300 rounds straight on *5 To Go,* a lot of people will shoot a "match run" of their best 4 out of 5, and it will be some amazing time that's hardly indicative of what their match performance will be. A lot of shooters lull themselves into the belief that a pace they've shot on their best possible run in practice will be their predictable pace. They get that pace in their heads and then try to recreate it in a match, and that's unrealistic. It's totally unrealistic to believe that and to place that kind of strain on yourself.

It's important to get a realistic idea of what you're going to do on a stage. The last few years I've started really paying close attention to keeping the feeling I have on match day pretty close to the feeling I have on cold runs at the range. It stays pretty close if I just show up at the range, strap on the gun, and attempt to shoot a match run for score. That's pretty much how I'm going to feel at the match as far as how tuned in I am. With that approach, it's hard to be really tuned in for your first run on a specific skill test. So if I'm practicing for something, I don't live with the illusion that the times I'm going to shoot in the match will be the same after I've practiced a stage for 300 rounds. Just walking up cold, it's hard to shoot to your maximum speed. It can happen; there have been times in the match where I've shot a stage as well as I could have ever hoped to in practice. Typically, though, you have just got to accept your state.

I've successfully done hundreds of Bill Drills, but to just walk out to the range and do one on the first 6 shots out of the gun is really difficult. So I started doing this as a little test. I'd walk out to the range and put my gun on and I'd try to do a Bill Drill on the very first 6 shots I'd actually draw and fire. For years, I never did one the first try. Then I finally did one and quit trying after that. Bill Drills are not that tough once you've made a few runs, made a few draws, fired a few shots. But that first 6-shot string is an accurate indication of what you can count on doing cold.

But you just end up pressuring yourself by picking your best times and your best runs and actually expecting to shoot them. You've got to get away from that. You've got to design your practices so you know what you're trying to do when you walk up to the line to shoot your cold run—you know you're simulating the match experience. And you should feel pressure in practice. You should feel like you're going to feel in a match. *This* is the time you've got to do it. *Now is the only time.* There are no throw away runs, no start-overs. What you do is what you get to keep for that day. And then when you see weak points or different targets you want to work on or different sequences you want to try, you can go back and practice those things. But to just stand and burn out on a stage you don't really learn anything. You just get grooved into that one stage at that one particular time.

Remember that when you're developing your shooting skills, you're also developing the awareness that will take you beyond them.

LEARNING THROUGH AWARENESS

I've learned a lot of technical things purely through being in a very aware, no-mind state as I'm practicing. Sometimes I notice things that I might not have noticed normally, like the gun coming up to the right of the target showing me a deficiency in my natural point of aim. I've even made changes by just becoming aware of some different pressure in my grip, for instance, where all of a sudden I had a major focus on it for no reason at all. It's amazing how your body works things out for you if you'll just let it.

Just let the scenario dictate what you want to do: *hit that target twice as fast as you can.* Once you've gotten beyond all your thoughts and ideas and the technical mistakes like jerking the trigger and trying and anticipating and tensing up and all the other garbage put on by those limitations, once your body is just simply trying to do that simple act—it's just seeing how fast it can do it—that's when you *really* begin to learn. That's when you see how fast the gun gets into your vision, what kind of a feeling you're having for your hand moving toward the gun or for the gun coming out. You'll start to feel the sensations of floating the gun or driving the gun onto the target that you've never really noticed before. Your mind is just really opening up and you're flowing freely.

If you will watch what the gun is doing when you fire it, that will show you where you need to place your attention to improve your technique.

If the intention is there, your body will find a way to work it out. When you know what you need to see, you will see it if you'll relax and keep yourself open. For example, when you know that you want to see the sight tracking up and down in the same place and on the same path for each shot, when you see that, then you know your grip is doing what it should. You should first know what you want to *see* instead of what you want to *do*. Learning begins with *visual* awareness, not physical awareness.

Watching the gun's movement and its position on the target will show you where you need to look for a better technique. And sometimes the answers aren't obvious, but they're always there. There are many subtleties involved in producing an aligned gun on target and keeping it aligned from shot to shot. Relaxation is the first step. Beyond that, be very sensitive to your perceptions when you mount the gun. Spend time noticing differences you perceive when you mount the gun with your eyes closed and with your eyes open, for instance, and when dry-firing and firing, and intuit your perceptions. If you're developing your freestyle platform, you may need to stop and see where the problem might be in pressures or positioning if you continually produce the gun to the left or right or out of alignment. It could be something as subtle as your shoulder alignment or your head position.

Don't be afraid to try different things; just make sure that you're keeping yourself open to your experiences and don't reject anything you discover, even if it's something that you're not "supposed" to do. If it works for you, then do it.

When you can produce the gun in alignment on the target, find it in alignment wherever you look or move, and see the sight tracking up and back to where it began, then what you're doing is correct. And remember that it's not how you look, *it's what you see.*

Just watch. See how much attention you've got. Sometimes you have to change your routine so that you are able to just watch. If you're hung up on shooting fixed scenarios from the Steel Challenge or Bianchi or IPSC, it's difficult to learn to just watch on something you've shot one-million times. Sometimes it's better to just fire into the dirt. If you want to watch every detail of gun movement, you've got to have no concern over whether or not you hit the targets. You may need to shift to that mode to really learn what you're seeing. Usually if you're in something that's too routine, you're not aware.

To really see the things I talk about seeing, you have just got to stop what you're doing and do something different. Stop doing your one-shot draws at 25 yards on a target—do your one-shot draws on a dirt bank or start with the gun in your hand and raise it. Just change *something* so that you can get to the point where you're watching it and seeing it for the first time again. The methodical routine just breeds habits; when you're in a routine, you're blocking yourself out.

Practice seeing what you see. How fast does your focus shift, how does the gun come onto the target? Pay attention.

Because I'm a technically-inclined person, when I notice my body start to make a mechanical change over time, I will stop—after the shooting—and try to take an objective look at that change. But it's not necessary for you to do that. People who aren't as technically inclined probably shouldn't even question the change if it seems to be working for them. But if a technical change seems to be working in the wrong direction for you, chances are that there's something else on your mind other than just relaxing and experiencing the shooting. Almost always, the changes your body will make, or the things you may be made aware of through shooting in a totally open state, will be beneficial. That's because you're very specifically focused on doing a very general thing then—shoot two shots on that target as fast as you can—and your body will find the best way to do that. You will only be limited by your present level of technical shooting skill.

Practice Seeing What You See

Even if you're at the range and run out of ammo, you can still learn a lot by just practicing *seeing what you see*. Be aware of when the gun comes on the target or what you're looking at when you go to the target. Are you looking at the target in focus, and at what point do you catch the sight in focus? When you're starting, are you just looking for the sight, and does it matter for different distances or where the target is or how small the target is? Once you've come onto the target and you've got a focus on the front sight and move to the next target, what do you see? Do you see the target clearly, do you see the center of the target, can you see the sight going all the way across? How far apart can you move the targets and still keep a pretty good focus on the front sight? At what point do you need to start looking to the next target to get the gun to move to that target quickly? You can practice seeing the target, sight, next target, sight—you can do all that without firing a shot. You can learn a lot just about how you can go. Does the gun come onto the target smoothly or does it come on tense? Does it come onto the center or are you always pushing it off one of the edges because you're overmuscling the gun? Experiment with different arm tensions and different sets and feels just to see how you can get the gun on the target the quickest and the smoothest. You don't have to shoot to do that. Never stop; always keep inventing new things that monitor your awareness.

AWARENESS EXERCISES

I strongly suggest that you spend whatever time it takes to progress through these exercises. I think that developing the intuitive awareness these will help instill in you is critical to reaching your potential.

Because you'll acquire the skills in increments, don't attempt to do the most difficult exercise until you can do the ones that lead up to it. Do these exercises in order. Make sure that you're completely satisfied with your ability to do each preceding one before you move on to the next. I've acquired these skills through my own awareness, so I really can't tell you how long you'll need to spend on each exercise before you can move on to the next. You'll just have to let your own perception of your progress determine what sort of training interval you'll need for each.

Pay attention. Observe yourself when your body makes a "mistake." Possibly your body might be trying to tell you something.

Don't attempt to do these exercises to gain any certain result because you're not going to gain any result that's going to be immediate enough to even matter.

Just pay attention to what you're doing and how you

are feeling and eventually your body will start following your own images.

Exercise 1

Start by holding the gun with your normal shooting grip and aiming at no place in particular. Lower the gun. With your eyes closed, raise the gun to what you feel is your normal shooting position, then open your eyes and verify sight alignment. Keep practicing this until you can raise the gun and always have the sights appear when you open your eyes.

Exercise 2

From that exercise, you'll move on to starting with the gun in either hand so that now you'll have to assume your grip before raising the gun. You again aim at nothing in particular. You can start with the gun in an aligned position, then take the gun out of your hand, reseat the gun, close your eyes, mount the gun, and see if you can verify sight alignment.

Exercise 3

Once you can do that consistently, move on to doing the same thing from a draw. Again, you're aiming at no place in particular. Start in your normal surrender or hands-down position, draw and mount the gun with your eyes closed, and then open your eyes and verify sight alignment. You at least want to see the sight in the notch; eventually you want to get to where you can see perfect sight alignment.

Exercise 4

Once you can do those three exercises and always produce alignment, you need to move on to producing the alignment and then *keeping* the alignment.

You might start with the gun aimed in on a blank area on a wall, verifying alignment with your eyes open, closing your eyes, and then pivoting to an imaginary target about 20 degrees to the left. Open your eyes and see if the sights are still in alignment. Then you can start over again and do the same exercise pivoting 20 degrees to the right.

Once you can do that exercise, you can keep increasing the distance you pivot, eventually moving 90 degrees to the left and right, keeping the sights in alignment.

To really work yourself up to this awareness, start with the gun aligned in the center, close your eyes, and pivot 90 degrees to the left, then, still keeping your eyes closed, pivot 90 degrees to the right and see if it's still in alignment. If you can do that, then you can pretty much keep the gun in alignment between your eye and the target no matter where you look.

You can also expand this to include variations of the exercises together. See if you can draw the gun, mount the gun, move it to the left, and then open your eyes—see if you can have a sight alignment without beginning with a verification of your original sight alignment. You can angle the gun down and up and all different ways to see if you can keep sight alignment.

Test yourself by coming up with movements and combinations of movements that could throw your alignment off, but practice until you see that the alignment is always there on demand.

Exercise 5

Once you can produce alignment on demand doing these exercises, move on to drawing and aiming at a specific target.

First get your body naturally and uniformly aligned on a reasonably sized target—at 3 or 4 paces, that's a spot about 1.5 inches in diameter. Then holster the gun, close your eyes, and attempt to draw the gun and find the sights aligned and on the target when you open your eyes.

Start by drawing at a slow speed, not a forceful speed—one that lets you feel all your body's movements, your grip, all the positions, and all the natural tensions or neutral things you've experienced in doing the previous exercises where you weren't actually aiming at a target. You can slowly increase the speed of the draw to where you're eventually going at normal speed. The more you do this exercise and the better you get, the more you can back away or make the target smaller.

When you can do this—reliably produce the gun in the target area with your eyes closed—it will give you a tremendous amount of confidence. As long as you're neutral, relaxed, and visually engaged with the target, if your sights are aligned by your grip, stance, and draw, wherever you point the pistol you'll hit. This awareness makes Types 1 and 2 shooting focus possible.

Take Note

All the time you're doing these awareness exercises, you're trying to develop slowly, piece-by-piece. Be aware of all your body's feels, of all the subtleties in the different parts of your fingers and of your hands on the grip.

The most productive thought you put into your shooting will be from a reflection on your awareness and observation.

Pay close attention to what you feel when you're working to devlop your skills. If you keep yourself open to your experiences, changes are automatic.

Notice how different tensions in different parts of your hands can produce the sights to the left or right and of the different tensions in either arm, tensions in your stomach, the way you hold your shoulders—just all the ways your body feels and how its parts work together in harmony to produce an aligned gun.

Every time you raise the gun, draw the gun, or pivot it, you need to be aware of the different ways your body feels in keeping the gun neutral—it's just feeding that information to your brain without actually trying to *attempt* to feel anything. Just pay very close attention to what you actually are feeling. It's especially important to make those observations not only on how you feel when the gun is not aligned and you bring it into alignment, but also how it feels when you do mount the gun in alignment.

Eventually, your visualization and imagery will bring the gun into alignment before you; it will become a "mindset" type of feeling that will have an effect over your whole body, as opposed to any specific feeling in any one of its parts that you might notice when you're breaking an exercise down.

Eventually you'll be able to visualize the sights in perfect alignment in front of your eye and then be able to mount the gun and have them there. This image will correctly guide your body. It just takes a lot of practice and a lot of awareness of what you're actually feeling when you're doing it.

For a really top-level visualization exercise, I practice shooting on a 10-inch plate at 15 yards with my eyes closed. I sight the gun on the plate, close my eyes, and holster the gun. Then I draw the gun and shoot the plate, keeping my eyes closed the whole time. To hit the plate, I have to hold the image of what I just saw before I closed my eyes.

The point is to allow the image to physically place the gun on target. I usually shoot within one second after I close my eyes; I've found that's about as long as I can hold the image clearly enough to allow it to guide my gun. Before I move to this I usually take it one step backwards to where I sight the gun, close my eyes, and then just lower the gun; I then raise the gun and shoot with my eyes closed.

OTHER EXERCISES

Bill Drill

An exercise I do a lot that really emphasizes a smooth draw and high-speed gun control is something Bill Wilson dreamed up. At 7 yards, starting from a surrender position, draw and fire 6 shots into an IPSC target. They have to be all As or it doesn't count. At the Master level the time limit is 2 seconds. If you can't make the 2 seconds at 7 yards, try 3 seconds, or with the modern timers, you can make it 2.7 seconds or whatever you want it to be. Use whatever limit is keeping you honest; whatever is keeping you on the ragged edge of keeping the shots in the A box. Don't make it too easy. When you first start out you may be able to keep all your shots in one-of-five runs, but when you can do it five-of-five, cut your time limit down. There is no time to think. The Bill Drill will show you how important it is to be aware of what you're doing—when you're doing it.

The Bill Drill emphasizes relaxation and timing. This is probably the most important standard exercise I do.

You can do variations on this exercise by moving it to 10, 15, 25, and 50 yards and making up your own time limits along the way. For real control, you can try the exercise by altering the time limit for the head box if you don't feel like moving the target back. You can do the exercise with a reload. A great Master-level exercise is to draw, fire 6 shots in the target, reload, fire 6 shots in the target in 4 seconds or less with all As.

My current practice times are as follows: 7 yards, 1.7 seconds. 15 yards, 2 seconds. 25 yards, 3 seconds. 50 yards, 4 seconds. Since I've gotten my Smith & Wesson, I have a new game I call the *Ultimate Bill Drill*. That's 18 shots at 7 yards in 3.5 seconds. From doing Ultimate Bill Drills, I noticed that my 10-shot break was almost always just under the 2-second mark. So my new "standard" Bill Drill is 10 shots in 2 seconds. The 10-shot Bill Drill is a game that any .38 Super shooter can play, and I recommend it as a more "advanced" drill after you've gotten to where you can do the 6-shot drill with some regularity. You just see that much more, and firing the extra shots just puts that much more emphasis on staying relaxed.

When I do a Bill Drill, my shooting focus is usually pretty much the front sight. If I'm using light loads and can see the slide cycling, sometimes I watch the whole top of the gun, or sometimes I'll watch the comp, but usually in my very best runs I'm glued right onto the front sight and am seeing its movement in every detail—just watching it bounce up and down.

As the gun is coming onto the target, I'm driving the front sight into the A-box; I'm picking up on the gun and the front sight very soon and am just staying with it all the way through.

This is a timing drill that puts your emphasis on shooting as quickly as possible and holding the gun in the A-box as best as possible. So the whole thing is that you need to be in control of the gun's muzzle direction; you need to get it into the A-box and keep it there. However you manage to do that is what you learn. And the best input there is watching the front sight's relationship to the rear sight. By watching it rise up and down you can just keep driving the gun right into the A-box.

As I mentioned in *Creative Shooting,* I sometimes work with a Type 1 focus in Bill Drills (although I may still see the sight very clearly) since I often just want to monitor my relaxation.

Master Level Bill Drill Times
7 &10 yards, 2 seconds
15 yards, 2.5 seconds
25 yards, 4 seconds
50 yards, 6 seconds

Calling Shots

Although you *always* do this, here's a way to practice it: shoot a 5-shot string at 25 or 50 yards in some reasonable time limit that doesn't allow you to shoot too incredibly accurately—enough time to just keep your shots in the A-box. Shoot those five shots and call all five before you walk down to look at them.

You might start out by calling one, then two or three, and then all of them. Being able to call all five shots will really help your imagery practice and help you in paying exact attention to where every shot breaks. And achieving this awareness will be critical to your development.

Reloading

A really good drill for just working on the smoothness of the reload is to draw and shoot an A and reload and shoot another A at 7 yards, not accepting anything that's not an A. A Master level time for that drill is 2 seconds. You could start at 3 or 3.5 seconds and work down.

This drill really emphasizes a nice smooth draw and shot, and a nice smooth reload and shot, because you're not going to accept anything that's not an A.

LOHF

Over the past few years I've kept a record of my LOHF—*Limits Of Human Function*—times. After I'm really grooved in to a course, the LOHF is my single, fastest run.

The Steel Challenge brought about the LOHF idea. We pretty much shoot the same courses and the same targets every year so we can all see where we're going and what we're doing from year to year. About four years ago, I noticed that I hadn't gotten any faster. And that was the first time I didn't see that I was shooting noticeably faster than I had the year before. I started mentioning that to the other top shooters and they all seemed to feel that it was the same for them. We felt like we had all hit a plateau. I wondered where there was to go after that. So I made up some specific tests and went out and tested what I could do predictably—cold, match-type runs—as opposed to the kind of run I could have on a practice day after I had shot quite a few rounds on a course and was tuned in and just had the best run possible, and then compare them to those times.

I've recorded these times over the years and keep looking at them to see if I'm any faster. I can be slightly measurably faster on some things, but it's not a major difference. The big difference I've seen is in consistency. I can shoot the predictable time more consistently and I can hover in the area between that time and the LOHF time more consistently. But the LOHFs are still accurate. My basic limit of human function in manipulating the gun out of the holster and across the targets in *5 To Go* is still 2.3 seconds. It's hard for me to move the gun and hit the targets any faster than that. It's hard for me to realistically hit a 10-inch plate at 7 yards much faster than .7 seconds, predictably, from a hands-up start. I can get in the .60s now and then, but .7 is a pretty fast number and it's been that way for about three years now.

But to keep all this in perspective, LOHFs just show me my current limitations—my speed barriers. I don't let my LOHFs tell me anything specific about my shooting. For me it's just interesting to see where my movement times have plateaued and to see if I can break those barriers.

But the main thing you can learn from charting your own times is to just appreciate the difference between the LOHF run when you're knee-deep in brass and the predictable run when you're cold. Too many shooters believe in the fallacy that they're going to shoot their LOHF run on match day, and that's a horrible attitude to have going into a match.

"All goals apart from the means are illusions." —Bruce Lee

I don't impose limitations on myself, or on shooting. Whatever the limits of human function are, they are always changing.

My Current Limits Of Human Function
(predictable runs are in brackets)
Steel Challenge
Speed Option: 2.5 [3.25]
5 To Go: 2.3 [2.9]
Triple Threat: 1.25 [1.50]
Showdown: 2.2 [2.6]
Roundabout: 2.0 [2.5]
Double Trouble: .90 [1.2]

IPSC (surrender starts)
10-inch disk at 7 yards: .7 [.85]
8-inch disk at 10 yards: .90 [.95]
8-inch disk at 15 yards: .95 [1.0]
10-inch disk at 25 yards: 1.15 [1.3]
2 As at 10 yards: 1.0 [1.35]
2 As at 15 yards: 1.15 [1.4]

BREAK OUT GAME

Rob Leatham and I play this game when we're practicing for the Steel Challenge. The way the game works is that before you shoot a stage you pick a time limit for a single run. It doesn't matter what the time limit is; it just has to be something that you think you can do. And in this game it doesn't matter who's faster or slower—what matters is who can come the closest to their time limit without going *under* it. Say you're going to shoot *5 To Go* and you're cold and don't think you're going to shoot too smoothly so you pick 3.2 seconds. You shoot your five runs and throw away one. The object is to hit exactly a 3.2 second average for your four keepers. If you average 3.19, you lose. You try to pick a pace that lets you see everything that you need to see and you'll find that you can see a lot more than you ever thought you could see at that pace.

In the last section, I warned against letting yourself turn into a pace or rhythm shooter on steel where you have just shot the course of fire so many times that you get into a rhythm of shooting at programmed time intervals. And we *do not* do this to try to program in a habitual pace. Playing this game keeps you from getting speed-headed and getting cocky after making a couple of fast runs. It keeps you focused on what you need to see to make your time limit and lets you see certain things that you may not be aware of seeing. Mostly, though, it will confirm your conviction that *you do have time to see what you need to see,* whereas normally you feel forced. But if you've trained yourself in practice with this game—when you're not going to let yourself to go faster than your time limit—you'll be surprized at what you'll start seeing. You'll see the gun whip onto a target and stop and you'll make refinements in the sight picture, you'll feel your finger on the trigger and feel the shot release and see the sight lift—you'll see things and feel things you haven't felt in years, or ever.

Eventually you get so good at it that it's not uncommon to hit the four-run average to one-hundredth. Your mind can adjust to what it sees; it's working like a clock and it knows what the timer is going to read. If everything went a little too smoothly on every string—the gun just moved and stopped and moved and stopped and lifted off the target on every plate—when you go to the stop plate you'll hesitate for one or two tenths while you just squeeze the trigger through. But the important thing is that you'll do that from what you *saw,* not from any ingrained, blind rhythm.

It's a fun game to play and it's really a whole new way to look at a stage that is normally only measured by your raw time. You always want to make your emphasis on what you can see and get excited about what you saw on a run, and on the next run you're going to see more.

On every run you want to improve on what you see, not on what your time is. By the time you've practiced on the Challenge courses for a while, your speed is going to be as fast as you're going to go. So it's not like you've got to wonder if you're fast enough—you are fast enough. The speed is there. What you've got to instill is the confidence that you can see what you need to see. In the match, that's what lets you go as fast as you know you can go. And "the speed is there" means the same thing for a C-class shooter as it does for a Master. You're shooting the targets as quickly as you can. So you can just quit thinking about that and put all your emphasis on what you can see. If you did that from the very beginning and never even looked at your times at all, you'd probably be better off for it.

AIR GUN

In my opinion, practice with an air pistol has limited *direct* value to practical pistol shooters. Most match air pistols are so radically different from the practical race gun that there's a danger in becoming too familiar with it. The super-light trigger, adjustable grips, and other international-style refinements can spoil you in a hurry. After a lot of practice with a full-race air pistol, your practical gun will feel pretty raw. So there is no point to using the air pistol in an attempt to simulate the speed aspects of practical shooting. Shoot the air pistol as it was intended to be shot: use

ISU targets and fire from the prescribed distances. Just don't ever confuse it with the real deal.

I'm really getting hooked on shooting my air pistol just in its own realm. Just like shotgun or rifle, it's just one more form of shooting that enhances my overall experience. If you have the setup at home, and you're not one of the fortunate few who live near ranges, the air pistol is always going to be there for you to pick up and shoot when you have that spare 15 minutes.

The real fundamental benefit of using the air gun is that you can narrow your focus down to looking the gun off. *No thought, front sight focus, gun fires.* And there is some recoil even with an air gun. You can pay attention to how the gun shifts in your hand, how the sight lifts, which direction it moves, the consistency of its movement.

You have the ideal opportunity to monitor the gun and call the shot. You'll also find that followthrough is very important in shooting an air pistol accurately. The speed of the pellet is slow enough to where even slight pressure changes or gun movement can affect the shot after the trigger is released for a longer duration than when firing a high-velocity .38 Super.

There is another benefit to practicing precision shooting, whether with an air pistol or with your practical gun. Shooting at a more relaxed pace on bullseye targets gives you a premium opportunity to experience awareness and focus. You'll see how flexible your mind and your focus actually are as you're preparing to fire. When you're watching the sights move around, feeling your pressure change on the trigger, monitoring the pressure you're gripping the gun with, the tension in your arm and shoulder, and your breathing, you're experiencing focus and awareness. There is no way possible for you to concentrate on all these things; however, you are constantly monitoring them as you're preparing to shoot. As the shooting moves away from the bullseye targets to the practical field, the speed increases but the monitoring and constant adjustments shouldn't stop. This is what you're working toward as a practical shooter. If you can experience it on the slow-fire range, so much the better.

Remember: Your thoughts are always one step away from the action.

One last word about practicing away from the range—be careful that you don't get lax when dry-firing. When you dry-fire, pay exact attention to where the sight is when the hammer drops. Calling your shots is always important, even when you're dry-firing at home. You can connect the audible click of the hammer falling with the front sight's position to call your shot.

APPENDIX A: THE SHOOTING TOOLS

Especially today, equipment changes probably faster than anything else in shooting. For that reason, it's hard for me to really recommend too many specific things. Just as soon as I did, chances are that something better would come out and I'd be using that instead of what I'd recommended here. There are a lot of general considerations, however, that I don't think will change because they all deal with the shooter's relationship to his gun. There really hasn't been much said about this subject, and that's what I'd mostly like to talk about. Although there will always be something different, right now there are enough different tricks available for the Government Model pistols that there is no reason you can't custom-fit it to whatever your personal preferences are.

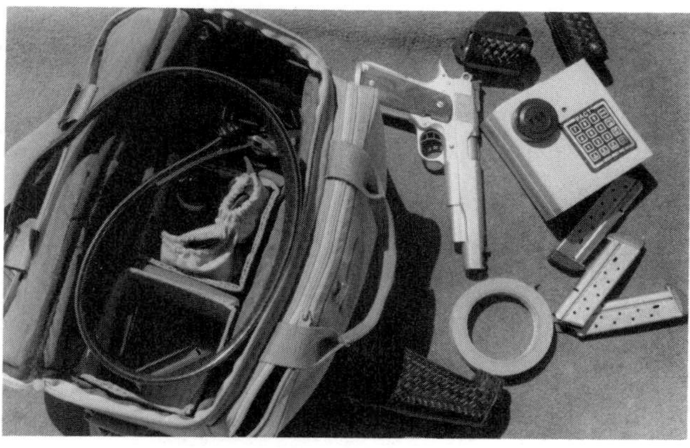

Any concern over equipment should always be with its effect on your performance.

I see no reason that we won't continue to have better and better equipment available to us. There's always a lot of experimentation going on with different guns, calibers, comps, and you name it. It also seems that experimentation often goes in opposite directions, so the choices you have become greater and greater. But with more choices always come more decisions. And for that reason, I think that it's more important than ever to address the really basic, shooter-oriented effects that different components, modifications, and philosophies have on performance. If you want to experiment, make sure that you know what result you're after. And no matter what form they might take, any component changes and modifications you make should be geared to improving *your* performance, not your gun's performance.

If you're new at this game, don't try to figure out all the details on your own. It's a lot easier to first try what seems to be working for the better shooters. You can bet that they've tried just about everything at some time, and regardless of the reasons they ended up using what they do, if you see most using a certain thing, try that before you go to something that you don't see anyone using. But one thing I can say for certain is if, in your mind, there is some-

**The gun fires.
You shoot.**

thing out there that you feel will work best for you, get it just so you'll have it. Anything less is a waste of money. The last thing you ever want to be saddled with is lack of confidence as to something as insignificant as equipment.

1. THE RACE GUN

Choosing a Gun

All the better-known pistolsmiths are capable of turning out top-drawer work. When you see what's offered by different builders, you're not so much looking at differences in quality, accuracy, or reliability, you're seeing differences in philosophies. Pistolsmiths all have their own ideas on what makes the perfect gun, which to them is the one that they build. Learn about the strong and weak points of the guns you're thinking about buying and try to find the one that will average out best for you. You may want a gun that capitalizes on your strengths or one that compensates for your weaknesses. If you feel your weak point is muzzle control, you may feel more comfortable with a heavier gun that will soak up more recoil. If you're blast sensitive you may want to sacrifice a little port area for a quieter gun. A shooter who isn't recoil sensitive at all and feels that his strong point is moving the gun from target to target could get away with a lighter, more responsive gun.

Whenever possible, shoot other guns with the features you're considering before you decide. Don't just pull the trigger and feel the jump; notice the effect the gun has on your timing and on your ability to go from target to target. Also shoot some groups at long range to see how well you can shoot the gun with precision.

Compensators

Generally, it seems that compensator designs using ports that are open at the top perform best. And, generally, the more ports and the larger the ports, the greater the effectiveness and the greater the amount of blast that is directed toward the shooter.

We'd all like to build a better mousetrap, but we don't want to get caught in our own.

Recoil reduction is the false goal. I've proven to myself, as I mentioned earlier, that the actual height the muzzle reaches during recoil isn't important. What is important is how quickly and precisely the gun can *return* for the next shot. A comp simply makes the gun easier to shoot by helping the gun to return on its own better.

I don't know if it was the comp itself, or that and the combination of 10 years experience, but I broke a speed barrier with a double-port gun on a simple Bill Drill. I could consistently shoot better Bill Drills than ever before compared to a single-port gun. And the fastest Bill Drill I've shot so far was 1.43 with my Smith & Wesson triple-port gun in the first week I had it, and I anticipate a major speed breakthrough with this gun. With the single-port gun, 1.70s were the fastest I could shoot with major loads; with the multi-ports, I get into the 1.60s consistently, and I've shot a 1.52 with major loads. I can occasionally shoot full-power 1.50s now, but I will never go above a 1.70. It's in this situation that the comp really makes a difference. Especially with the multi-chamber designs, I have the sensation that the gun is just floating there and that it's doing all the work for me. With the multi-port designs, on one shot on a target, there's no difference, and on two shots, there might be a very slightly noticeable improvement. So while the amount of muzzle flip is never a determining factor in how you place in a match, it's better when there's less of it since the shorter upward movement makes timing easier. Even if it doesn't make a measurable difference in a stage at the Nationals, if I can go out in practice and see that a certain design is better, I have got to use it. And the lower muzzle flip is all from the comp—it's not something that I'm doing.

This is my Smith & Wesson steel gun. The slide and barrel were extensively machined to reach a 35-ounce weight. Our goal was to make the gun cycle crisply with light loads. The pistol is based on a Model 5906. My IPSC gun uses this frame with a longer, heavier Model 52 slide. (Smith & Wesson photos by Nyle Leatham.)

Although my own comp versus no comp tests have shown the actual shot split differences to be in the hundredths of seconds, the comp makes the gun all around easier and better to shoot. Major .38 Super in a stock gun is a very unpleasant gun to shoot. With a comp it's still unpleasant, but now its functional ability far outweighs its unpleasantness. Letting the gun do the work is the central thing with .38 Super. When you switch from a .45 to a Super, the whole recoil impulse is different. The Super is much more obnoxious because it blasts more and kicks more so you try to hang on to it harder and muscle it more. But the real deal is that the .38 Super works much better for you—*if you'll just let it work.* The higher pressure works the comp better, and even though the gun is louder and more violent in your hands, it's actually returning better on its own. If anything, you have to back off the tension from what you'd use to hold a .45. I finally figured out that if I just let the gun do the work for me, I could shoot the Super much faster and much better than if I tried to contain that blast and recoil. And what really shines in a 1.50 Bill Drill is the feeling that the gun is just doing all the work. You're definitely driving the gun, but you get the feeling of the gun being suspended and it's amazing how fast it can keep the shots in the A-box.

Aside from the benefits of better balance and a greater distance between the sights, a main effect of the comp is that it allows you to mount the front sight on the barrel. If the gun isn't fitted up that well, you can aim the gun more accurately because the sight is staying with the barrel. But the really important thing that gets missed out on by people who mount their front sight on the slide instead of on the comp is that the comp-mounted sight doesn't cycle with the slide. It's easier to keep the sight in focus if it's only moving up and down instead of also back and forth. It can appear that you keep a slide-mounted sight in focus, but it's much harder and requires a much more refined focus than it does with a fixed sight just popping up and down. The very first thing I noticed when I shot my first comp gun was the non-cycling front sight.

I've experimented with all the different comps throughout their evolution, and I see no reason to believe that development will slow down. I can see all types of possibilities toward the ultimate aim of eliminating the upward movement of the gun. My Smith & Wessons use a triple-port comp with decreasing-size chambers. On my IPSC gun, the first two ports are each angled slightly to the right. That's done so the comp will steer the muzzle to the left to offset the sight movement to the right that I've mentioned seeing. I'd like to see the sight go straight up if it will do that without having to sacrifice anything by my trying to force it to move straight. But it really doesn't matter to me how the sight moves as long as it moves back to where it started; it just has a more uniform look if it's tracking vertically. If you're shooting doubles on small steel disks, for example, it looks more symmetrical to your eye to see the sight go straight up and down rather than trying to track it at an angle.

Weight

Before there were compensators, a few guys shot the 7-inch "longslides" because the guns weren't so violent. But when we started setting up specific tests that measured gun movement, like the *Speed Option,* they found that gun could slow them down by as much as .5 seconds a string compared to a 5-inch gun.

The first compensators were basically weights with no real porting. They were so heavy that you had to put a 7-pound spring in the gun to make it function with a major .45 load. The guns didn't have a lot of muzzle flip as such, but they just cycled too sluggishly. Anytime I've got the sensation of the slide cycling, I don't like that at all. It takes away from the crispness of the feedback from the gun. I like to have the gun set up so that its moving mass is light enough and can move fast enough so that I'm not conscious of its operation.

A lot of guns are still built with an emphasis on heavy weight. While the weight does dampen the lift and kick, the big, heavy guns have drawbacks. That much weight is too hard to move and stop quickly target to target, and when you've got that much weight coming up in recoil, although it doesn't come up that far, you've also got to stop that weight and get it into position again for the next shot. Anything that goes up is going to have to return, so you've got to strike a compromise somewhere. I'm not really in favor of light guns that are so violent to shoot that they're intimidating, and I don't like heavy, slow, sluggish guns. With whatever power factor load I'm using, I like to have the gun set up in weight to where it feels like a real compromise between short muzzle flip and fast return. When you're deciding on a comp setup, it's really important that you see how that setup either supports or upsets your timing. Your own timing will control more recoil than anything you can screw onto the end of a barrel.

For an IPSC gun, the zone between 41 and 43 ounces seems to be a decent compromise between soaking up the beating the .38 Super gives out and being able to move the gun quickly. I've done specific tests involving target acquisitions with 45-ounce guns and I'm not measurably slower than with, say, a 43-ounce gun. In the past, I switched to a lighter weight, bushing-type gun for the Steel Challenge; however, in '89 I shot the match with my 43-ounce IPSC cone gun. I've compared my movement times from target to target with shooters of equal skill levels who are using guns 6-8 ounces lighter and there doesn't seem to be any difference that you could attribute to gun weight. But my Smith & Wesson steel gun only weighs 35 ounces. We ended up with such a low weight because we wanted to get the moving mass of the gun down to where it would cycle very sharply with a light bullet. Usually when you're shooting as light a load as possible, the cycling feels sluggish, so we're experimenting with different weight slides to eliminate that. I again haven't seen any difference in target acquisition times, but I definitely notice that the gun has a much better feel running steel loads. My S&W IPSC gun weighs 41 ounces.

For me, the balance of a pistol is as important as its overall weight. I don't want a gun that's either muzzle heavy or muzzle light; I like to feel that the balance point is just forward of the trigger. As I mentioned in *Creative Shooting,* the ultimate sense of awareness in my own shooting is having the feeling that the gun is floating between my eye and the target. Although this sensation comes from within, I'm certain that the balance in my pistol has a lot to do with reaching it. Regardless of its actual weight, a gun can be balanced however the shooter wants it. Heavier grips or different weight guide rods will dramatically shift a gun's balance.

Having half the width of the front sight showing as light on either side is a good compromise between having a precice sight picture when you need it, and less distraction when you don't.

Sights

I've always been happy with Bo-Mar® sights. With a standard sight radius of 7.5-8 inches and a standard rear notch, I suggest using a front sight that's about .100-.115 wide. I use a .100.

A major point made by some bullseye experts is that the front sight should fill up half the space of the rear notch as your eye perceives it. Most top practical shooter's front sights aren't that narrow though, and a bullseye shooter's sights are drawn around a little different base—their rear sight notches are wider. But I've found that it's hard to get a better combination than having half the width of the front sight blade seen as light on either side. That combination gives a basic sight picture to shoot accurately with and it also gives you plenty of room so you can look *through* the rear sight to the front sight in faster shooting when the emphasis is either on staying with the front sight or on seeing the targets clearly. The narrow front sight looks better to me on plates and on tight shots. The narrower you make the front sight, the less conscious you are of that forced "textbook" picture of sight alignment, or of the rear sight at all, and for me that's better. But the important thing is how it appears to you. Depending on your arm length and the sight radius of the gun, the actual dimensions of your sights will vary to give the image that you like.

The whole idea of getting your sights drawn around a base as I've suggested is to achieve more of a "ghosting" effect where you easily and clearly see what you need to see of the rear sight, but it's not taking your attention away from what's beyond it.

Inputs

I deepen the rear notch as far as I can without having to file off the top of the screw head. The reason is also to get that "look-through" feeling. As you can see in the photos, I also change the shape of my rear sight notch by widening its base into a triangular shape. That lets me see even more. I find this is especially helpful when I'm crowding close up against a no-shoot, for instance. As my hold moves onto the shoot target, I can see through the bottom of the sight and sometimes can see the different colored target, whereas normally that would be totally blocked out.

Your eye can easily center and align this design. As a matter of fact, I've found that my eye can align the front sight faster in the wider gap. In Type 2 shooting it's also a lot easier to keep the sights in sharper peripheral focus. The wider gap shows more distinction between the front and rear sights and gives a less blurry look to the sights.

I modify my rear sight to see as much of what's downrange as possible without destroying a precision sight picture when I need it. In Type 2 shooting where I'm looking through my sights to the targets, or in Type 3 and 4 where I want to be conscious of a front sight focus, this rear notch allows me much more visual input and far less visual distraction from a forced sight picture.

The triangular rear sight notch simply allows more input. The rear sight can really be a limitation to the amount of visual input you can get. If you could shoot without any sights at all you'd be unbeatable. You could approach things that haven't been done because the sights are just too limiting.

Rob Leatham and I discussed this one year at Bianchi. All we had seen for the month we practiced that match was a red dot on the target. At the match, we took the speed guns out for the shootoff on Saturday, and after we finished our qualification runs we were talking about how it felt to be shooting those guns after not shooting them for a month. The major sensation we both got was how huge a section of the target the rear sight and gun blocked out. They blocked out everything below the the top of the front sight. After shooting the red dot, the conventional sights on the speed guns seemed so limiting; they were blocking out way too much visual input. We couldn't believe that we could actually shoot targets and be able see so little. We felt like it really put a limit on our speed, because when it comes right down to it, you can only shoot as fast as you can see.

But at the same time, when we're practicing for a speed match like the Steel Challenge, we get a feel for where the top of the gun is and where the gun is pointed without the sights seeming to block out the targets. After practicing for the Challenge, then the conventional sights seemed to be more unlimiting because the electronic sight is so bulky and because you can only see the target through the scope. After you shoot a couple more times, then you don't even notice it again. And you do as well as you can do. The limitation is still there but you don't see it. It takes an extreme example sometimes to see the limitations you're dealing with, whether they're mental, physical, or technical.

For most IPSC shooting, we could actually use sights that are a lot more crude than what we use. But we like to have them all dressed up nice—all square and blacked. Lately I've been shooting matches with no sight black; there's a little red paint on there, they're all shining, but who cares? It doesn't really matter. If I'm seeing the glare and the shine at least I'm getting some input off of it.

Sight Color

The color may change if the environment or targets change. If the background is dark between targets, I'll usually paint red on the front sight. At the Masters, the area behind the range where we shoot the *Speed Event* is wooded and dark. Even though the targets are white, you can lose the sight between targets when you're trying to follow it for some of the shots. I use red for dark backgrounds instead of orange because orange can glow so fiercely in direct light that you don't have any idea where the top edge of the sight is.

TRIGGERS

The triggers on my guns never pull more than 2 pounds. I did all my own Government Model trigger work and learned how from trigger guru Jack Breskovich. My triggers are totally safe and reliable—I can drop the slide or do anything I want to. There's .020 engagement on the hammer, but with the proper leverage and proper angles I can get the trigger down real safely to 2 pounds. I don't ever have to tune it or re-do it; if it's done correctly it will last forever.

I really wouldn't recommend a 2-pound trigger for the beginning shooter. I would recommend at least a 3-pound trigger just to help develop the fundamental of followthrough. Feeling the weight of the trigger on your finger and being aware of overcoming the weight is what builds followthrough. The heavier the trigger, the more you have to follow through to make a good shot. I think that when you reach a higher level, though, you'll want to move to a lighter trigger.

Every trigger, regardless of how "crisp" it breaks, has some amount of travel. Some shooters like more or less travel either before or after the shot breaks. To me, the main thing that makes a good trigger is that it has to have a small amount of *total overall movement*. By that I mean it's got to have very little movement in it to release the hammer and, most importantly, very little movement to release the disconnector so you can fire again.

This was the major area of work we did on the Smith & Wesson and we were able to get the overall movement down to the minimum I've experienced. That no doubt contributed to firing my first-ever .11 split after shooting that gun for just one day. I can cycle this gun faster and more consistently than I've ever been able to cycle a Government Model. Several times I've drawn and fired 10 shots into an IPSC target at 10 yards in under 2 seconds with all the breaks being .12s or .13s, with occasional .11s. I've never been able to approach that level of speed or consistency with a Government Model gun.

My preference for small trigger movement is not from an accuracy standpoint; the small overall movement just reduces the chance of not being able to release the trigger and having to double-clutch it to get the shot off. And the amount of overall movement your gun has is going to be in the fit of its parts. I really don't care how "crisp" a trigger is.

COMPONENTS

Following is a breakdown of what I think about some popular modifications and additions that you'll find on most race guns. While my preferences may not agree with yours, maybe some of my opinions will get you to stop and take a look at your own reasons for using what you do.

Grip Safety

The grip safety should make your hand feel like it's locked very securely into the gun and should help position your trigger finger where it can work the best. Not all grip safeties are shaped alike, so you should try different ones. On my Smith & Wesson I was able to have the back of the frame contoured exactly to fit my hand; that makes a big difference in how the gun feels to me.

The only style of grip safety I really don't have any use for are the extremely high ones. First, I'm not a real big believer in the idea that just using some device that turns down muzzle flip is going to increase your shooting ability. But mostly, I just don't like the way they position my hand on the gun; it feels like I should be pulling the trigger with my middle finger. With a Government Model, my trigger finger is already touching the frame the way it is, and with the high safeties my finger comes into contact with the frame even more. If I were going to experiment with that gun, I would come up with a way to relieve the area on the frame where my finger rubs. I've noticed that my finger moves out away from the frame a little bit when I shoot it, and the faster I'm shooting the more my finger moves away.

My Smith & Wessons use a triple-port comp. My IPSC gun has the first two ports angled to offset muzzle movement to the right in recoil.

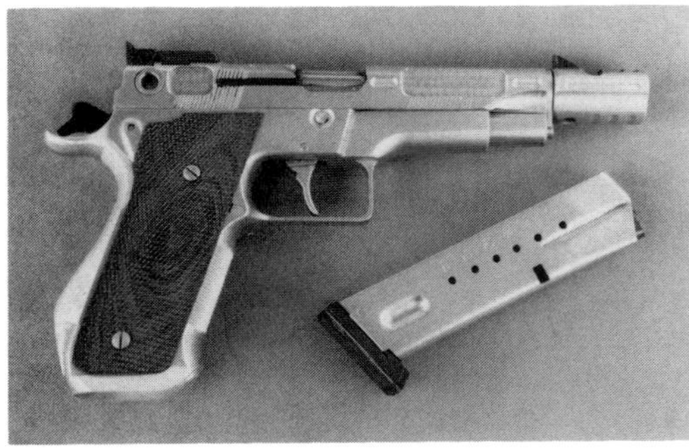

Gun components should all be selected with an eye on improving the gun's relationship with you. On my Smith & Wesson, the frame was contoured to exactly fit my hand. The trigger geometry for this gun was also designed around my preference for a trigger that's positioned farther forward.

Cutting up underneath the trigger guard is another popular modification. For me, it's the same story as with the high safeties. The combination of a high safety and an undercut trigger guard would position my hands so high on the gun that any advantage from lower muzzle flip would be far offset by moving my trigger finger into a position where control there would suffer. I can get my hands up plenty far using a standard grip safety and frame. I just don't think that those types of modifications are going to help me shoot a Government Model any faster.

Ideally, the trigger finger position should be a straightaway type of thing so that the finger is not angling down or up. Someone with extremely small hands might even want to look for a grip safety that places his hands lower on the gun than most do; someone with large hands may benefit from the higher safety and undercutting the trigger guard. The point is that you want your finger to extend and rest naturally on the trigger and be able to move freely and precisely without touching any part of the gun.

There's also plenty of room for experimentation with the position of the trigger itself. I like to have between 2.75 and 3 inches distance between the closest point on the grip safety and the front of the trigger. That puts my hand in the best position to operate the trigger accurately since it moves my point of contact with the trigger naturally to my finger tip. With the Government Model style pistol, it takes an extra-long trigger to reach this length. With the Smith & Wesson we were able to engineer the trigger geometry to get this distance.

Grips and Checkering

I use the grips made by Craig Spegel for my S&W. I had him make them just a little bit thinner than the stock grips, and for my particular hand that just takes away some of the round feeling of the gun caused by the thickness of its double column magazine.

On a Government Model gun, I used custom grips that were slightly thicker than the stock grips. The rounder feeling they gave to that gun was more comfortable for me. The way your grips are contoured and how thin or thick they are can definitely make a lot of difference as to how the gun feels in your hand.

I use 30 lines-per-inch checkering because it's just easier on my hands than 20 lpi. 20 lpi tends to be more sharp and usually needs to be dulled. I don't think that 20 lpi adds any control and in an extended practice session it's just more painful on your hand and makes the gun more unpleasant to shoot.

Accuracy

My guns will shoot around 1.5 inches at 50 yards; 3 inches is about as much as you should tolerate. You may never actually use all the accuracy that's built into a race gun, but it's important that the gun will shoot exactly where it's pointed. An accurate gun gives you a little more margin for error and might bring a few near-hits inside the lines. Besides, it helps you in developing the fundamental of accuracy. You never want to wonder if a poor group is you or the gun. It should always be you.

Magazines

I don't make any distinction between match magazines and practice magazines. I use the same ones all the time. I always number them and if I have a problem with one I just quit using it. The first problem is the last problem. And buy good magazines. They're every bit as important to the function of your gun as any of its other parts.

We built the S&W around a setup that holds 18 rounds total. Not that you need the shots for misses, but it saves you time by not having to reload when it's not mandatory. It takes about 5-6 steps of shooter movement for the reload to not be a factor. You can stay up with a guy who doesn't have to reload if you're able to make sharp, perfect loads, but it's much more difficult; besides, if you're of equal skill levels, you'll never make up the time on him. I can also alter the gun's balance and weight when shooting steel by varying the number of rounds I keep in the magazine.

Magazine Release

For my Government Models, I made my own extended magazine release buttons by having someone weld a piece on a stock button and then I checkered it. For that gun, I prefer the straight button to the mushroom type. And the reason for that is simply that you don't have to disassemble the magazine release to take the gun apart.

I installed a stop in the release so that I couldn't push the button in far enough to snag the magazine. I made the stop by cutting a decapping pin so that it fit inside the spring. The stop has to be cut to *exactly* the right length.

Magazine Wells

There are a lot of different styles on the market for the Government Model. I like those that are combined with the mainspring housing because they're the most simple.

One thing, though, is that while most magazine wells are designed to fit flush with the stock opening, that's not nearly good enough. You also need to have the frame-portion of the magazine well opened up and relieved well back into the gun because that's where you'll get the most leeway in putting the magazine in. Blowing a reload and losing a match because the magazine snags is an experience we can all do without.

Springs

For minimum felt recoil, I like to run with the lightest spring I can get away with without battering the gun and, of course, making sure the gun feeds. For the lighter loads I used a 10-pound spring in the Government Model; for major I used a 13. If your gun has a lighter slide and comp assembly you might want to use a 14-pound spring. And always use Shock Buffs® or something similar.

2. AMMUNITION

First, to contribute my thoughts to the Great Caliber Debate, .38 Super is the best cartridge for *all* the different matches you can shoot with a Government Model. That's not to say that Super is the best cartridge for everyone. If you're a die-hard IPSC shooter and like your life less complicated, the .45 works well. It's easy to find the perfect load and cases last for years. If you shoot exclusively steel, 9mm can work fine. But if you're into shooting both steel and paper, the .38 Super really shines. With the Government Model, we use the Super in the lighter-load matches mostly because it's just more convenient than switching to a 9mm. The different 10mm rounds have some promise for IPSC—especially the .40 S&W; however, in my mind, the 10s aren't the hot setup for steel. In my Smith & Wesson IPSC gun, I'll be using a specially-developed 9mm cartridge which is roughly equivalent to major .38 Super. The round will be a proprietary cartridge that has no SAAMI specifications attached to it and, unfortunately, there won't be any information available about it.

Power Factor

A real good point to understand is that I can shoot the courses at the Steel Challenge just as fast using my major load as I can using my steel load. I use the steel load just because it's less annoying since there's not as much blast. Also, on match day, your room for error seems to increase with lighter loads, especially if you're not feeling too connected.

For IPSC shooters, there's always the question of whether they should use major loads in practice. When I was first learning to shoot and was using a .45, I practiced with major loads because I felt that I got too sloppy from using light loads and that I needed to develop my fundamentals well enough to handle any load. Other shooters say that they never shoot major loads until the match. That might work for some people, but with a .38 Super there is just too much difference in blast between light and major loads for me to want to deal with.

If I'm preparing for a match, I never want to shoot a lighter load in practice than what I'll be shooting in the match. If I'm practicing seriously for an upcoming IPSC match I'll definitely be shooting major. But for just general IPSC practice, I wouldn't shoot full major loads with the Super. I'd recommend shooting about a 150-160 power factor so it still takes about the same control but is a little easier on the gun and just a little less painful on all things involved.

For a steel match, I follow a similar idea. I feel that I get much more benefit if I just drop the load down a little bit before a match. Before the Challenge, my practice load runs 50 fps faster than my match load. Since the match load runs a little bit slower, there is a slightly noticeable improvement from a little less recoil. And that little bit less recoil always seems to give me a confidence edge. When I switch to the lighter load on my last practice runs, my control seems to be a little more precise.

For IPSC, I load to a 180 power factor for a major match. And I usually give myself more of a cushion if I have to travel. You have to consider the temperature where you'll be shooting because that can affect the velocity and pressure. For instance, since I live in Arizona, I have to keep my ammo in a cooler at the range when I'm practicing for the IPSC Nationals. Basically, I want to correct the ammo to the proper temperature range I anticipate shooting in, and then I want to be able to fire 20 rounds in a row and not have one go below the power factor.

The base composition of different powders is different and can actually affect pressures and velocities totally differently in the same temperatures. You should check with your powder manufacturer for some insight into what to expect from different temperatures. If you back off your loads for a safety margin, you can get an idea of how your powder reacts to different temperatures by artificially changing the temperature of the rounds before you chronograph them. Don't get extreme, but try to test some that are cool to the touch, at normal outside temperature, and some that have been in the sun for a few minutes—make it realistic. Check the difference in the spreads to get some idea as to the direction you might have to take your powder charges to correct for different environments.

When you're working up your major loads, you have to use a chronograph. Period. There's no other way to know where you stand, and it's a pretty foolish thing to not know where you stand when you're dealing with unique loads. I use a supported-chamber barrel and small rifle primers for major Super loads. These have become common-sense precautions and you should observe them. Due to the necessity of pushing .38 Super over "industry standards" to make major, I really can't go into specifics on data beyond telling you that my current favorite powders are Winchester-Western® 540 and Accurate Arms® #7.

Actually, the whole issue of "pressure" is a little abstract. SAAMI specs are established to make ammunition safe for the most marginal stock pistol sold in this country. My race gun is far from a stock pistol, and far from marginal. With its quality components and fitting, and with the design enhancements that the comp and supported chamber barrel add, my race gun can safely handle a lot more pressure than it could "out of the box." But everyone's gun is different, and the shooter *must* take responsibility for understanding that too. Differences in chamber dimensions, barrel lengths, and a lot of other things, can make one load safe in some guns and dangerous in others.

Super Bullets

For major .38 Super, you have two basic choices: lighter bullets going faster or heavier bullets going slower. Both work, but I favor the lighter bullet approach. If you want to try lighter bullets, make sure that your bullet can handle the extra velocity without leading. Shoot some groups before a practice session and compare those to groups shot after the session. If they're still within a cluster to your satisfaction, you can rest assured that accuracy will hold up at a match. If you have trouble with leading, going to a plated or jacketed bullet is the only solution. Some barrels favor jacketed or lead bullets over the other, so check with your pistolsmith if you can't use what you want.

I recommend using jacketed bullets, if only in matches. They are more reliable and consistent than lead, but the main reason I use jacketed bullets is actually because of the "smoke factor." You just don't get the smoke with jacketed bullets that you do with lead. A lot of the matches we shoot now, like the Steel Challenge and the IPSC Nationals, have ranges set up so they face the sun at some time during the day. If you get stuck out there on a calm day when the sun is low, you're going to be losing with lead bullets.

I like lighter bullets because the higher pressure makes the comp work better and the sharper cycling gets rid of the bumping sensation you get with the heavier bullets. The standard specs for .38 Super barrels also seem to favor the lighter bullets for accuracy. I've shot really well with heavier bullets, but I've steadily worked down in weight. Every time I went to the next lighter bullet it took some time to adjust to it. When I'd first try a lighter bullet, I'd shoot quite a bit worse on standard, measurable tests, like Bill Drills. Then my body started to get used to each step down in weight, and then I'd like the lighter bullet better than anything else. It takes a while to get adjusted down to light bullets just like it takes a while for a new shooter to get adjusted to a .38 Super from a .45.

Although you *never* rely on it, when shooting steel you sometimes use hearing as a backup. For steel loads, I run a faster bullet than many shooters. I like the feedback I get off the target from a faster, lighter bullet. For instance, when I shot heavier bullets, on *Outer Limits* I used to shoot the 40-yard target last, but with the lighter bullets I shoot the 25-yard plate last before I step out of the box just because I can hear the hit so much faster if I need to. If you've called a borderline, questionable shot on the far target on *Outer Limits*, you're going to need to hear the hit before you step out of the box.

Sighting In

Your pistol should be zeroed with the same care a bullseye shooter would use. If your gun is one-half-inch off, you may be losing on shots that fall close to the scoring lines, or those that barely miss the edge of a plate. Also, you may show up at a match sometime and be faced with a lot of long-range shots, 4-inch stop plates, or other shots that demand exact precision. If your gun is absolutely zeroed, it can make a difference in both your score and your confidence.

I use a 40- or 50-yard center zero, depending on what I'm preparing to shoot and on which gun I'm using. I shoot 10-shot groups to get more accurate feedback from the target. The center of my group will be exactly at the point where the top of my front sight was. With a .38 Super that puts the gun less than one-inch high at 25 yards, so you can virtually hold exactly where you want the bullet to go at any range out to 50 yards. With a .45 there is a little more mid-range trajectory difference so you'll have to aim a little lower at 25 yards if you're doing extremely precise shooting; otherwise, you can follow pretty much the same formula for an IPSC-type match.

I haven't been able to tell a difference in my point of aim and point of impact from shooting offhand or from a rest, but if the pressure you exert on the grip is different when you bench the gun, impact can change, so pay attention to keeping your feels the same as when you're shooting freestyle.

You've got your gun sighted in—you know where it's pointed. Do you know where *you're* pointed?

APPENDIX B: REVOLVER SHOOTING

Whether you're an NRA Action Pistol competitor or enjoy shooting the revolver in IPSC, practical shooting fundamentals are the same for a revolver or automatic. However, there are certain skills that must be developed and emphasized to perform your best with the revolver. Through awareness and focus, shooting the revolver doesn't have to be an entirely different sensation. I'm able to switch back and forth between revolvers and automatics without difficulty. That's because I've learned that it's necessary to use a different focus for revolver shooting. By knowing what that focus is for each type of shooting I do with the revolver, my awareness takes control of my gun. By being aware of the proper focus, I've made the "transition" from automatic to revolver even before I fire my first shot.

It's really difficult to get equal support from both hands with the revolver, but it's important. The best way to do that is to position the support hand so it's more on the gun. The shooting hand is as high on the gun as is comfortable. My grip places the support hand slightly lower than for an automatic, but that also gives me a little more leverage to counter this gun's massive weight.

REVOLVER FUNDAMENTALS

The Grip

Compared to the automatic, the revolver is more difficult to grip effectively. By effective, I mean that the grip must be neutral. In the last few years I've taken a serious look at a better way to grip the revolver, and, in essence, I feel that is to place the support hand more equally on the gun as compared to the shooting hand. I've really worked to move my support hand more into the same position it's in with the automatic. The heel of my shooting hand is just left of center on the rear of the grip. If the grips on your pistol have an open back, the heel of your shooting hand would be flush with the left edge of the backstrap. This way the supporting hand has a more equal gun surface to contact and can actually touch the rear of the grip, not just the side. Now my supporting hand can "work" itself more into the grip and offer much more help. If you want to try this you should be able to remove your shooting hand and hold the pistol using only your support hand. This change in my grip resulted in my support hand being slightly lower on the pistol. Consequently, my support arm is bent slightly lower than my shooting arm and that gives me just a little increased leverage there to hold the massive weight of a

Bianchi-style pistol.

The shooting hand is placed as high on the gun as is comfortable. The thumb of my shooting hand presses against the pistol grip and is pulling slightly back. The thumb of my support hand presses slightly against my shooting hand thumb and lies at a 45-degree angle across my shooting hand thumb. The point of contact for my support hand thumb is right at the outside edge of the shooting hand's thumbnail. You might want to begin work on your own grip by emulating those positions; however, there are infinite possibilities for where your thumbs rest, the pressure you apply with them, etc. The basic goal, though, is to offer at least equal gripping force with your support hand. Keep that in mind and you'll find what works best for you.

Trigger Control

Trigger control is of ultimate importance, and I consider it to be the main focus in revolver shooting. Trigger control is far and away the most critical aspect of shooting a double-action revolver. For optimal double-action trigger control, two principles have helped me: the hammer should rise and fall with no change in speed or motion; the trigger must be pulled straight to the rear in one continuous motion and without hesitation.

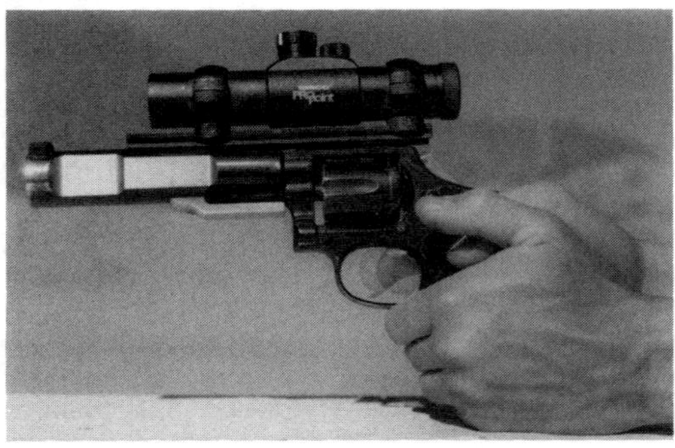

Trigger control is the main focus in shooting a revolver. Pull the trigger through with no hesitation, no change in speed.

The speed with which you press the trigger doesn't matter as long as it's consistent. The speed of the trigger pull has no relation to the quality of the trigger control. A difficult shot does not need to be pulled slowly, and many shooters make the mistake of slowing their trigger pull, or even stopping it, when they face a shot they perceive as being difficult. Pull the shot straight through without hesitation, without thought. *Let the trigger pull your finger.* The last tenth of the trigger stroke is the most critical.

Pull the trigger with only exactly enough force to overcome its movement. If you need to shoot faster, just stroke the trigger faster. But regardless of the pace you're using, the release speed to return the trigger should be the same as it was stroking the trigger through.

With the revolver, the first joint of my finger rests right on the trigger; I use a narrow trigger to help position my finger there. Having my finger in that position gives me the best leverage and control at that final point just when the hammer is released. But that's for me—everyone needs to experiment to find the position that gives the best control.

Regardless of where your finger rests on the trigger, make sure that the trigger is the only thing your trigger finger rests on. Don't let your finger rest on or rub along the frame or trigger guard as you stroke through.

THOUGHTS ON BIANCHI

Each shooter must realize his own needs for improvement in various basics, so what I'll do here is share my thoughts on the focus I use for each separate stage at Bianchi as well as offering a few tips on preparing to shoot them. Overall, I've found that it's more productive for me to practice the match itself less and the individual events more.

I like to be comfortable on my first shot. Excepting the *Mover,* on any string we shoot at Bianchi I always set up to favor the first target.

Each stage at Bianchi requires a different focus. Pick the right one and stick with it.

Falling Plates: The wobble zone (area the sight or dot covers) is much smaller than the plate, so you must have the confidence to just pull the trigger straight through.

I don't rush the draw as getting the perfect grip is extremely important. I confirm my body and sight alignment on the first plate, no matter how long that takes. Once they're correct, I roll through on my first shot and begin pulling the trigger immediately for the next one.

Depending on the distance and the time limit we're down to, I'll be operating the trigger at different speeds. The pull stays the same, that is, the effort with which I pull the trigger stays the same; however, the speed will change for every string of fire.

I look at the very center of the target. My eye is aware of the dot's relationship to the center of the target and is trying to keep the dot there—steering the dot. I'm visually aware of the dot's relationship to the target and I'm also mentally aware of the way my finger is pulling the trigger to influence wherever the dot is. I'm not actually focused on trigger control or on the dot; I'm focused on the *relationship* between the trigger pull and the placement of the dot—it's just a total observation process.

Pull the trigger straight through as if you have no idea when the gun will fire.

Barricade: I like to grip the gun as high as possible, especially when shooting weak-side.

I use the technique of holding the barrel with the weak hand when shooting weak-side. I use a medium pressure to do so; about the same as if I had my hand on the pistol.

There are a few different ways you can hold the barrel with your weak hand. I put my index finger over the front part of the barrel right at the finger's lowermost joint. The muzzle sits in the web of my hand to the left of the thumb and under the index finger. The bottom three fingers and thumb actually grip the barricade (which is made of 2-inch angle iron at Bianchi). Since I'm able to actually grip the barricade and essentially clamp the gun to it, the angle iron construction makes it unnecessary to lean into the barricade. When the barricades were made of 2x4s, we had to lean into the barricade for stability. My support arm is straight with little or no pressure on the barricade.

This is the grip I use for the *Barricade.* I grip the angle iron with about the same tension I would use if my hand were on the gun.

For the shooter who has learned trigger control with his weak hand, that position should be reversed for shooting the barricade strong-side. The only difference is in the draw. On the right-side barricade, as well as on the weak-hand practical, you draw the pistol with the strong hand by gripping the scope. As soon as the pistol is clear of the holster, you acquire the shooting grip with the weak hand and mount the gun. A word of caution: if your scope is electronic, it's possible to switch it off during the draw. You may want to tape the switch in position.

My focus on the *Barricade* is on the aiming area on the target. Recoil is always a factor on the *Barricade* and the most important thing is that you don't fight it.

I roll the trigger through on the first shot with the exact same speed that I use on the second shot; I imagine that I'm firing my second shot.

Practical: Compare this stage to shooting plates at the same distances. And at 50 yards, f-o-l-l-o-w through!

My focus is on watching the dot lift on recoil. I'm forcing my visual followthrough on the dot to where I try to recall the exact spot where it was before I saw the dot lift.

Grip the gun as high as possible with your weak hand for better control. Focus on rolling the trigger straight through when shooting weak-hand. It's important in weak-hand, and on all unorthodox strings, to pull the trigger straight through on the first shot at the same tempo as you would if you were on your second or third shot of the string. The tendency that we're fighting is that of raising the gun onto the target and starting to pull the trigger while the gun is still not quite in the aiming area, or even still coming onto the target. I've found that it works much better for me if I get the sight into an acceptable aiming area without putting any pressure on the trigger at all, and then rolling the trigger straight through to the rear in one smooth, continuous motion.

Mover: This is the stage that usually makes or breaks the match. There are a couple of corners you can cut that will give you more time for shooting.

One that I have found to be effective is drawing to the point where the target will be when the sight reaches my eye level. This takes practice and a consistent drawing speed, but even if you miss (miss early, not late) you're still working from a head start. This eliminates sight tracking while drawing.

The most important thing is keeping your focus on your lead area. I don't like to think in terms of lead *point* because, just like on any other target, there is a wobble zone on the mover too. Thinking of lead *area* helps you to realize that there is as much room to score on that target as for any of the others. I see the lead area until the gun is reholstered. *Never* look for your hits; don't shift your focus back and forth. Get started shooting as early as possible and *roll the trigger through*.

My overall stance is about the same as with my automatic. For precision shooting, it's really important for the stance to be relaxed and neutral.

Final Thoughts

Shooting the revolver with the scope or red dot sight allows a unique focus. To try to classify the focus types I use at Bianchi so you can relate them to what I covered in Section 3, I suppose that Type 5 is as close a description as I can offer. Since the trigger pull is always the critical element, and also since the dot allows you to take some attention away from your "sight picture," a focus on trigger pull can work very well there. On most all the shots at Bianchi the dot is almost always in an acceptable aiming area; the wobble zone is always on the plate or 10-ring, and with the dot, the visual focus can seem to take care of itself. So if I say that I look at the target on some strings, that's not really a Type 2 focus because the dot is *always* there—it's not like you're able to look *through* it.

On many strings of fire, I use more of an aiming-area

focus where I'm more focused on looking the dot into the 10-ring until the dot lifts; I'm steering it in and keeping it there with my eyes and my trigger control. What you're actually seeing in a "dot focus" is hard to describe because, technically, the dot in the scope is focused on infinity, so you're not supposed to be able to actually focus on it. But sometimes it appears that I'm looking at the dot; I may not actually be focused on it, but I am looking toward it because I don't have a conscious recall of a clear target focus. In that awareness, I'm just watching and wanting to see the dot lift, and that controls the followthrough. And I've also noticed sometimes that I'm very aware of the target focus where I'm aware of the dot on the target and am holding the dot in the aiming area with my visual attention and my trigger pull.

APPENDIX C: GROUP SHOOTING

Since I've made such a point of the importance of learning to shoot accurately and of making group shooting a big part of your practice, I'd like to tell you just exactly how I shoot a group. I usually shoot my groups at 50 yards because that's a distance where you can't get away with any imprecision. I use 9-inch paper plates like what you find at the supermarket. Sometimes I staple a smaller black aiming circle in the middle of the plate, usually the 4-inch circle I use for practicing the Masters *Precision Event*. That seems to give me a better aiming reference. The normal procedure I follow is to look right at the center of the target where I want the bullet to hit and then line the sight up on that as precisely as I can. I run my visual focus back and forth from the sight to the target, sight to the target until I'm happy with how the gun is positioned. At that point I bring my focus back to the sight and see the textbook top center of the front sight while I very carefully release the trigger, watching for the sight to lift.

I put sand bags on the hood of my truck and just lean slightly into it so my shooting position is extremely stable. I rest the gun on the bags. I set the bags up high enough so that the gun butt is resting on a blanket that goes across the truck; the frame of the gun actually cradles in the bags.

Even when the gun is totally stable on the target, you still want to have the feeling that you're aiming *while* you're pulling the trigger, releasing the shot within a time frame that's going to give you a surprise break. You don't want to have the feeling that you're aiming the gun and *then* pulling the trigger. That can lead to picking the shot off and will affect your groups even when firing off sandbags.

You'll notice that your vision is clearest on the first shot. That's when you have the best perception of seeing the sight placement and alignment. After about the third shot, your vision starts to deteriorate. I usually won't shoot more than six shots before I let my eye rest.

I use my normal freestyle grip and keep the same tension in my arms and hands as I use offhand. I just let the gun recoil up and down off the bags as it does when I'm standing. I'm careful to not put any downward force on the bag; I get it so that the gun is just sitting there perfectly lined up on the center of the target. I don't have to muscle it or steer it to keep it there; I let the bags do all that work for me. Pay very close attention to the relationship between trigger pressure and sight movement. You know you're doing what you should when you see the sight lift and return, settling right back to where it started. When I shoot my best groups, I don't have to shift the gun's position at all to realign it from shot to shot.

ACKNOWLEDGEMENTS

I'd like to thank my publishers, Glen and Kris Zediker, for their tireless and unceasing work and prodding to help me turn this book from just an idea that I've always thought about to an actual reality. Without their help and encouragement, and certainly their talents, it would have never happened.

Everything in this book could be wrong...

Check it out for yourself. *It's you who has to learn.* You won't learn by copying an idea—you have to experience it for yourself. When you become the experience, you will have learned, possibly without understanding.

Steel Challenge course reference

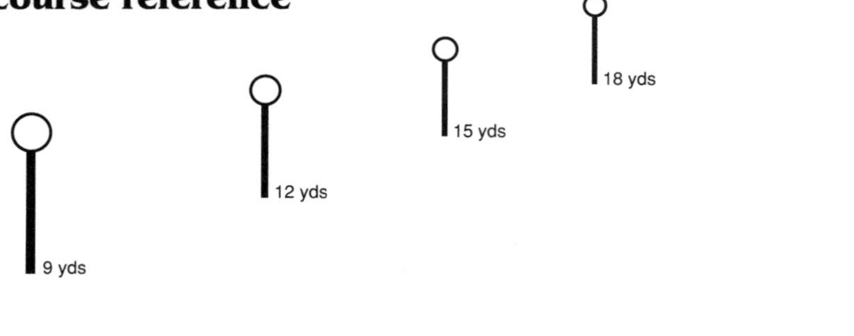

5 To Go
10-inch target plates
12-inch stop plate

Shooter's Box

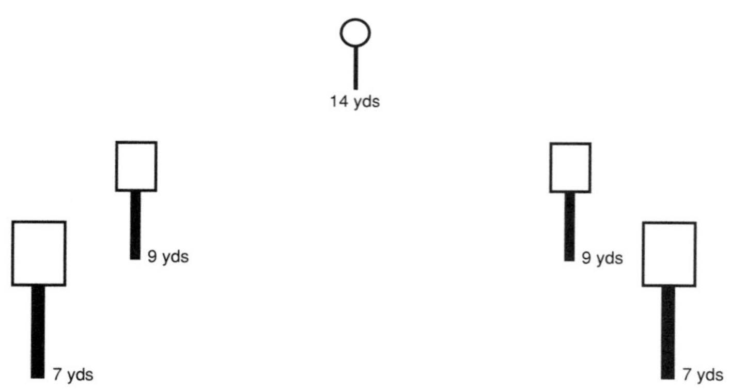

Smoke & Hope
18x24 target plates
12-inch stop plate

Shooter's Box